GERMANY'S STEPCHILDREN

Also by SOLOMON LIPTZIN

ARTHUR SCHNITZLER

RICHARD BEER-HOFMANN

SHELLEY IN GERMANY

THE WEAVERS IN GERMAN LITERATURE

LYRIC PIONEERS OF MODERN GERMANY

HISTORICAL SURVEY OF GERMAN LITERATURE

FROM NOVALIS TO NIETZSCHE

HEINE

GERMANY'S STEPCHILDREN

by

SOLOMON LIPTZIN

College of the City of New York

PHILADELPHIA

THE JEWISH PUBLICATION SOCIETY OF AMERICA

5704–1944

To

My Parents

CONTENTS

PART V

THE RENAISSANCE OF A PEOPLE

LIST OF ILLUSTRATIONS

GERMANY'S STEPCHILDREN

INTRODUCTION

GERMAN AND JEW — two souls within a single breast — this tragic duality, which faced hundreds of thousands of individuals, has become a subject of increasing interest in recent decades and has given rise to endless discussion, both oral and written. The present study, a modest contribution to an apparently inexhaustible theme, attempts to answer the following question: what was the attitude towards this problem on the part of the most sensitive spirits directly affected? In other words, how did German writers of Jewish origin, creative poets, novelists, dramatists, essayists, react towards this duality?

It was not until the nineteenth century that this duality took on tragic proportions, necessitating complex psychic adjustments. For in earlier centuries the members of the Jewish cultural community were normally excluded from the German religious and cultural fellowship. If, however, a Jew did not feel at home in his spiritual environment and if he preferred to leave the community of his birth and ancestry, the transition to a new social and cultural life generally involved the comparatively simple expedient of baptism. Thereupon he was received with open arms by either the Lutheran or the Catholic Church as a full-fledged member of the Christian majority and allowed to participate in all fields on the same terms as other Germans.

Since the rise to power of the National Socialist move-

1

ment in 1933 and especially since the promulgation of the
Nuremberg Racial Laws in 1935, all efforts at a spiritual
fusion of Germans and Jews yielded to a strict severance
of the two groups. The slogan German *and* Jew was
replaced by the implacable command German *or* Jew.
Baptism of a Jew no longer admitted him to the ranks of
the Germans, who looked upon themselves as primarily an
ethnic group, and marriage of a Jew outside of the Jewish
fold was banned as *Rassenschande*, racial defilement. Jews
were compelled to assume distinctive names, such as Israel
and Sarah, so that even in correspondence Germans might
know whether they were in contact with ethnic kin or
with ethnic aliens.

The outbreak of the Second World War brought about
an extension of German racial doctrines and practices to
all German-occupied lands. Jews were again herded in
ghettos, as in medieval days, and the Yellow Badge was
reintroduced in order to make their presence unmistakably
visible to their neighbors. In the early 1940's the final step
was taken: the mass-deportation of Jews from the Reich
and their complete exclusion from all its cultural activities.
Hitler thus put a violent end to the German mirage that
had dazzled Jewish eyes since the Age of Enlightenment
and, by dissipating a tragic duality, quickened the tempo
of Jewish regeneration.

This duality of German and Jew, which has now become historic, was faced throughout the century between
Napoleon and Hitler by all Germans of Jewish origin or,
if a different phrasing be preferred, by all Jews residing
within German-speaking territory. Solutions ranged from
baptism en masse to *Los von Europa* — "Away from
Europe." A critical analysis of these solutions, as they

appear and reappear in the lives and works of German-Jewish men-of-letters during the century of emancipation, may cast some light on this still debatable problem of Jewish duality in all Diaspora lands. Such an analysis may unveil insufficiently known difficulties, may perhaps influence overbold theorists to be more wary of facile generalizations, and may in some measure help point the way towards a more fruitful approach. For, although historical phenomena are unique and similar causes do not necessarily bring about similar results, nevertheless a study of the soul-searchings undertaken by German Jewry may help avert some errors of judgment and may further to some extent a better understanding between Jews and their neighbors.

PART I

FROM EMANCIPATION TO BAPTISM

RAHEL VARNHAGEN, 1771–1833

CHAPTER I

RAHEL VARNHAGEN

FOR a thousand years Germans and Jews lived as strangers near each other. Medieval ghetto walls formed not merely physical barriers. They were also symbolic of spiritual barriers separating two distinct cultural groups. Now and then individuals might undertake excursions into the world of the alien group. But not until the eighteenth century did Germans and Jews in appreciable numbers really discover one another.

Enlightenment was the spiritual force that helped to break down prejudices and superstitions which had long prevented mutual understanding. Enlightenment spelled the victory of tolerance in both camps. Clarity of thought on religious and temporal matters rendered possible a better acquaintance between leading representatives of the German and the Jewish ways of life. The intimate friendship between Gotthold Ephraim Lessing and Moses Mendelssohn was the finest expression of the spirit of cooperation which was replacing long prevalent distrust and suspicion. The intellectual élite among the Jews sought to contribute to the stream of German culture, and the élite among the Germans for a time welcomed these new allies in the battle against unreason and obscurantism. Ever since the 1780's Jews and Germans mingled in the Berlin salons, exchanged opinions, and influenced each other's religious, philosophic, and aesthetic expressions. The prominent place in the social life of the Prussian capital, which the Jewish salons were able to maintain for more than a generation, can be traced back to political and economic conditions resulting from the Seven Years' War.

This war, which lasted from 1756 to 1763, necessitated financial operations of great skill and magnitude. Frederick the Great had to turn to experienced financial agents in order to be assured of sufficient war materials for his campaigns on all fronts. Since Jews of Berlin, Breslau, and Königsberg were best able to meet his wants, he often assigned war contracts to them. As a consequence, a few Jewish families in these towns accumulated considerable wealth. The populace of Prussia, groaning under the burden of a long drawn-out struggle, attributed its hardships to the Jews, even though most Jews remained in abject poverty and economic insecurity. When the war emergency came to an end, the King yielded to popular clamor and turned over the handling of Prussian finances to Christian bankers. Jewish capital, no longer utilized for the state treasury, was thereupon invested in trade and industry. Factories arose, and Berlin increased rapidly in population and prosperity. Special exemptions and privileges were granted to Jews who furthered the welfare of their Prussian fatherland. These few wealthy Jews before long received their Christian clientele of aristocratic rank not only in their offices but also in their drawing rooms. Cultured wives and vivacious daughters charmed all visitors. By the end of the eighteenth century, admission to these Jewish salons was regarded as a valued favor. Here informality, frankness, warmth attracted the young princes and enlightened noblemen who were bored by the stiffness and conventionalism of feudal homes. Here diplomats and actresses, bankers and poets, Protestants and Freethinkers, Catholics and Jews conversed on terms of equality. Charming hostesses, excelling in beauty, learning, and wit, were keenly alert to all new literary and artistic developments. The rationalism of Berlin, the classicism of Weimar, and the rising tide of romanticism found a sensitive audience in these circles, where men and women of spirit and intellectual achievement were ever welcome, no matter what their origin, German or foreign, Christian or Jew, aristocrat or commoner. For more than half a century, from the 1780's through the 1830's, the Jewish salons exercised a civilizing influence in Berlin. The most famous of the salons were those of Henriette Herz and of Rahel Varnhagen.

Henriette Herz, who lived from 1764 to 1847, was the daughter of a Jewish physician of Hamburg, whose family had originally emigrated from Portugal. At twelve she was engaged to Marcus Herz, a prominent physician of Berlin and a follower of Moses Mendelssohn and Immanuel Kant. At fifteen she married. Her husband attracted to their home the leading representatives of German and Jewish enlightenment. Her youth, her extraordinary beauty, her social charm, her aesthetic education, her knowledge of foreign languages, enabled her to fascinate all visitors, and especially the passionate pioneers of romanticism. Her salon was frequented by Mirabeau and Friedrich von Gentz, Alexander von Humboldt and Wilhelm von Humboldt, Nicolai and Fichte, Tieck and Chamisso, August Wilhelm Schlegel and Friedrich Schlegel. Young Börne glowed for her and Schleiermacher found in her his soul's mate.

As the greatest theologian of his day, Schleiermacher moulded the religious views of Berlin's romantic circles.

He interpreted Christianity as a religion of the heart, as the submission of the individual to the infinite, as the abandonment of the self to a higher power sensed by all who contemplated the phenomena of nature and history. In his eyes, Judaism was a petrified corpse, a venerable mummy. In his opinion, a Jew who wished to embrace German culture in its totality should be required to adopt the religion of the majority population. Henriette Herz was deeply moved by Schleiermacher's public and private sermons and genuinely convinced of the truth of the Protestantism he expounded; yet she did not yield to his constant urging and did not seek conversion — as long as her mother was alive. In 1815 she even refused an offer to tutor Princess Charlotte, afterwards Empress of Russia, because this position required her to accept baptism. But after her mother's death in 1817, she saw no reason for remaining any longer within the Jewish fold.

It was in the salon of Henriette Herz that Friedrich Schlegel, the impetuous genius of Early Romanticism, first met Dorothea, the oldest daughter of Moses Mendelssohn and the wife of the Jewish industrialist David Veit. Under the stimulus of Schleiermacher's religion of the heart and the romantic doctrines of free love and experimental love, she eloped with Friedrich Schlegel, even though she was his senior by more than eight years and the mother of two children. From Paris she wrote to Schleiermacher in 1802 that she was at heart a Protestant, but that she did not deem it necessary to make a public display of her faith. A reading of the Old and the New Testaments had convinced her that Protestant Christianity was purer than Catholicism and therefore to be preferred. The latter had, in her opinion, too many similarities to ancient Judaism, which she had come to despise utterly. She felt that any cultured person, who studied the Bible with understanding, must arrive at similar conclusions. Her acceptance of the new creed in her heart of hearts ought to suffice. Solemn abjuration of Judaism and public profession of her religious transformation smacked too much of Catholic ostentation, imperiousness, and vanity. She wished to avoid such action. In 1804, however, when she was able to marry Friedrich, she consented to baptism as a Protestant. Four years later, she and her husband were converted to Catholicism. The couple settled in Vienna. There the Schlegel home became a social and intellectual center. While Friedrich, the ex-revolutionary and ex-atheist, devoted himself to the service of Metternich's reactionary policies and to lectures on literature, Dorothea, the ex-Jewess and ex-Protestant, busied herself with religious and charitable tasks. Her ostentatious Catholicism, her missionary zeal, her fanaticism exceeded normal bounds — which did not prevent Jakob Grimm from writing to his brother that she still retained her Jewish face. She wrestled with her two sons, until she weaned them from Jewish orthodoxy to Catholic piety. Their father, David Veit, begged her to refrain. He wrote that it would be the death of him if both sons were to desert him and go over to Christianity. She replied that no power on earth could stop her. She was soon so successful in her proselytizing efforts that one son wished to enter the clergy and even sought to get his father to worship the Trinity. Both sons finally ended as pious painters of religious pictures, as prominent members of the Nazarene Group in Rome. Dorothea herself remained ever a model of piety until her death in 1839 and the envy

of many a Jewess who could not equal her devotion to the
Church.

The most brilliant member of the Jewish salon hostesses,
however, was undoubtedly Rahel Levin, the wife of the
Prussian diplomat and author, Karl August Varnhagen
von Ense. Rahel, who was born in 1771 and died in 1833,
is generally acknowledged to be the greatest woman that
German Jewry produced. Her home was for a generation
a pleasant and informal meeting place for aristocrats and
scholars, Classicists and Romanticists, radicals of the
"Young German" vintage and statesmen of the Holy
Alliance. Here Goethe found his most understanding readers and his most ardent worshippers. It was the Jewess
Rahel who opened the eyes of her lukewarm contemporaries to the uniqueness of this supreme German personality
and who assigned to him a rank equal to that of Moses,
Socrates, and Jesus. A word from her made and unmade
reputations. A veritable Rahel cult flourished throughout
her life and her influence continued undimmed long after
her death. Her praise was sung by Jean Paul and Friedrich
Schlegel, Wilhelm von Humboldt and Heinrich von Kleist,
Karl Gutzkow and Theodor Mundt, Prince de Ligne and
Prince Louis Ferdinand of Prussia. She was referred to by
her husband as the third luminary of Judaism, equalled in
radiance by Jesus and Spinoza only. Heine spoke of her as
the most gifted woman of the universe. Carlyle introduced
her to English readers. The historian Ranke, who knew
her in his young days, characterized her as a seeress with
the instinct of a Pythia. Georg Brandes called her the first
great modern woman in German cultural life. As late as
1907, the Swedish writer Ellen Key remarked that, except

for the works of Elizabeth Barrett Browning, no book by a woman was more indispensable to her than Rahel's *Letters*.

What was the attitude of this human magnet towards her German-Jewish roots? How did this lovable literary seismograph, that could record spiritual vibrations still imperceptible to others, react to the duality within her soul? Her glowing German patriotism was always stressed by German scholars of pre-Hitler days, but her viewpoint towards her Jewish roots was formerly glossed over. Undoubtedly, her Jewishness was a source of embarrassment for her. The first young man to whom she was engaged, Count Finkenstein, broke off his engagement with her because his aristocratic family objected to an alliance with a Jewess. Although Rahel never denied her Jewish origin, she felt it as a stain on her personality, as a stigma with which she had been branded by an infamous fate. It is true that at Paris she sometimes mentioned that she was a Jewess from Berlin, but in the Prussian capital itself she avoided all references to this humiliating fact. Only from rare passages among her voluminous correspondence can one gain a glimpse into her secret grief: the sullying of her personality by linking it to a despised people, the ignobility of her birth that placed an insuperable obstacle in the way of her complete amalgamation with the aesthetic Germans. "How loathsomely degrading, offensive, insane, and low are my surroundings, which I cannot avoid. One single defilement, a mere contact, sullies me and disturbs my nobility. And this struggle goes on for ever! All the beauty that I meet with in life passes me by as a stranger, and I am compelled to live unknown among the unworthy!"[1] To her friend David Veit, who must not be confused with his namesake, the first husband of Dorothea, she wrote in

1793 that she could never adjust herself to the fact that she
was a Jewess, and again, in 1795, as follows: "I imagine
that just as I was being thrust into this world a supernatural being plunged a dagger into my heart, with these words:
'Now, have feeling, see the world as only a few see it, be
great and noble; nor can I deprive you of restless, incessant
thought. But with one reservation: be a Jewess!' And now
my whole life is one long bleeding. By keeping calm I can
prolong it; every movement to staunch the bleeding is to
die anew, and immobility is only possible to me in death
itself."[2]

Since Judaism had at first no positive content for Rahel,
even as it had none for Henriette Herz, Dorothea Schlegel,
and hundreds of other enlightened or romantic women, she
saw no objection to baptism. She advised one of her friends,
who hesitated to change his Jewish sounding name and his
Mosaic faith, to drop his scruples: "You have no reason for
wishing to remain in the glare of the religion of your birth.
You must assimilate yourself externally as well to the great
class with whose customs, opinions, culture, and convic-
tions we are one."[3] Her own conversion to Protestantism
took place on her wedding day, September 27, 1814. She
was then forty-three and Varnhagen barely thirty.

Rahel's acceptance of Christianity was in the beginning
merely an external act, a necessary formality that had to
precede her marriage. Hardly was she converted, however,
when she commenced to treasure the Jewish heritage, which
she had until then despised. The more she immersed herself in her new faith, the more conscious did she become of
its Old Testament basis. She read and reread the Bible.
"The human soul is by nature a Christian,"[4] she remarked,
but she saw the revelations of Christianity as stemming

from the revelations of the biblical patriarchs. She was angry at the Christian rabble, which desecrated the name of Jesus by using it lightly, for she looked upon Jesus as her dearest brother, as the supreme example of humility and love, as a model which she ought to follow and imitate. She spoke of God as her friend and father, with whom she was on excellent terms. This personal relationship to the deity, which struck observers as unusual, was fundamentally biblical and reminiscent of the Jewish Bible covenants between God and man. Rahel became aware of superindividual streams that coursed through her from a distant ancestral past on to some unknown intimate future. She wrote in 1825: "Where we stem from and where we flow towards are just as many limbs of us as the limbs we have for our daily use."[5] The writings of the seventeenth-century German mystic Angelus Silesius and of the eighteenth-century French mystic Louis Claude de Saint-Martin were her favorite religious texts.

The anti-Jewish riots of 1819 caused Rahel more grief than similar agitation before her conversion.[6] She spoke of herself as an unhappy Cassandra, who foresaw the breaking of the storm but could do nothing about it. She felt that at least the Christian clergy, which prized the Old Testament, ought to speak out when synagogues were burned and Torah scrolls torn up. She wanted to know what was to happen to the mass of Jewish refugees fleeing from the incited mobs. Were they to return to the hate-filled communities to be further abused and tortured, despised and exploited, kicked around and thrown down the steps? An abominable, poisonous sentiment was sweeping the country. The rage of the normally peace-loving, moral, obedient Germans against the Jews in the prov-

inces was, in her opinion, an aftermath of the Romantic
revival of medievalism. Berlin was still calm. Apparently
the rabble feared to attack the native Jews, some of whom
had seen service at the front and many of whom were either
baptized or married to Christians. But the continuing
agitation was none too pleasant. The linking of politics
and religion was bad. The Jews had made this mistake in
their ancient theocratic kingdom. The same mistake was
now being made by those European monarchies that had
a state religion.

Rahel's early dissatisfaction with her Jewish origin gave
way at the end of her life to a happy acceptance of her
ancestry. Five days before her death in 1833, she referred
to herself as a refugee from Egypt and Palestine, who had
found help and affection in Germany. "With supreme delight do I think of my origin and this entire interconnection
of fate through which the oldest memories of the human
race are bound up with the newest happenings, and through
which the furthest reaches of time and space are linked.
That which for so long a period of my life seemed my greatest disgrace, my bitterest pain and misfortune, namely to
have been born a Jewess, I would not now dispense with
at any price."[7]

Varnhagen von Ense, Rahel's husband, related many
instances of her quiet intercession in behalf of Jews and
especially of her gentle influence in weaning her German
aristocratic friends from early ingrained contempt for her
former coreligionists, so that association on terms of mutual respect and genuine equality might be possible. Once
she even induced Prussian officers to rescind their declaration that Jews were not *satisfaktionsfähig*. This expression

signified that Jews, being devoid of honor, could not seek amends on the field of honor and that therefore their challenges to duels need not be accepted or seriously considered. This change of attitude on the part of Prussian officers took place after the notorious public scandal centering about the poet and aristocrat Achim von Arnim, who was beaten up by the Jew Moritz Itzig.

It was in the year 1811, soon after Arnim's marriage to Bettina, the sister of his poetic collaborator and friend, Klemens Brentano, and a poetess in her own right, that the Romantic poet had his memorable encounter with Jews. Among the Berlin salons frequented by Bettina was that of the wealthy Jewess, Sara Levy. Arnim, who boasted of his hatred of Israelites and who often entertained his companions with anti-Jewish gibes, was of course never invited to Jewish homes and never accompanied his wife on visits where he would have to associate with the despised creatures. One day, however, when a splendid musical festival took place at Madame Levy's and Bettina was among the many guests, it suddenly dawned upon Arnim that he would like to go there to call for his wife. Without further ado and without bothering to change his street attire — since he was not going to an Aryan home — the uninvited poet appeared among the numerous elegantly dressed men and women; and without a word of explanation, apology, or polite greeting, he gave vent to his caprices, insulted those present with inappropriate jokes, and spoiled the entire elaborately prepared evening. When he finally retired, there was general muttering among the guests at his horrible behavior. Madame Levy had been mocked and disgraced in her own home. Her nephew, Moritz Itzig, undertook to act for her. He wrote a letter to Arnim calling his

attention, in serious and carefully chosen words, to the
impropriety of his conduct. Instead of ending the unpleasant matter with an apology, Arnim sent a scornful reply.
Thereupon Itzig challenged him to a duel. This was too
much for the aristocrat: the brazenness of a "Jew-boy"
teaching manners to a Prussian officer and demanding
satisfaction! Arnim called together his comrades in the
officers' quarters, showed the challenge, and obtained from
them written statements that a duel with a Jew was un-
thinkable and not provided for in the code of honor. This
document, abounding in arrogance and further insults, he
forwarded to Itzig along with his own derisive reply, which
stated how sorry he was that he could not spare the Jew any
insults, but that a Jew must learn humility and submission
to the necessary laws of the universe which made one person a pariah and another a nobleman; the Jew-boy was still
young, however, and could still improve; meanwhile Arnim
wished to help him along by dictating to him by means
of this letter an assortment of slaps, strokes of the cane,
and whip-lashes. Itzig, in righteous indignation, warned
Arnim that, if the latter was too ignoble and too cowardly
to cross swords, he would have to expect chastisement with
the cane. Arnim laughed at this threat from the gutter of
society, strutted about his usual haunts as a superior being,
and considered the incident over. One afternoon, however,
Itzig appeared before him at a Berlin bathing pavilion and
in the presence of many witnesses began to beat him with
the promised cane. The tall and powerful officer cried for
help and was saved by the spectators. Itzig, upon being
overpowered and apprehended, explained that he had no
other recourse since the nobleman had persisted in insulting him and had refused to duel with him. Soon thereafter,

Arnim, in an attempt to save his tarnished honor, turned the case over to the court, invoking its protection against the "insane Jew-boy." The court, after due deliberation, found no trace of insanity in Itzig's action, but of course had to punish the assailant, although it recognized extenuating circumstances and considerable provocation. The officers' corps felt disgraced by the actions of Arnim. They, too, now looked upon him as a coward and avoided him. He retired to his estate in the province, while Moritz Itzig, upon being released, remained in the Prussian capital.

In the circle of Rahel, the Arnim affair was frequently discussed and the brilliant hostess took every occasion to stress to the Prussian officers who visited her the injustice of their attitude, as expressed in the memorandum they gave to Arnim. She pointed out that their declaration concerning the Jews' innate lack of honor was anything but honorable. Every individual, Jew or Gentile, who was ready to answer with his life for his principles, must be recognized as a man of honor. Whoever offered to fight a duel was worthy of having his challenge accepted, no matter what his racial origin. But, even if officers, because of their exaggerated pride, held to the erroneous opinion that they could not fight with a Jew, then they must be especially careful not to hurt his feelings. It was unchivalrous, ignoble, common, and vile to deride and insult a person whom they considered beneath them. When one Prussian officer, named Barnekow, who was convinced by Rahel's arguments, asked her what he could do about the declaration, which he had already previously endorsed, she advised him: "Sit down and write to Moritz Itzig, you have realized that the memorandum you had given to Herr von Arnim was based on erroneous reasoning and that far from maintaining any

longer the opinion that a nobleman need not duel with a
Jew, you yourself were now ready to offer him satisfaction
with weapons of his choice for your previous declaration,
in so far as it conveyed an insult to him." Barnekow followed Rahel's advice and wrote this letter. Moritz Itzig,
surprised and moved by this offer, expressed his gratitude
and stated that a letter with such sentiments was satisfaction of the finest type. Barnekow's example was followed
by others and Jews were accepted as *satisfaktionsfähig*.
In 1813 Itzig volunteered to serve his Prussian fatherland
in the war against Napoleon and died a hero's death in
battle. In contrast to this Jew, Achim von Arnim continued to stay at home on his Prussian estate, an object
of universal scorn and pity throughout the war and in the
years following. An epigram on the death of the Jew at
Lützen and the life of the poet beside the warm stove cir-
culated in Berlin: *Itzig und Arnim seien beide geblieben,
jener by Lützen, dieser hinter dem Ofen.* Arnim remained to
the end of his days one of the bitterest foes of the Jews, in
contrast to his wife Bettina.

Varnhagen, who related this incident in his memoirs,
was himself without any anti-Jewish bias. Under Rahel's
daily influence, he gained sympathetic insight into the
Jewish soul and acquired lasting immunity to the prejudice rampant in his circle of diplomats. Astonishment
and admiration possessed him when he contemplated the
vitality and endurance of this remarkable people, a people
which gave titanic figures to the stream of culture, and
which, in his opinion, was daily still contributing thousands of talented baptized and unbaptized individuals,
without in any way depleting its own vitality. Thus

awakened by Rahel, he held that the Jews were in truth
God's chosen people, a unique phenomenon in universal
history; the progenitors of two religions, one for themselves and the other for the entire world; a people whose
history was sacred to Christians and Mohammedans,
and whose literature was translated into all languages;
a people so gifted that their very oppressors and torturers
sang their psalms, honored their patriarchs, and elevated
one of their condemned to the rank of a God.[8]

It pained Varnhagen to see how the contempt everywhere
visited upon Jews, despite their high achievements, undermined their self-respect and lessened their self-esteem. An
experience at Homburg, a summer resort near Frankfort on
the Main, revealed to him to what degree of slavishness a
Jew might degenerate under the influence of an unhealthy
environment. Wanting to rent a room, he casually asked
the renting-agent, a Jewess, whether the landlord's wife was
not of Jewish blood. "God preserve us! You don't have to
be afraid!" came the quick answer. The expression "God
preserve us!", which a Jewess in his presence felt obliged to
use about her own people and faith, made Varnhagen aware
of the vile pressure under which Jews were forced to carry
on their daily work and which they came to accept as a matter of course. He rebuked the renting-agent and assured her
that he would have been pleasantly surprised, if she had
confirmed his suspicion. This attitude of Rahel's husband
must have been quite a shock to the woman, who in her
business dealings with her clients had learned by bitter experience that these were rarely pleased to associate with Jews
when on vacation. Especially was this aversion true of
Christian clients of Jewish origin.

Varnhagen often commented on the irresistible desire of

German Jews to flee from their religion and their past. His
diary contained the following entry under the date of October 20, 1842: "The King was asked what he really wanted
of the Jews. He answered: I wish them well in everything,
but I also want them to feel themselves as Jews. These words
are a key to a great deal: — I was asked, what the Jews
really wanted. I answered: to leave them time to become
Christians."[9]

Flight from Judaism, which set in at the close of the
eighteenth century, showed no sign of abating through much
of the nineteenth. A veritable epidemic of baptism swept
the Jewish communities of Germany. As early as 1810, the
Prussian king had to take steps to slow down the rate of con-
versions, which threatened to deprive the royal treasury of
valuable special taxes levied upon Jews. A decree was issued
forbidding pastors to baptize Jews, unless these could produce a police statement certifying to the seriousness of their
intentions. The procession to the cross was begun by the
financial aristocracy and the intellectuals. The lower bourgeoisie followed. The will to complete assimilation was so
strong among the emancipated Jewish youth that not even
threatened disinheritance prevented sons from embracing
Christianity and thus meeting their fellow Germans on an
equal footing. Many a father had his children baptized
during their minority, though he himself might refrain from
submitting to this rite. Baptism was not regarded as apostasy
but as a corollary of assimilation. The Jewish father of Felix
Mendelssohn-Batholdy explained to his children that he
raised them as Christians because this religious form was
common to most educated people and hence a social necessity. He himself hesitated to desert the faith of his ancestors,
but was urged to do so by his brother-in-law Salomon, who

had taken on the name of Bartholdy at the time of his conversion: "You say, you owe it to the memory of your father — do you really think you did something wicked when you gave your children the religion which you regard as better for them? It is rather a form of homage which you and all of us are rendering to the efforts of your father in behalf of true enlightenment. He would perhaps have acted as you did for your children and I for my person. One can remain true to an oppressed, persecuted religion, and can even force it on one's children with the prospect of a lifelong martyrdom — as long as one regards it as the sole means of salvation. But to do so, when one no longer believes this, is barbarism."[10] When Dorothea Schlegel, in her missionary zeal, suggested to her sister, Henriette Mendelssohn, the desirability of joining the Catholic Church, the latter at first flared up in anger, but did not long persist in her indignant mood. While the Protestant composer Felix Mendelssohn-Bartholdy wrote Church music, little suspecting that it would one day be banned in his native Germany as non-Aryan music, his aunts vied with each other in their devotion to Catholicism. Henriette lamented in her will that God did not deem her sufficiently worthy to effect the conversion of all her brothers to the only blessed Church, but she hoped that Christ would listen to her prayer and shed the light of his grace upon them. She begged that on her tombstone there be engraved her baptismal name, Maria, and that there be erected for her a cross with the words: "You have redeemed me, O God of Truth!"

In contrast to the Jewish salons, where conversion to Christianity was assumed to be fashionable and desirable, it is interesting to call attention to the attitude of Bettina von Arnim, the most talented authoress among the Berlin

women of non-Jewish origin. As the sister of Klemens
Brentano and wife of Achim von Arnim, two of the bitterest
foes of German Jewry, she yet managed to retain a sober
approach to the Jewish question, as can be judged from her
dialogue on the Frankfort Ghetto in her book *Gespräche mit
Dämonen*, published in 1852 but recording impressions that
reached back to 1808.[11]

Bettina held that it was not wise to proselytize the Jews,
for they were more than merely a religious community. They
were a nation. Their religion was deeply rooted in their
psychic structure. It was the last pillar of their independence
as a group. It was their will to survive. It assured their
national existence in exile. The synagogue or temple was
their resting place in their journeying as fugitives through the
wide world. The bitter distress that the dominant religion —
the religion of love — imposed upon them could not consume
their marrow. They still adhered to their past and regarded
the Christians as usurpers. Let oppression be removed from
them and they would become a healthy force in society. Let
human rights be restored to them and they would enter into
free competition with the Christians to usher in the golden
age on earth. Jewish children must be given access to all
avenues of knowledge and allowed to follow all scientific and
philosophic pursuits. They must be permitted to learn
riding, dancing, music. The brighter side of Jewish character
would then come to the fore instead of the darker. The
beautiful sunlight would again stream through the Jewish
soul and waken it to sublimity. Surely, the Jew was not
contemptible who on the eve of the Sabbath shook off the
filth of the week's work on his doorstep and entered his house
as a priest, invoking God's blessing upon his family and his
people. Surely, scorn should not be visited upon the Jew who

remained faithful to his stern creed in exile, amidst privations and servitude. The Christian was more contemptible who incited the children and the unthinking rabble against mankind's oldest tribe.

Similar sentiments were voiced by Prince von Pückler-Muskau, a Silesian aristocrat who frequented Jewish and non-Jewish salons and whose opinions carried considerable weight in literary circles during the Metternich era. Commenting in 1834 on the discriminatory treatment still meted out to the Jews of his native land, he exclaimed: "I know not what the feelings and opinions of those who term themselves Christians may be upon this subject, but for myself I can truly assert that, since I arrived at maturity, I never conversed with a well-informed Jew without experiencing shame and humiliation, or without being impressed with the conviction that we have no right to despise the articles of their faith, but that we have afforded them too much reason to doubt the charity of ours."[12] Pückler-Muskau expressed veneration for the English because they had in the preceding year emancipated the Jews of Britain. He hailed this step as a glorious token of the advanced state of English intellect and culture, as a splendid victory of justice and humanity, and as a proud example to other nations. "Hail to thee, noble, illustrious people! How numerous are the clouds of error which have vanished before thy enlightening influence! And now thou hast laid the ax to the root of that remnant of barbarism — the persecution of a numerous class of our fellow-creatures, which has so long existed to the eternal disgrace of civilized Europe!"[13] As an Hegelian disciple, Pückler-Muskau recorded his faith that the progress of events towards a more logical world-order could not be arrested indefinitely and that the nineteenth century, which trampled in the dust prejudice upon prejudice, would soon sweep away persistent anti-Jewish laws and usher in the empire of reason.

In surveying the attitude towards the German-Jewish duality during the post-Napoleonic generation, it thus becomes apparent that writers of non-Jewish origin, such as Varnhagen von Ense, Bettina von Arnim, and Prince Pückler-Muskau, displayed a deeper sympathy and a better understanding of the tragic aspects of the problem than many of their contemporaries of Jewish stock. The latter fled from Judaism. They hurled themselves madly, hysterically, into the arms of an overidealized German culture. They wanted to be Germans, nothing but Germans. Their dangerous experiment unleashed forces that raged with undiminished intensity throughout the nineteenth and twentieth centuries.

LUDWIG BÖRNE, 1786–1837

Chapter II

LUDWIG BÖRNE

LUDWIG BÖRNE may be regarded as the symbol of a certain type of emancipated German Jew during the first generation of the nineteenth century.

Born in 1786 in the ghetto of Frankfort, he was subjected in his childhood, boyhood, and youth to all the degrading restrictions imposed upon his coreligionists by a political and legal system that had not yet broken with medieval inequalities and religious intolerance. In his early manhood he profited from the abolition of these ancient disabilities by an enlightened regime that stood under Napoleonic influence. He found himself accepted as a citizen and an equal by his compatriots and appointed to an official position by the government of his native town. In his mature years, after the defeat of Napoleon, he had to give up his position because of the restoration of the old order and had to face the successful re-imposition of degrading distinctions between Jew and German. To escape being hurled back into the ghetto, after having moved about as a free individual amidst the German intellectual élite, Börne accepted baptism in 1818. But soon he was made to realize that this act merely removed him from the Jewish community with which he wished to have nothing in common, while at the same time it did not bring him any nearer to the German community to which he felt a real inner attachment. In his last years he could no longer hide from himself the insight that his affection for Germany was not being reciprocated, and he transferred his hopes for a more amicable relationship between Germans and Jews to a none-too-distant better future that would dawn after the victory of an inevitable political revolution. Only death, which came in 1837, saved him from complete disillusionment and from the final recognition that his faith in Germany was misplaced.

The experience of Börne is typical of his entire generation of German Jews. His very name bears testimony to the shifting emphasis that he placed upon the two souls within his breast. The Jewish child was known as Loeb Baruch. The young man, who sought to enter into western culture and to retain at the same time his Jewish heritage, preferred the name of Louis Baruch. The mature individual, who desired the complete effacement of his Jewish background and complete acceptance within the German fold, chose the name Ludwig Börne. The final failure of his efforts to woo Germany is evident in his death in exile and his burial on French soil.

When Loeb Baruch was born, the Jews of Frankfort were still restricted in their residence to a single street, the *Judengasse*, afterwards known as the Börnestrasse. In this narrow lane, the Jews were locked in after sunset on weekdays and as early as four o'clock on Sundays. On certain holidays and festive public occasions, they often had to remain indoors during the day and were let out only in the evening. A strict watch was kept at the ghetto gate. The boy Baruch is said to have remarked: "I don't go outside, simply because the soldier over there is stronger than I am!" When high dignitaries passed through Frankfort, arrangements were made so that their eyes would not be polluted by the sight of Jews.

Thus, at the coronation of Emperor Leopold I, the Jewish leaders, who wished to pay homage to him, were arrested and kept under a police guard during the ceremonies. On walks outside of the ghetto wall, Jews were not permitted to use the footpath but had to share the gutter with the vehicles. No Jew was admitted to any scientific, artistic, or cultural society. Even the most prominent Jew in this city of Rothschild had to doff his hat to any street urchin who cried: *Mach Mores, Jud!* — "Make your obeisance, Jew!"

Prince von Bülow, German Chancellor during the first decade of the twentieth century, narrated in his *Memoirs* that his father often walked through the streets of Frankfort with Baron Mayer Anselm Rothschild and that the latter would occasionally tell queer stories about his childhood, when he and his parents were still locked up every night in the *Judengasse*, and how one day, as he begged to be let in just when the gates were being closed, the sentry seized him by the ear and in language none too polite warned him that this was the last time the "Jew-boy" would be allowed in so late.

In one of his satiric aphorisms, Börne listed some of the regulations that the government of Frankfort kept in force ostensibly for the benefit of its Jews. "On Sundays, they were not allowed to leave their street, lest they be beaten up by drunkards. Before their twenty-fifth year they were not allowed to marry, so that their offspring might be strong and healthy. On holidays they could not take a walk outside of the gate before six o'clock in the afternoon, for fear that the excessive heat of the sun might harm them. They were prevented from using the public sidewalks and were forced to betake themselves through the fields, so that their agricultural talent might be stimulated. If a Jew crossed a street

and a Christian called out: *Mach Mores, Jud!* the former
had to take off his hat and through this courtesy cement
more closely the love between the two religious groups.
Certain streets had to be avoided by Jews, probably because
of the poor pavement."[1]

During the Napoleonic period, the Jews of Frankfort
obtained their freedom from civic disabilities, but not entirely as a gift from an enlightened government. The sum
of 440,000 gulden was collected from them as the price for
guaranteeing them the right of civil equality, supposedly an
inalienable right of human beings, according to political
theorists of the Enlightenment. But hardly had Napoleon
been defeated and hardly had the sound of the retreating
French artillery died away, when the cry immediately arose:
"Jewish insolence must be curbed!" Before the peace conference at Vienna had a chance to pass upon the matter,
Jewish rights began to be whittled down. In all the drafts
of the projected Frankfort constitution, it was assumed that
Jews were no longer to have the same civil rights as others.
The Jewish community thereupon sent a delegation to
Vienna to complain to Metternich. Börne's father was a
member of the delegation, but Börne himself lacked faith
in the efficacy of legal memoranda and paper petitions.
"Good God!" he exclaimed, "For thirty years a sea of
human blood has flowed in behalf of truth and justice, and
is it still necessary to bring proof of one's righteous possession
of the sacred inheritance of humanity, as though possession
of a disputed cabbage field were up for discussion?"[2]

In 1819 Börne published an essay in defense of the Jews,
entitled *Für die Juden*. He had faith in the good will of the
Germans. Without justifying their anti-Jewish attitude, he
tried to understand it and to explain it as a pardonable

weakness. He pointed out that the Germans, who had suffered much at the hands of Napoleon, hated everything the French brought. And just as one scorns the good which hostile hands offer, so Germans scorned the improvements that the French legal code brought to the fatherland. Since the Jews owed their civil liberties to the French, the Jews were looked at askance as friends of the former invaders and it was therefore perfectly natural for the feeling to arise among the unthinking populace that the Jews should not be permitted to retain benefits bestowed upon them by Germany's foes. This pardonable prejudice on the part of the masses could be overcome by clarifying the issue and transferring it from the realm of feeling to the realm of reflection.

Börne therefore undertook an appeal to reason. He reminded his readers that in former unenlightened centuries Jews and heretics were burned because of mistaken religious zeal but that now in an enlightened age, when no government dared to say that it persecuted the Jews on account of their faith, what justification was there for continuing ancient malice? Formerly the idea prevailed that Jews were not admitted to heaven and hence should not be tolerated on earth, but now that they were no longer denied admission to heaven, why were efforts continued to annihilate them from the earth? "The most shameless hypocrisy is practiced toward the Jews; false assertions are made with such boldness that even well-intentioned people are deceived, because they cannot imagine that anyone should want to deceive them so brazenly. — The people will discover that they were designated as jailors of the Jews, because jailors as well as the jailed may not leave prison. The only difference is one gate more or less, but neither group is really free."[3]

Börne called upon the commoners, irrespective of religious affiliation, to form a united front against the rulers and the privileged aristocrats and patricians. Religion should not be a barrier between human beings. According to him, the very word denotes, etymologically, a binding together. Religion stands for love and reconciliation. Were all men equally wise, equally gifted, of equal sentiments, religion would be unnecessary. Religion is the binding together of what is diverse, the eternity of what is transitory, the fixation of what is unstable. Religion pardons guilt and dissolves sin in universal radiance. But, alas, what have human beings made of it! "A bloody stream flows down eighteen centuries and on its banks dwells Christianity. How have they desecrated the holy of holies! Religion became a weapon in rapacious or treacherous hands. How have they abased the God of love and misused his teaching as a justification for their tyranny and their avaricious morality!"[4]

Börne confessed that he was sensitive on the subject of Jews, but he denied that the slightest spark of hatred against Christianity glimmered in his breast. He was no less ill at ease when people praised him because of his origin than when they reproached him or pardoned him for it. He wanted to be thought of as an individual apart from his Jewishness and was chagrined when his utterances were referred to the hereditary strain within his personality. His sensitiveness cropped out when he, the apostle of freedom, wanted to limit the freedom of comedians to caricature his coreligionists. In reviewing a Frankfort performance of a successful farce, entitled *Unser Verkehr*, which sought to attain comic effects by ridiculing Jewish traits, Börne justified the objections raised by the Jewish community to this play. He analyzed the apparently logical argument that, since comedy aims to amuse and since the nobility, various professions, and even the clergy are often subjects for farces, the Jews had no justification for objecting. He pointed out that the analogy was fallacious. A dramatist seeks to arouse laughter by ridiculing not the nobility as a class but only certain excesses of aristocratic pride, not the lawyers as a professional group but legal quibbling, not the clergy but certain clerical foibles. Nobody in the audience will generalize from any funny idiosyncrasy and as a result hold the entire group in disrepute. But when Jewish mannerisms are brought on the stage and the whole play is devoted to ridiculing these mannerisms, then the audience does not merely laugh and amuse itself. It carries home the impressions it received on such an occasion and imputes these weaknesses to all Jews and more particularly to the nearest Jewish resident or competitor. After listening to a narration of evil traits, supposedly characteristic of Jews of different ages and countries, the Frankfort burgher projected these traits upon the head of the particular Jew who happened to be close at hand.

If the stage must deal with Jews — and Börne was not at all happy at the thought — then tragedy was a far more appropriate vehicle. Richard Cumberland's drama, *The Jew*, successfully performed for many years both in England and Germany, furnished him with a good illustration. Börne reviewed this tragedy rather favorably. He pondered on the strange experiences that Cumberland must have gone through before he could attain to a sympathetic understanding of this people. "How many thousands of unfortunates must Cumberland have seen suffering until he could suspect the immense *Judenschmerz*, a rich dark treasure handed down from generation to generation, before he could discern

the sorrows that are silent because they are unaccustomed
to find a listening ear? How many thousands must he himself have unwittingly condemned before he finally found a
single innocent Jew to portray sympathetically to an audience?"[5]

An ordinance of the Frankfort Senate, setting aside June
27, 1819, as a memorial day commemorating the great conflagration of a century earlier, offered Börne a welcome
opportunity to attack a government that made distinctions
between its inhabitants on the basis of religion. In an article,
entitled *Zwangs-Gottesdienst*, he noted that for the Christians
the Senate of the Free City suggested the holding of divine
services, while for the Jews it commanded memorial prayers
in the synagogue. He called attention to the different tone
used in addressing both sections of the population. The
Jews were to engage, not in divine services, but only in
prayers. Moreover, these prayers were not suggested but
ordered. With considerable emotion, he exclaimed: "Ordered
prayers! Do you heed them, Father of Light? Will you not
know how to distinguish between the warm, fervent prayers
of the heart and the prayers commanded by the police? Do
you not surmise the bitter curse of the oppressed, which they
sugarcoat with blessings because of fear of the oppressors?
A Frankfort Jew is to remember lovingly the decayed bones
of his foes, who a century ago, when alive, met with misfortune! He is to remember with brotherly affection the
people who slandered him, mistreated him, trod him under
foot! He is to recall the time when he had no fatherland and
when his birthplace was more foreign to him than any foreign
land! Does not the description of that fire state that daily
a hundred men — artisans, peasants, soldiers, and Jews —
had to work at the scene of the fire to remove the wreckage

and to clear the ground, and that the Jewish master-builders received strict orders to draft as many as possible for this work? And the memory of that time should fill a Jew with benevolence? He should lament the misfortune of those whose descendants still persecute him today and degrade him as much as they can? O poor fatherland in which such things occur! For, hate the Jews or love them, oppress them or elevate them, be good to them or persecute them: all this is left to your caprice. But I tell you one thing: see how far you get with the freedom of Germany so long as this freedom is not to be for all."[6]

The theme that the freedom of all is inextricably bound up with freedom for the Jew recurs throughout Börne's polemic writings. He opposed all efforts to isolate the Jews from others. He refused to acknowledge the existence of a Jewish problem as distinct from the general problem of human emancipation. When God created the world, he created man and woman, but not master and slave, Christian and Jew, rich and poor. Hence, our love should embrace all mankind, without differentiating between serf and lord, poor and rich, Jew and Christian.

In his student days, in 1807, when Börne applied for a passport and the clerk wrote in the document: *Juif de Francfort*, Börne gnashed his teeth in helpless rage. In later years he attacked with equal vehemence Jewish religious separatists like Gabriel Riesser, who wrote a pamphlet lauding him, and Christian anti-Semites like Dr. Holst, the author of a vitriolic pamphlet defaming him. He held that it was, on the one hand, absurd on the part of the anti-Semites to divide the world into two parts and to call one Judaism and the other non-Judaism, to regard the latter as

terra firma, on which flowers blossomed, birds sang, brooks
murmured and harmless shepherds spent idyllic days, and
to regard the former as a tempestuous sea where sharks
preyed and hypocritical crocodiles deceived. It was, on the
other hand, equally absurd for Jewish nationalists to speak
of a special mission of the Jews and to insist that their preservation as a people was necessary for the fulfilling of their
task. He felt that the Jewish mission had been accomplished
long ago. It was to teach the world cosmopolitanism. The
Jewish nation perished in the most beautiful and enviable
manner: it was merged in universality. The Jews did indeed
dominate the world in accordance with God's promise unto
them. They dominated through their offspring Christianity,
this beautiful butterfly that emerged from the ugly caterpillar
of ancient Judaism. The Jews were the teachers of internationalism and the entire world was their school. They
were the apostles of freedom, and freedom could not come
into complete realization as long as there were nations.

If only the Jews were not continually being jarred and
mistreated, they would quickly assimilate and disappear
from the face of the earth. "You ask me what you are to do?
You will find the answer in an old moral tale for children, the
fable of the sun, the hurricane, and the wanderer. The
hurricane and the sun disputed. Each claimed to be mightier
than the other. The hurricane tried to remove by force the
coat of a traveler. In vain! The fiercer it raged, the tighter
did the traveler pull the coat about him. And now the sun
came with its light and its mildness. Thereupon the wanderer took off his coat. The Jews are such wanderers;
orthodoxy is their coat; you are the hurricane; and the sun —
will now radiate in America."[7]

America, Börne felt, will solve the Jewish question and

point the way for Europe. America will make assimilation desirable. America will be the melting-pot of nations. There the Jew may lose that sensitiveness which he cannot escape in Frankfort; for in this German city he was forever reminded of his origin and the word Jew was the inseparable shadow of all events, all relations, all conversations, every joy, and every discomfort. If a Jewish businessman suspended payment, the court emphasized that it was a Jewish firm that failed to meet its obligations. If a Jew was a doctor or a lawyer, the directory listed him as a physician or an attorney of Jewish nationality. If a Jew stole and one inquired after the thief, the answer was invariably: it was a Jew. If a Jew excelled in any field, the ill-natured remarked: he remained a Jew all the same; while the good-natured commented: he reflected honor upon his nationality. If a Jew went to a tailor and ordered a coat, the tailor never failed to mention that Jacob or Isaac had had a similar coat made. If a Jewess bought flowers, the gardener told her that a customer by the name of Esther had bought a rosebush from him a few days ago. If a Jew died, or was born, or was married, the gazette recording the event always separated the Jewish cradles, coffins, and wedding bells from those of the Christian.

This separation irked Börne. All men are born free and equal, and therefore no one was entitled to any superior advantage of any kind simply because of the accident of birth — neither the aristocrat in his relation to the commoner nor the Christian in his relation to the Jew. "I do not love the Jew or the Christian because he is a Jew or a Christian; I love them because they are human beings and born to freedom. Freedom is the soul of my pen, until my quill is dulled or my hand paralyzed."[8] He pitied the

German rabble that comforted itself for a miserable existence in the cellar of society with the thought that there was
still a sub-cellar in which Jews dwelt. He found no less
arrogance in this attitude than in the aristocrats' arrogance
towards plebeians. But the masses will learn better in the
course of time. The spirit of man is always progressing,
despite the barricades of stupidity. The human heart is
constantly being ennobled, despite the example of the degenerate. The new persecution of Jews is not the revival
of old hates. It is but the last flicker of the flame of hate
before dying out completely. Many absurd laws have yielded
to the march of enlightenment. "A time will come when in
Hamburg it will seem as ridiculous that formerly a Jew could
not become mayor of the city on account of his religion as
it now seems ridiculous that as late as the reign of Frederick
the Great a Jew had to wear his dagger on the right. — I
hope that I shall live to see the day when even in a Hanseatic
town one will not be allowed to write an inciting or stupid
book against the Jews without being committed to a prison
or a madhouse."[9]

Börne suspected an economic motive behind much anti-
Semitic agitation. He observed that writers who incite
against the Jews begin by rising to dizzy moral heights; they
try to prove that sun, moon, and stars participate in the
Jewish question. Soon afterwards, however, they tumble
from these heights and fall into a barrel of sugar, a banker's
office, a drygoods store. After speaking of death and immortality, of man's destiny, of theocracy, of ethics, and
after showing that Judaism is an atmospheric poison embracing the entire earth, they end by remarking that the
air is, after all, different in each place and they undertake

to defend a special anti-Jewish ordinance not for every city
but for a particular city and for a particular street in that
city. In this one street Jews may live, in another they may
not. In this street they may live on the right side but not on
the left. On this right side they may build houses but not
corner houses. In houses that have two exits, they may
trade at one door but not at the other; at this door they may
deal with goods of one kind but not with goods of another
kind — and thus the thick clump of unreason is cut up into
a thousand splinters. It is easy enough to prove that the more
Jews are restricted in their trade, the more their Christian
competitors will profit. This may be desirable from the
point of view of a section of the population, but it is still no
proof of the justice of the anti-Jewish cause. "You complain
that all the Jews devote themselves to usury and yet you
hinder the spiritual development of those who want to escape
from usury. I will not be brushed aside, I insist upon an
answer: tell me, gentlemen of Frankfort, why are only four
Jewish physicians to be permitted to practice and why no
Jewish lawyers whatsoever? Please answer me: do the Jewish
physicians write their prescriptions in Hebrew? Do they heal
skin diseases according to the rules of the Old Testament?
Do they charge usurious bills to their patients? Don't the
Jewish lawyers know the legal code or do they practice according to the Talmud?"[10] Börne branded as a superstition
the widely held impression that the Talmud influenced the
conduct of the average Jew. The entire Jewish youth, inso-
far as he himself had come in contact with it, knew little of
the Talmud and most certainly did not live in accordance
with its precepts. In thirty years, the Jews, in his opinion,
would recall the Talmud only to laugh at its contents.
There was no moral justification whatsoever for anti-Jewish

legislation. There was at most an economic justification in the eyes of some Germans. Rothschild was the symbol of Jewish wealth. Rothschild, by his very prominence on the European stock exchange and by his financial assistance to the reactionary states, rendered a complete understanding and cooperation between the Jewish and the non-Jewish masses more difficult. If a revolution were to break out, the liberty-loving masses would look upon the Jews as allies of the oppressive governments, but these governments would do nothing to protect the Jews. On the contrary, the Jews would be turned over to the hate of the populace. They would be sacrificed, just as in India an ox is sacrificed to the boa constrictor. After the snake has had its fill and cannot move, it is then killed. Similarly, the Jews would be the first to be hurled into the ravenous jaws of the coming revolution.

Though Börne adhered to his belief that the inevitable political revolution would ultimately bring about the complete dissolution of the Jews as a minority group within the German cultural body, it dawned upon him that the transition period would take a greater toll of his coreligionists than of others. Without allowing himself to become embittered against the Germans, he began to doubt that even the noble masses would be very noble in their treatment of Jews. In the last years of his life he questioned whether a democratic Germany, which would grant civil equality to all human beings as an inalienable right, would be so very happy to include Jews, who were, after all, human beings. "It is bad for the Jews that in this matter as in everything else the German is ruled by his heart. Even to be just, a German must love. But it is a fact that the Jews are not loved."[11]

The fear that the Jews would not be justly treated even in a more progressive state led Börne to overcome his psychological aversion to the group from which he had for a time deemed himself emancipated. After the Revolution of 1830, he wrote that, in spite of his feeling towards his co-religionists, he had always come to their defense. In 1832, five years before his death, he referred to his origin with greater pride than in his younger days: "I would not be worthy of enjoying the light of the sun, if I repaid with vile muttering the supreme grace which God bestowed upon me in letting me become both a German and a Jew — just because of ridicule, which I always despised, or of pain, for which I have long since consoled myself. No, I have come to prize my undeserved fortune in being at the same time a German and a Jew, so that I can strive for all the virtues of the Germans without sharing any of their faults. Yes, because I was born a slave, I love freedom more than you. Yes, because I know the meaning of servitude, I understand freedom better than you. Yes, because I was born to no fatherland, I yearn for a fatherland more fervently than you. And because my native soil was no larger than the *Judengasse* and beyond its locked gate foreign territory began for me, therefore neither a city nor a province suffices me as a fatherland."[12]

Börne's increasing disillusionment with his fellow Germans led him to an ever higher evaluation of Jewish contributions and Jewish possibilities. Despite his hatred of chauvinism and of claims of national superiority, he goaded the Germans with the rebuke: "You are thirty million Germans and amount to about thirty as far as your influence in the world is concerned; give us thirty million Jews and the world would

not count beside them. You have deprived the Jews of air;
but this saved them from putrefaction. You have strewn
their heart with the salt of hate; but this has preserved it
fresh. You have locked them up all winter long in a deep
cellar and stuffed up the cellar hole with dung; but you yourself, exposed to the frost, are half frozen. When spring
comes, we shall see who blossoms earlier, the Jew or the
Christian."[13] Börne even found some justification for the
small part that the Jews played in the Revolution of 1830.
If the Jews had learned to be careful before taking sides in a
political struggle, no matter how ideal the cause, it was due
to the fact that they once did take up arms in a so-called
War of Liberation, the war against Napoleon, and that,
when they returned as victors, they were not given the
promised equality but were rather deprived of what rights
they still possessed. Börne remembered the experiences of
his own family. While his own brother marched with the
Frankfort volunteers and while his own mother worried day
and night, Börne lost his job as police actuary because he
was a Jew. "A Jew may be stupid once, but he is rarely
stupid twice."[14]

Börne was tired of wooing Germany. Attacks leveled
against his radical principles would have spurred him on to
champion them even more vigorously. But, alas! the attacks
were directed not against his principles but against his origin.
His conversion to Lutheranism had not helped him to escape
being constantly reminded that he was a Jew. Nor could the
Jews escape paying for the fact that he once belonged to
them. The pamphleteer Eduard Meyer attacked them as
the people of Börne. The Jewish religious leader Gabriel
Riesser felt called upon to reply, even though Börne was an

apostate from Judaism, and this reply was held up by the censor for many months before it finally appeared in 1832 under the title *Börne und die Juden*. In the year after his conversion, Börne had scoffed at the doctrine broached by an anti-Semitic specialist that Jewish blood needed for its cleansing a threefold filtration and that only the grandchild of a baptized Jew could be accepted within the German fold, provided that this descendant married into a Christian family. But in his last years Börne did not laugh at such absurdities. He was irritated, hurt, embittered. When Wolfgang Menzel, who had been his ally in a common struggle against Goethe, turned upon him in the course of a Jew-baiting crusade, Börne answered with a vitriolic diatribe, entitled *Menzel der Franzosenfresser*, in which his disappointment with Germany was clearly evident. Nations were, in his opinion, no less egoistic than individuals and generally cared little for the suffering of others. Perhaps the Jews would have to wait for the disappearance of nations before they themselves would be allowed to disappear and to forget their past.

Börne was definitely disillusioned. There is, however, no evidence to warrant the belief that this final disillusionment would have led him beyond mere despair or that he would ever have reconciled himself to the desirability of the continued existence of the Jews as a separate entity among the world's peoples. Until his dying day he remained an assimilationist and an internationalist.

Börne began by assuming the possibility and practicability of a complete fusion of Germans and Jews. His baptism was his personal contribution in this direction. It was to remove even the religious barrier to such a fusion.

But before long he encountered the stern refusal of the
Germans to accept the ardent wooing of Jews, baptized or
unbaptized. He ended by hoping for Jewish assimilation
to the mass of humanity after the disappearance of individual nations. America, the melting-pot of nations, would
show the way.

DAVID FERDINAND KOREFF, 1783–1851

CHAPTER III

JEWISH CHRISTIANS

BÖRNE'S disciples were a group of writers, Jews and non-Jews, known to literary history as Young Germany, whose works were banned throughout most of Central Europe by a sweeping decree of the German Federal Diet which met in 1835 at Frankfort under the auspices of Count Metternich. These writers advocated a united Germany, democratic forms of government, social equality without any distinctions of birth, and religious tolerance that would embrace even the irreligious. Allied to this group were the political poets of Jewish origin, Karl Beck and Moritz Hartmann. These lyricists continued the radical cosmopolitan traditions of Börne, but it was Beck who more particularly relived Börne's Jewish experiences.

Beck, who was born in 1817 and died in 1879, is hardly remembered today. Yet for a time he was looked upon as a poet of supreme ability. In 1839, Gutzkow, the uncrowned king of Young Germany, placed upon his head the laurels of Byron. Arnold Ruge, a collaborator of Karl Marx, praised him unstintingly. A host of rhymsters imitated him. Friedrich Engels wrote of him as the resurrected Schiller and recommended him to his friends as the future Goethe. His lyric, *Das Lied von der blauen Donau*, was set to music by Johann Strauss and, as *The Blue Danube Waltz*, attained an international vogue. The literary public was intoxicated by his glowing rhetoric, his passionate imagery, his consuming love of freedom. Beck mocked at the poets who yearned like sweet little birds to fall asleep in the safe harbor of a maiden's bosom. He wished to go out upon the horrible battlefields, where nations bled, ideas clashed, and human hearts broke. He called for a new Samson to burst the chains of the Philistines, for a new David to fell the Goliath of prejudice, for a new Bible and a new Bill of Rights.

Beck's imagery was to a large extent derived from the Old Testament. His most tragic poems were not, however, those in which he thundered against political and social injustices, but rather those in which he gave lyric utterance to his *Judenschmerz*, the Jewish pain within his soul. In a poem, entitled *Das junge Palästina*, he spoke through the lips of Börne and told in heart-rending verses that he loved Germany as one loves a bride, but, alas, this bride did not want to have anything to do with the all-accursed Jew. He fled, but was not permitted to rest anywhere. He was constantly asked: where is your fatherland? Though he climbed to the highest mast of hope, he could not discover any strand that he could call home. He gave up his Jewishness in the expectation of finding friendship and understanding among others. But despite his ardent wooing, he could not persuade others to reciprocate his affections. Beck took his readers to the narrow *Judengasse*. He let various ghetto types pass in review before them and then exclaimed: if fate wants to mock a human being, it creates a soul of dynamic energy and glowing will, a soul that strives to divine heights, and then lets this soul be born of a Jewish mother. Such a soul is then imprisoned in the dungeon called Judaism and tries in vain to break through the iron bars. The intensest suffering of Beck, the emancipated Jew, was not, however, due so much to the fact that his love was not returned by the Germans as to the fact that he must, alas! feel contempt for his own people, whom he would so much wish not to have to despise.

Beck's biblical drama, *Saul*, published in 1841, reached its climax in David's prophetic vision of his people's future: eternal wanderers, whose fame will extend to all ends of the earth and whose fall will be as deep and as gloomy as the abysmal ravines. In disgrace and self-inflicted despair, they will flee from place to place, resting never. Their home will be the entire world and yet they will be everywhere homeless. Like vermin, they will creep along, scorned and worthy of scorn. Posterity will see only the derisive caricature of a people that was once pure, simple, and glorious.

On May 27, 1843, Beck severed all bonds with the Jewish religious community and was baptized as a Protestant. But the Jewish fate continued to haunt him. He prefaced his *Lieder vom armen Mann* (1846) with a satiric dedication to the house of Rothschild. In this dedicatory poem, he rebuked Rothschild for not liberating his own people, who were ever waiting for redemption. The Jews had buried their proud past and their ancient realm, but they retained their longing for a king. Rothschild was their present monarch. He might have restored honor to them and directed their vision to a nobler activity than the filling of gold sacks. But instead of redeeming them, he joined them in dancing before golden calves and silver clods, and as a result the lot of King Rothschild and of his Jewish people remained utterly hopeless.

The generation of Beck, Börne, and Young Germany was
the post-Napoleonic generation, the first generation to leave
the ghetto walls and to hurl itself with passionate ardor
into the literary life of Central Europe. It was also the
generation of Karl Marx and Ferdinand Lassalle, Jewish
leaders of German Socialism. The attitude of Börne and
Beck towards Jewish emancipation must not, however, be
confused with that of Marx. The latter's pronouncement,
that the social emancipation of the Jews was the emancipation of society from Judaism, had its roots in hostility
towards his Jewish origin. In the most embittered descrip-
tions of Jewish life and Jewish traits of character on the
part of Börne or Beck, however, one still feels a heart
pulsating with pain and an undertone of deep sympathy
for a people degraded and, alas! worthy of degradation.
This attitude should not be characterized as *Judenhass*.
It is much more complex and much more pathetic. It is
Liebeshass, or love-hate, a tragic emotion discernible among
many intellectuals of Jewish origin even unto the present
day, an emotion to which literary men were especially
addicted a century ago.

The most unpleasant manifestation of this unfruitful
approach to Judaism may be seen in the plaintive lyrics of
Joel Jacoby, a poet of considerable talent, whose personality disintegrated as a result of the tragic duality into which
he was born.

It is difficult to reconstruct the life and career of this
strange individual, who was both Jew and Catholic, idealist
and political renegade, democrat and agent-provocateur.
A native of Königsberg, he was born of strictly orthodox
Jewish parents in 1810 and ended his career in 1863 as a
Catholic official of the Prussian propaganda service. His

literary activity was restricted to the 1830's. Eternally at odds with himself, he was at the beginning of this decade the ally of the Young German liberal reformers and at the close of this decade the target for their most vicious attacks. Although Jacoby has not yet found a biographer, nevertheless his political metamorphosis may be studied in the memoirs of Gutzkow, Laube, Varnhagen von Ense, and in his own pamphlets, from the revolutionary *Politisches Büchlein für Deutsche*, which appeared in 1833 when he was hounded by the police, to the reactionary *Frevel der Revolution*, which appeared five years later when he was himself in the service of the Prussian regime.[1] Jacoby's political pamphlets, both those calling for the violent overthrow of the established order and those defending the status quo, impressed his contemporaries less than did his Jewish elegies, which appeared anonymously in 1837 under the title *Klagen eines Juden*.

Heinrich Graetz, the famous historian, regarded Jacoby's Jewish poems as the truthful representation of the somber views of those Germans of Jewish origin who, while admiring Judaism in its ancient and venerable form, yet entertained doubts as to the possibility or desirability of its continuance. Jacoby held that the Jewish religion, when it ceased to be the sole possession of the people first professing it, was transformed into Christianity because in this rejuvenated form it could more easily spread to all ends of the earth and could more readily be accepted by all peoples. During the many centuries, while its missionary offspring advanced from victory to victory, Judaism became fossilized, and the Jews, excluded from the stream of progress, remain in bondage to their ancient ritual until such time as the gracious will of an inscrutable God shall liberate them from their

inflexibility. All tampering with the traditional rites was
therefore sacrilegious. The mixture of liberalism, free
thought, and aesthetic folly, which went by the name of
Reform Judaism, was, in Jacoby's opinion, a pathological
aberration of the age, since the wheel of history may not
be turned backward and Judaism cannot be reformed or
resurrected as a vital progressive creed. It must be revered
as a museum-piece, as a relic of a past civilization. The
Christian religion and the institutions of the Church were
the pillars of contemporary Europe. These must grow in
splendor and power, and Jews should lend their support
to the progressive edifice erected thereon. The Jews might
and ought to continue to congregate in their venerable
synagogues, but as a distinct group they were to have no
share in the historic process now or hereafter. Their day was
definitely over. Any attempt on their part to participate in
the coming social and political struggles would be sheer
folly. It was true that the radicals promised them complete
equality and emancipation. But even if the revolutionary
groups were sincere in their promises, the Jews would be
liberated as Jews, only to be guillotined as owners of capital.
If the robe of the king was purple, the robe of the sovereign
populace, or mob, would be blood-red. There was no hope
for the Jews as a group save in extinction and death. Others
experienced ups and downs, perished as peoples, and were
rejuvenated in a new racial mixture. Others might hope,
for they had attained salvation at the hands of a God of
love. The Jews alone were without such a God. If they
could only find their way to him, how they would cling to
him, how blessed they would be! For then they would be
liberated from the ancient law, they would no longer have
to drag the chain of the past down all the ages; they could

exult and participate in the historic happenings. Such a bold wish was, however, impossible of fulfillment and thence sprang the poet's despair.

The spirits of all nations pass before the poet. Each is young, vigorous, beautiful. The spirit of the Jew, however, is embodied in Ahasverus, the weary wanderer who grieves for a grave and cannot find it, who yearns for rejuvenation and cannot attain it. "Thou hast scattered us among all peoples and hast extinguished our radiance. Thou hast made our body immortal in history and we wander corpselike among these blossoming mortals . . . Lord, let us go hence! We are weak, we are tired, we yearn for the burial-vault. Other peoples are interred after completing the work of their days."[2] Why not we? Permit us to perish, so that we may be re-incorporated in the stream of progress under a new name, perhaps even as Germans.

"How I do love you, Germanic life, Germanic thought, Germanic history! You, my second fatherland — how I love your iron discipline, your moral seriousness, the word of your sages and the character of your peoples! As in my divine homeland do I feel myself amidst your old temples and a spirit of kinship wafts over me in these halls. Often have I unwittingly pressed my hot, tear-bedewed countenance to your cold marble, and a marvelous, homelike greeting floated down from your pillars, and I heard the merciful God say: you are redeemed, you have redeemed yourself! Will the day ever come on which my brethren will enter the Christian-Germanic temples and receive the sacrament of rebirth? Will that festive day come?" The poet himself doubts it. The Germans may be induced to assimilate the individual Jew, but they will not and cannot assimilate the entire Jewish people. These are doomed to misery and unending pain, for they are an inferior people, no matter how splendid their past may have been. "We are not worthy of sitting in the council of the wise and the mighty, and we have no desire to partake in the tribunal that determines the weal and woe of peoples. Fools have made such demands, fools with insolent dull minds."[3] Jacoby asks for much less. "Extinguish scorn and hate from your spirit and do not begrudge us the grave and the bread in exile. Do not torture and oppress our immortal soul and do not make it forlorn and cowardly. Do not dishonor our holy creed and do not tell the populace monstrous fictions about it, thus strewing seeds for future murder and future autos-da-fé. If your world begins to sink to dust and ashes because of Christian crimes, do not hurl the blame upon us and do not say that we have poisoned the well of life."[4]

The chief concrete complaint that Jacoby singled out as a subject for lamentation was, oddly enough, a decree by Frederick William III of Prussia forbidding Jews to bear Christian names and ordering the police to make sure that the decree was vigorously enforced. It was hoped that, as a consequence, those Germans of Mosaic faith who felt humiliated by the compulsion to revert to such names as Israel and Sarah would more readily be converted to Germans of the Christian faith. When this decree was made known, consternation reigned in assimilated Jewish circles. The historian Leopold Zunz, in a scholarly work on Jewish names, brought proof, in 1837, that his coreligionists had at all times borne names current among the native population of the country wherein they dwelt. The Prussian government yielded to pressure and modified its original ordinance and not until a century later were the Jews of

Germany compelled by law to assume names that would definitely identify them as non-Aryans.

Jacoby's elegiacal psalm on this subject illustrates one type of reaction which was genuine, even if entirely too sentimental: "The children of my people came to me, wailed and wept. The graybeards and the mothers drew near and anxious pain was depicted on their features. I asked the little ones: Why do you weep so early? And to the gray-beards I spoke: why do you moan so late? The children lisped: Alas! — we may no longer bear the bright and beautiful Christian names, but only the dark and ugly Jewish ones. We are to be branded at our games. And the graybeards said: The quiver of wrath is again emptied, misery and danger threaten our children. Then did I make reply: O children, it is well that you weep, for your eyes are to learn this daily work early. O graybeards, it is well that you moan, for you follow your old custom. Be comforted, be silent, and bear proudly the proud names of your ancestors . . . For he himself, who came to earth in order to redeem the world in glory, bore the name of a Jew! And when the West was still sunk in barbarism, your names flourished in immortal splendor, dominating the world, enlightening it, and delivering it . . . For I will say this unto you: before the hand of the clock of history has revolved, many splendid names of the Occident will be mowed from the earth as stubble by the sharp sickle; but as long as time endures, there will always be royally enthroned the names of Abraham, Moses, Isaiah."[5]

The apologetic approach, revealed by the psalms of Jacoby, was characteristic of those Jews who were on the verge of solving their practical difficulties and spiritual homelessness by choosing baptism for themselves and their

children. This was the end prophesied for Jacoby, immediately upon the appearance of his Jewish lamentations,
by Solomon Ludwig Steinheim, the Hamburg physician,
philosopher, and poet. As the author of plaintive Jewish
lyrics, Steinheim feared that he might be taxed with the
composition of the anonymous *Klagen eines Juden*. Hence,
he included in the second edition of his own elegies, which
was issued later in the same year of 1837, a violent attack
upon the anonymous poet, whom he accused of self-debase-
ment and self-estrangement.[6] He saw in Jacoby's elegies
an expression of fear, moral cowardice, distraught sensi-
bilities, and contemptible sentiments utterly foreign to the
Jewish temper. He protested against the desecration of the
Jewish name by a person who stood between two religious
bundles of hay, unable to make up his mind which one to
choose. Steinheim ventured the prediction that the poet
would turn to the bundle that had the least thistles.

Within a year or two this prediction was fulfilled. The Jew,
Joel Jacoby, became the Catholic, Franz Carl Jacoby. In
his book *Kampf und Sieg*, published early in 1840, he laid
bare the story of his conversion. But as early as August 3,
1837, when he wrote the preface to *Religiöse Rhapsodien*,
his decision to embrace the cross was apparent. He pictured
in florid language the advent of a glorious day on which
Israel would approach the cross, place the Torah at its feet,
and receive permission to perish in happy adoration of the
sublime symbol of the redeemer. He confessed that he had
always looked upon Judaism as a burden and that in his early
days he had been tempted to escape to neo-paganism. With
greater maturity he had, however, come to the conclusion
that worship of the flesh, as advocated by his former, Young

German friends, was an error and a delusion. Hellenic temples cannot be a substitute for the pillars of the Church. Referring to his past association with Gutzkow, Laube, and St. Simonian ideas, he exclaimed remorsefully: "I too wooed the Gods of marble and was enticed by their glitter. But all my youthful passion could not warm the naked marble bodies; all my glowing songs could not breathe life into them, and my outstretched arms embraced the dead and beautiful forms in vain. My yearning heart remained as cold as the marble I embraced: until the bells of the Church recalled me to the home I had forsaken, the home of my soul, the word of God."[7]

Jacoby's life story is not pleasant to review. As an individual he well merits the oblivion into which he has fallen; as a poet his talent was not of the highest; as a political thinker he lacked originality; but as a symbol of the homeless German-Jewish intellectuals of the post-Napoleonic generation he reveals more clearly than Börne or Beck the utter confusion, unrest, and moral decay which gripped thousands. Neither the self-abasement of the renegade Jacoby nor the more violent reactions of Börne and Beck pointed the way to a desirable solution of the tragic duality, German and Jew.

The dilemma in which the neo-Christians found themselves a century ago was most poignantly characterized in a sonnet by the dramatist Ludwig Robert, the brother of Rahel Varnhagen: "If a Jew be a person who in his mother's womb was already condemned to vile slave-status, who lives in his fatherland without rights as a target for the mudslinging rabble, whom nothing can help — neither deeds nor sacrifices, and whose cup of sorrow and disgrace remains full to the brim — then I am a Jew and know that I shall forever remain a Jew. And if a Christian be a person who seriously essays to bear his earthly cross in humility and to love those that hate him mortally, a person who believes his heartbreaking experiences are but trials set for him by the Lord, then am I a Christian and may justly bear this title."[8]

Ludwig Robert's best drama, *Die Macht der Verhältnisse*, was based upon the Achim von Arnim-Moritz Itzig controversy, which had brought to the fore the question of a Jew's right to demand satisfaction on the field of honor for insults received. Robert had obtained from Julius Eduard Hitzig, a court official and a baptized relative of Moritz Itzig, the legal files pertaining to the sensational trial of 1811. He at first intended to publish excerpts from the court documents with all the names and titles of the aristocrats who participated in the unsavory dispute. Realizing the impropriety and danger of such a step, however, he dramatized the material, changed the time of the action to the eighteenth century, and substituted a Prussian colonel for Achim von Arnim and a commoner for Moritz Itzig. This commoner, the writer Weiss, seeks to avenge his sister's honor, compromised by the officer. When he challenges the latter to a duel, the officer refuses to engage him in arms on the ground that Weiss, being of less noble birth, was not *satisfaktionsfähig*. Thereupon Weiss is forced to shoot him down like a dog. Through the mask of the commoner there looms the face not only of Moritz Itzig but also of Ludwig Robert, the over-sensitive Jewish-Christian, who was never permitted to forget that he was born Robert Levin and who suffered keenly because of his ambiguous position between religions and peoples.

No less tragic but more sensational was the life of Robert's friend, the poet, physician, mesmerist, professor, statesman, and Jewish-Christian, David Friedrich Koreff. His meteoric rise and fall during the years following the Congress of Vienna illustrates the new possibilities opened to talented baptized Jews of the early nineteenth century but also the dangers that forever beset them because of their non-Christian origin and the ineffectiveness of their efforts to obliterate every trace of early association with an unwelcome ethnic group.

In all the literary and scientific works of Koreff, in all his correspondence, in all the records of his conversations — save in his declaration on the day of his conversion — he did not once mention the word Jew. Unlike others, who gave vent to their *Judenschmerz* in prolific lamentations, he maintained silence, absolute silence, defiant silence. And yet, friends and foes, in their correspondence, in their conversations, and in their publications, insisted on referring to him as the Jew Koreff.

Born on February 3, 1783, the son of a wealthy physician of Breslau, Koreff continued in his father's profession and soon attained great skill in the art of healing. As a young man in his twenties, he aroused astonishment and envy at Berlin because of the uncanny accuracy of his diagnosis of difficult medical cases. But Koreff did not content himself with well-established medical techniques. He became the most successful practitioner of Mesmerism, then in great vogue, and effected several sensational cures of mental patients. In spare hours, he translated Hippocrates from the Greek, Plautus and Tibullus from the Latin, and composed original poems that found their way into Romantic literary almanacs or anthologies. He became one of the

founders of the Berlin Romantic School. Introduced into
the *Nordsternbund*, a circle of young poets, he soon became
the soul of this group where aristocrats and commoners,
Jews and Gentiles, fraternized without distrust and without
any sense of inequality. Adalbert von Chamisso, the author
of *Peter Schlemihl*, and Varnhagen von Ense, the husband
of Rahel, were his intimate friends. He settled in Paris when
Napoleon's might was at its zenith and quickly succeeded
in making his way to fame both as physician and as man of
letters. He mastered the French language in a very brief
time and wrote for French journals on German science and
poetry. His patients in the French capital included Napoleon's family and noted ambassadors from many realms.
Making use of mental therapy, he soon came to be known
as a miracle-man and effected cures after other physicians
had abandoned hope. His personality radiated confidence.
Women idolized him. He enjoyed his profession to such an
extent that he persisted in refusing payment for his services
from rich and poor, as long as the money he inherited from
his father lasted. And when he tired of Paris, he traveled
through Italy and then transferred his activity to Vienna
just as the congress of European plenipotentiaries got under
way there in 1814. His brilliant conversation charmed the
Austrian Chancellor, Prince Metternich, and the Prussian
Ambassador, Wilhelm von Humboldt. Diplomats vied for
his services. When Napoleon escaped from Elba and began
the Hundred Days' Campaign, the Prussian Chancellor,
Prince von Hardenberg, obtained an appointment for Koreff
as physician at General Army Headquarters. After the
Battle of Waterloo, the aging prince sought to retain Koreff
as his personal physician and adviser. King Frederick
William III of Prussia issued a royal decree granting Koreff,

then only thirty-three years of age, a full professorship at the University of Berlin and held out to him promises of further advancement.

Now, however, that Koreff's star was in the ascendant and his influence growing by leaps and bounds, whispers became audible that he was a Jew. The University faculty, unable to oppose the King's wishes and yet unwilling to receive the intruder into its midst, seized upon this rumor and spread the report that Koreff had no right to occupy an official post since he was still unbaptized. The King, apprised of this rumor, demanded an explanation from his Chancellor. Then only did Koreff confess the unpleasant truth to his aristocratic patron. The Prince was at first put out, but, on regaining his composure, he gave orders that this fault be immediately corrected.

The story of Koreff's baptism is not without humorous aspects. The secretary of the Prussian Legation at Dresden related that von Hardenberg, passing through the Saxon capital, called him into conference and told him: "I am faced with a disagreeable situation. I didn't ask Koreff about his religion and he never spoke to me about it. I like the man; I prize him highly; I don't want to lose him. Envy, disfavor, and stupid intolerance have exposed that he was still unbaptized, but the cabinet-order for his appointment has already been issued. After all this horrible gossip, I must have Church evidence that he is a Christian; a baptismal certificate, even if he were now to be baptized, is no longer sufficient. He will stay with you until you have found ways and means of sending him back to me with a document certifying that he was a Christian. How you arrange this is up to you; I don't want to hear any more gossip."[9]

When the Prince departed, steps were immediately taken

to comply with his command. Koreff was asked to sign the following statement: "My father, who was addicted to the Mosaic faith, ordered me not to acknowledge adherence to any religious group before my thirties, but thereafter to accept whatever belief I found to be the best after a thorough investigation. I have therefore studied carefully both the Mosaic and the Christian religious systems, as well as all other creeds; I have convinced myself that Evangelic Lutheranism offers true freedom of conscience, equanimity of soul, and happiness; and I am determined to accept it and to let myself be initiated into Christianity." The baptismal ceremony took place immediately after this declaration. Church authorities of Saxony were then able to certify that Koreff was a Christian, without mentioning how long. This statement completely satisfied all formal requirements for his royal appointment to the University.

Still the Berlin faculty continued its hostility. Koreff repeatedly gave assurances that he was a Lutheran. It availed him little. The King conferred on him the Iron Cross. Someone thereupon remarked that Judas Iscariot also gave lip service to him who first bore the cross. Students tried to interrupt Koreff's opening lecture with whistling and stamping of feet, and University colleagues sought to embarrass him in his academic activities in a hundred petty ways. Since von Hardenberg frequently consulted him, Koreff's intercession was sought by many professors and courtiers, but these petitioners resented their humiliation in having to flatter an ex-Jew. Many apparent friends, who accepted favors from him, hated him because of his origin and sought to undermine his influence. A dissatisfied diplomat wrote that the Chancellor's Jew was responsible for all troubles. Another reported: "The Chancellor has a Jew as his personal physician; the latter has hypnotized him frequently but has been unable to get him to be clairvoyant." Jakob Grimm informed his brother, Wilhelm Grimm, that Koreff was as unpleasant and as forward as were all baptized Jews. The family of Wilhelm von Humboldt never mentioned Koreff's Jewishness as long as they were attached to him, but, the moment friendship cooled, the blemish of his Jewishness occurred to them.

His teacher and only sincere friend at the University of Berlin, Professor Christoph Wilhelm Hufeland, called his attention to the general disapproval among the faculty of his efforts to force himself upon the academic body by means of royal commands and against its expressed will. Koreff's reply revealed his awareness of the prejudices he had to overcome and, though he avoided the expression Jew, he was not unmindful of the fact that his difficulties stemmed in large measure from opposition to his origin: "I, fool that I am, thought innocently enough, one would receive with joy a person who, like Odysseus, had wandered much among the cities of men, who had sacrificed half his wealth to attain knowledge, who in his unceasing striving for truth had ever served mankind and never his own advantage, who had cast all prospects overboard when his fatherland rose up in arms, who still envies those that died the death of heroes at Lützen, who would again expose himself for his fatherland if it were in danger, who even now asks for nothing more than to devote himself in quiet solitude to his beloved scientific studies, who has no intention to practice, who deprives no one of any position, and who did not think he stood in the way of anyone's ambition or envy. I scold myself a fool, because I assumed that the friendly reception I received abroad would

also be mine in my native land. In Paris, where I practiced
for six years, I can't recall a single unpleasant quarter-of-
an-hour at the hands of my colleagues. In Geneva, even
though a prisoner-of-war, I was received as a brother by
everyone . . . In Rome and in Naples there was a unanimous
wish to hold on to me. What a difference in reception! Yes,
had I suspected that so much envy, so much malicious
persecution would fall to my share at the hands of friends in
my own country, I, who was born here, whose paternal
house was demolished by bombs, whose heritage of wealth
was lost in the general catastrophe that overtook my fatherland, truly I would now be sitting at the foot of Vesuvius
and would be writing as my epitaph: *ingrata patria, ossa mea
non habebis* (ungrateful fatherland, thou shalt not have my
bones.)"[10] Koreff's Prussian patriotism got the better of his
momentary resentment, however, and he concluded his reply
with a plea that Prussia be preserved as an asylum for pure
science, as a sanctuary for worthy ideas, as a hospitable
hearth on which the flame of truth might burn, as a welcome
haven for all heroes victimized by fanaticism and unjust
ostracism. He reminded his reader that the spirit of free in-
quiry had saved Prussia from annihilation; this spirit made
Prussia the fatherland of mankind. Human generations
come and go, opinions rise to the surface and fade away like
the ripples of a stream, passions burst into blossom and
then wither away like the leaves on the trees; but the spirit
of truth marches triumphantly and incessantly over the
face of the earth, crushing with the force of an avalanche
all ephemeral existences that try to block its progress.

In 1818 Koreff was called upon to assist in the founding
of the University of Bonn and in the selection of a distinguished faculty. Some of Germany's best scientists and

literary personalities applied to him in their own behalf and in behalf of friends. At the same time they sought inner compensation for their humiliation in having to direct their pleas to a Jew by secretly abusing him in their private correspondence. He was *le Juif corréferent* and by a twisting of syllables he becomes *Coref, le Juif errant*. The very persons he helped to important positions used their newly acquired authority in order to slander and degrade him, and by 1822 they finally succeeded in stripping him of his power. Prince Pückler-Muskau, son-in-law of Chancellor von Hardenberg, then wrote: "Koreff has been unseated and at table one hears only tirades against Jews and jokes about Jews."

Forced to leave Berlin, Koreff again betook himself to Paris and sought to resume medical practice. Now he, who encountered hostility in Berlin as a Jew or ex-Jew, found himself attacked in Paris as a Prussian; and it required the intercession of learned scientists, among them Baron Cuvier, the founder of comparative anatomy, to obtain for him permission to carry on his cures. Heine, who once eulogized Koreff's opera *Aucassin and Nicolette* in a sonnet, won in him a friend whose help proved indispensable during frequently recurring illnesses. For the composer Meyerbeer and the latter's brother, the dramatist Michael Beer, Koreff paved the way to Parisian fame. Association with these Jews and ex-Jews meant more to him in the years after his downfall than in his years of splendor at Berlin. Poor, lonely, disillusioned, he lived on in exile until 1851 and was then buried in the cemetery of Père-Lachaise, the final resting place also of Ludwig Börne, his more famous Jewish-Christian contemporary and brother-in-exile.

Börne, Beck, Jacoby, Koreff — each in his own way

illustrates the difficulties faced in the springtime of Emancipation by the Jewish intellectual élite, as it strove with might and main to solve by complete and thoroughgoing assimilation the tragic duality into which it was hurled by the accident of birth. A more titanic spirit and a greater poet than these was also to come to grips with this problem, a warrior of the pen who embodied the yearning, the despair, and the dawning hope of his entire generation — Heinrich Heine.

PART II

FROM ASSIMILATION TO NATIONALISM

HEINRICH HEINE, 1797–1856

CHAPTER IV

HEINRICH HEINE

THE Dutch-Westphalian Jew, whose bones rest in Paris and whose sole surviving statues found a refuge in the United States, should have borne the name of Chaim Bücke-burg, according to Adolf Bartels, chief literary historian of the German National Socialists. For over a century, how-ever, this strange and tragic figure has been known to the world as Heinrich Heine. His spirit has profoundly influ-enced German thought, German literature, German music. Homage has been paid to him widely beyond the boundaries of his native land. England, France, America, Russia, Scandinavia, and many other realms have felt the force and spell of his personality. The youthful lover in early spring still finds in Heine's verses the perfect expression of his dawning emotions, and even the aged cynic at a winter fireside feels himself in harmony with certain moods of this poet. The inarticulate human soul that weeps in the excess of joy or laughs because of unbearable pain finds tongue in him and learns to understand itself. Matthew Arnold spoke of Heine as the sardonic smile wandering over the lips of the spirit of the world, but this designation applies to merely a single aspect of a very complex personality. It is doubtful whether any formula, no matter how beautiful or apparently lucid, can encompass the many contradictions within the soul of this German and Jew.

Heine was not a chance figure such as often crops up on the literary horizon to enchant with sweet lyrics or sparkle with scintillating wit or add works of art to a language rich in masterpieces. On the contrary, we encounter in him the prophet of a nation at the turning point of its political development — the German nation as it neared the end of its thousand-year-old struggle for unification; we see in him the embodiment of a most paradoxical age — an age suckled on outworn medievalism and dreaming of liberation through science and industrialism; we behold in him the pioneer of a people at a crisis in its history — the Jewish people as it burst forth from the ghetto confines clamoring for knowledge and joy and power long withheld from it; and finally we discover in him the best personification of the jagged modern soul, torn with unanswered doubts, wrestling with despair, complex beyond analysis, and hypersensitive to the point of morbidity.

Heine's character was a product of his Jewish heredity and his German environment. His Jewish background was his fate, the cause of his greatness, and the origin of his tragedy. He ever sought to escape from it. He always returned to it. Now he fled from its ascetic severity to the fleshpots of a gay world; and now, filled with remorse, he retreated to seek refuge in its stern serenity. In him East met West, the Orient clashed with the Occident; nay more, in him Jerusalem, Athens, Berlin, and Paris struggled for supremacy. He was the frail vessel that must break under a great mission. He was the Jew awakened from his medieval dreams who, in his mad haste to adjust himself to the modern world, overstepped himself and rushed on without halt or pause for breath until he found himself alone on the threshold of the twenty-first century, just as much out of harmony with his neighbors, just as little understood by his contemporaries as ever before.

Upon this Jewish substratum was superimposed the heritage of a great cultural nation. All the intellectual and emotional currents that swept over Germany from the close of the sceptical eighteenth century to the idealistic revolution of the mid-nineteenth century exercised a profound influence upon him. Düsseldorf — the town of his birth, Hamburg — the city of his tragic love affair, Frankfort — the seat of his brief business career, and Munich — the artistic capital of Bavaria, introduced him to varying aspects of German spiritual life. At the Rhenish university of Bonn he fell in 1819 under the spell of August Wilhelm Schlegel, the famous scholar, critic, and founder of the Romantic Movement. At Berlin from 1821 on he joined the disciples of Hegel, the idolized philosopher of the academic youth. Romanticism with its reverence for the Middle Ages, nascent modern Realism with its devotion to the present, Messianic radicalism with its vision of a Utopian future, *Weltschmerz*, pantheistic optimism, and the deepest tones of social cynicism — all found responsive chords in his personality. Heine experienced Germany in all its phases. If his manner of reacting was Jewish, the situations to which he reacted were German. If, again, his method of approach towards reality was Jewish, the facts of reality with which he grappled and about which his activities circled were German. Perhaps we say that the steel beams upon which the structure of his personality rested were Jewish, but the structure itself was German.

Heine early recognized this dualism in his nature, but he did not shrink from it. Unlike Börne and other assimilated Jews of that generation who wanted to be Germans, nothing

but Germans, Heine never really severed his inner relation
to Judaism, despite his many harsh comments about its
practices and practitioners. Even his baptism must not be
interpreted as such a severance. Nowhere did he express
any craving for the baptismal rite. Never did he voice any
pride that he did become a member of the Lutheran Church.
On the contrary, he defined baptism as a ticket of admission
to European culture and he resented the apparent necessity
of having to obtain such a ticket. For years he sought to
avoid conversion and was the only member of his family to
raise objections when this matter was discussed at his
parents' home in Lüneburg. In a letter to his friend Moses
Moser, dated September 27, 1823, he listed the motives that
might lead him some day to accept the new religion and
remarked: "From my way of thinking you can deduce that
baptism is a matter of indifference to me, that I do not even
attach any symbolic importance to it, and that in my situation and in the manner that I might go through with it, no
one else need attach any significance to it. The only effect
it might have upon me would be that I would dedicate myself all the more to the struggle for the rights of my racial
comrades. Nevertheless, I regard it as beneath my dignity
and as a stain on my honor, if I had myself baptized in order
to accept a position in Prussia. In Prussia of all places ! ! !
I really don't know how I am to help myself in my bad
situation. In chagrin I may yet become a Catholic and hang
myself . . . We are living in a sad age; rogues get to be the
best people and the best of us must become rogues. I understand well the words of the Psalmist: Lord, give me my daily
bread, lest I blaspheme Thy name."[1]

For two years longer Heine resisted the pressure exerted
upon him to accept baptism as the best way out of his eco-

nomic plight. When he finally yielded to the cross, on June 28, 1825, he did so frankly for economic reasons and never defended his apostasy on moral grounds. He once remarked that he would not have had to resort to baptism if the laws had permitted the stealing of silver spoons. At another time he commented that he would not have become a Christian if Napoleon had had a better teacher in geography; for such a teacher would have emphasized that the winters were very cold in Moscow; hence Napoleon would not have gone to Russia and would not have been defeated and the Jews would still be enjoying the political equality guaranteed by the Napoleonic regime and could dispense with baptism. When Heine was informed that his friend, Eduard Gans, after conversion, seemed enthusiastic about the new religion, he castigated his former associate in a poem entitled *Einem Abtrünnigen*: "And so you crawled to the cross that you despise, to the cross that only a few weeks ago you thought of treading under foot ... Yesterday a hero and today already a rascal." There is no doubt that Heine was castigating himself no less than Gans. He confessed to Moses Moser that he often arose at night, placed himself before the mirror, and scolded himself for his apostasy. After his conversion he attended the Jewish temple at Hamburg when the rabbi preached against the baptized Jews who let themselves be lured by hope of a job to abandon the faith of their fathers, and was so thrilled by the sermon that he wanted to visit the rabbi in order to voice his approbation. On January 9, 1826, half a year after his baptism, he wrote: "I am now hated by Christian and Jew. I regret very much that I let myself be baptized. I don't see that I am any better off since then. On the contrary, I have met only misfortune ... Is it not foolish: hardly am I baptized, when I am decried

as a Jew?" In the *Harzreise*, he was undoubtedly referring
to his baptism in that passage in which he describes his
climb to the peak of the Ilsenstein. On this mountain peak
he was seized with dizziness and would surely have plunged
down into the abyss, if in his soul's distress he had not
clung to the iron cross. He felt that he deserved forgiveness
for embracing the cross, in view of such a critical emergency.
The testimony of the pastor who performed the baptismal
ceremony to the effect that Heine embraced the new faith
because of inner craving and pure religious devotion does
not seem credible, especially if we consider the many expressions of hostility to Christianity dating from the very year
of his conversion. In September 1825, he exclaimed: "The
Japanese hate nothing so much as the cross. I want to become a Japanese." A few months later he begged Moses
Moser to write an article about Christian vileness in proselytizing Jews and Jewish vileness in using baptism as a
means of economic advancement.

Heine's attitude towards his Jewishness becomes clearer
if this concept, as it existed in his mind, is subdivided into
its chief components. Judaism was to him both a religion
and a racial fellowship. As a religion he was at first indifferent to it; then after his baptism he hated it because it
was the progenitor of Christianity, his pet aversion; and
finally in his dying days he came to revere it. As a racial
fellowship it always filled him with pride and gladness and
he was unremittingly active in furthering its welfare.

During his student days at Berlin he joined, in 1822, the
"Society for the Culture and Science of the Jews" (*Verein
für Kultur und Wissenschaft der Juden*), an organization
aiming to promote the cultural emancipation of the Jews.

His chief associates were Leopold Zunz, Ludwig Marcus, Eduard Gans, and Moses Moser. He participated in its meetings and taught German, French, and history under its auspices. He gained an insight into the Jewish past, of which he had until then known little. He gathered material for his novel *The Rabbi of Bacharach*, a novel that was to glorify medieval Jewish life in the manner of Walter Scott's poetic idealization of medieval Scottish history. He traveled to Poland and studied conditions in eastern ghetto towns. He recognized that the Polish Jews performed the functions of a middle class in a territory inhabited almost exclusively by nobility and peasantry. He saw the danger lurking in their economic rôle of buffer between the other two classes. He expressed the wish that the Polish Jews would be encouraged by the government to devote themselves more extensively to agriculture. The lack of a Jewish peasantry was not a healthy condition. In the past there was little inducement for a Jew to return to the soil because the lot of the serfs who tilled the soil was entirely unenviable. But, with the abolition of serfdom, the peasant's standard of living was bound to improve and the Jews should therefore gladly turn to the plow.

The poverty of the Polish Jews stirred the poet to profound pity. He recalled that these half-starved Jews were in preceding generations far superior to the Polish nobility in culture and education, since the noblemen understood only the rude profession of war-making and lacked all refinement, while the Jews, on the other hand, had a scholarly tradition which was linked to their religion and which they carried along with them whenever they had to abandon their previous fatherland and comforts. This tradition had, alas! become stagnant and fossilized in the nineteenth cen-

tury. The weeds of superstition were ruining the garden of
Hebraic culture. Nevertheless, the Polish Jews, with their
ill manners and their ungrammatical dialect, must be prized
far above the German Jews, who were dressed in accordance
with the latest fashion and who were conversant with the
latest best-seller. There was something whole and sound
about the former which the latter lacked.

Heine could more easily imagine himself as an orthodox
Jew, despite his indifference to all organized religion, than
as a reform Jew. Orthodoxy was, in his opinion, the best
antidote to the "poison" of Christianity and the best pre-
servative for the Jewish people. He was vitriolic in his
comments on those assimilated Jews of Hamburg who wished
to emasculate Judaism of its ancient forms and who therefore revised the traditional services so that these might
resemble more closely the services of their Christian neighbors. He found more genuine religious feeling in old-fashioned
unassimilated Jews who still wore long beards and shabby
coats, whose German was atrocious in grammar and pro-
nunciation, and who ran about with packs on their back in
all sorts of weather in order to earn a bare pittance. Such a
Jew is Moses Lump or Lümpchen, who lives in the slums of
Hamburg amidst filth and poverty. "But when Moses Lump
comes home on Friday evening, he finds the seven-armed
candelabrum lit; the table covered with a white cloth; he
puts away his bundles and his worries and sits down with
his unshapely wife and still more unlovely daughter; he eats
with them fish cooked in a pleasant white garlic sauce and
sings the most splendid songs of King David; he rejoices from
the bottom of his heart at the exodus of the children of Israel
from Egypt and is happy that all the tyrants who plotted
evil for them have died, that King Pharaoh, Nebukadnezzar,

Haman, Antiochus, Titus, and all such folk are deceased, but that he, Lümpchen, still lives and eats fish with wife and child. This man is happy; he does not have to torment himself with an education; he sits, contented with his religion and his green robe like Diogenes in his barrel; he looks with satisfaction upon his lights, which he himself does not even clean. And I tell you, though the lights burn somewhat dimly and the Sabbath-woman, who is supposed to clean them, is not available, even if Rothschild the Great were now to enter with all his bankers, brokers, shipping-agents, and department chiefs, with whom he conquered the world, and were to say: 'Moses Lump, ask for a favor; whatever you wish, shall be granted,' I am certain that Moses Lump would calmly reply: 'Clean the lights for me!' And Rothschild the Great would exclaim in amazement: 'Were I not Rothschild, then I should like to be such a Lümpchen.' "

Heine maintained that orthodox Jews are more likely to be happy than their assimilated brothers because they live with the Bible. This book is for them an inexhaustible treasure, that compensates them for all the ills heaped upon them. It is their fatherland and a fatherland which migrates with them. For its sake they gladly endure disgrace, hate, and even death. Its every page has cost them blood and tears, yet they refuse to part with this most sacred heritage of Jehovah. "What a book! as great and as wide as the world; rooted in the depths of creation and jutting into the blue mysteries of heaven; sunrise and sunset, promise and fulfillment, birth and death, the entire drama of mankind is contained in this book. It is the book of books, *Biblia*. The Jews may easily console themselves for the loss of Jerusalem and the Temple, and the Ark of the Covenant, and the golden utensils and jewels of Solomon; such loss is slight in comparison with the indestructible treasure saved by them, the Bible. This book is their fatherland, their possession, their ruler, their good fortune and their misfortune. Concentrating on the reading of this book, they little notice the changes that have taken place about them in the real world; nations rose and fell; states flourished and disappeared; revolutions stormed across the globe — the Jews, however, sat bent over their book and paid no attention to the wild chase of time that passed over their heads."

Heine did not question the desirability of Jewish survival. His political radicalism was tempered by the fear that the German radicals were likely to usher in their revolutionary activity by cutting a few thousand Jewish throats. The best Jews would probably be the first victims. While disclaiming any love for the Jewish religion, Heine was ready to fight for the Jewish people and their right to continue as Jews. "In evil days which are bound to come, the Germanic rabble will hear my voice, so that it reëchoes in German beer-halls and palaces." The Jews must under all circumstances be preserved as an antidote to Christian civilization, which brings so much suffering to mankind. Never would he forget his people as long as Heine remained Heine. The oath of the Psalmist — May my right hand wither, if I forget thee, Jerusalem — was often quoted by him. He repeated it in 1824 as the expression of his eternal adherence to his people, even while contemplating baptism.

Heine saw the Jews and the Germans as two distinct peoples who were drawn to each other by spiritual affinity. This affinity had its roots in the dim past and will extend into the future. In ancient days Jews and Germans were the most inexorable foes of the Romans and therefore natural allies. Furthermore, the Bible, the great family chronicle of the Jews, served the entire Germanic world as an educational text, appreciably moulding the Teutonic soul. More important still, both the inhabitants of Germany, which might be designated as the occidental Palestine, and those of Palestine, which might be termed the oriental Germany, lacked attachment to the soil and were not afflicted with the disease of patriotism. Unlike the Greeks and the Romans, who were filled with intense fervor for their fatherland, the Germans knew only loyalty to the leader or chieftain, migrating at his behest from one territory to another; while the Jews had even advanced beyond this stage and acknowledged loyalty solely to the moral code, the abstract principle of justice, universal law as embodied in the Torah. Perhaps in the course of time not only Germany but also all Europe may rise to the spiritual level of the Jews and may accord highest reverence, not to the soil from which one sprang nor to the person of the ruler or *Führer*, but to the Law as the embodiment of man's yearning for freedom and equality. Cosmopolitanism and republicanism arose in Judea, and Jesus, a teacher in Israel, originated the first International and was its most zealous propagandist. In the figure of a gentle youth, Jesus walked under the palm trees of Palestine and preached *liberté, égalité, fraternité*, slogans later adopted by the greatest thinkers as in accord with reason and incorporated in the enlightened gospels of the French.

It may well be that the mission of the Hebraic tribe has not yet been wholly accomplished. From a people that once directed the world into new channels of progress, further initiatives may still be expected. Golgotha was not the only hill on which a Jewish god bled for the salvation of the world. The Jews are made of the stuff of the gods and whosoever steps on them today may perhaps kneel before them tomorrow. Perhaps they will again give to mankind a supreme liberator, an earthly Messiah comparable to the heavenly one with which they have already blessed others, and this new Messiah will bring salvation not only to Israel but also to the entire suffering race of man. The Jewish mission will end whenever this earthly Messiah appears on the scene preaching the gospel of industry, the dignity of work, and the right to joy. The railroad will usher him in and roses of gladness will be strewn along his path. Jewish emancipation will then proceed hand in hand with Christian emancipation, for the Jewish cause is fundamentally identical with the Christian or the German cause. The emancipation of the Jews is part of a social movement embracing the entire earth. The Irish, the Greeks, the West Indian Negroes, and other oppressed peoples are facing a similar struggle for liberation. Europe itself is only now attaining to maturity and is only now cutting itself loose from the leading-strings of the privileged aristocracy. Heine exclaimed: "The Jews are angry at me because I do not draw the sword for their emancipation in Baden, Nassau, or other Gotham states. O the shortsightedness! Only before the gates of Rome can Carthage be defended!" The war for the liberation of humanity must be waged on a far vaster scale and, alas, every inch of progress costs streams of blood.

In Heine's opinion, religious opposition to the emancipation of Jews was only a surface expression of a more deep-seated antagonism to Jews as owners of wealth on the part of the masses who were deprived of all means of acquiring wealth. By excluding Jews from agriculture and handicrafts and hence compelling them to limit themselves to trade and finance — professions which the Church proscribed for true believers — governments legally condemned the Jews to be rich, hated, and ultimately murdered for plunder. Despite Christian insistence upon humility, renunciation of earthly goods, and devotion to spiritual salvation, the common people continued to long for the means of enjoying the present and hated those who possessed an overabundance of such means, especially if religion permitted the exercise of this hatred. In former centuries the pretext for plundering Jewish homes and massacring Jews was that they had crucified Jesus. This pretext was about as logical as that of the black Haitians who, during the massacre of the white inhabitants on the island of Santo Domingo, ran about with an image of the crucified Saviour and shouted: "The Whites killed him; let us kill all the Whites." The real incentive for the Negroes' acts of violence was desire for the wealth of the whites. Similarly, the chief motive for all anti-Jewish acts on the part of the Germans is desire for the possession of the Jews' wealth. Such acts will recur, according to Heine, whenever Jewish habits of industry and Jewish commercial talent will enable Jews to attain a higher level of prosperity than their neighbors. It is unfortunate that in the Middle Ages the importance of industry was not recognized, that trade was regarded as ignoble, and that financial transactions were disdained by Christians. The Jews alone were thus able to develop skill in banking and business. They alone were compelled to acquire riches and were then hated because of their riches. Although Christians have since then also learned to engage in these lucrative economic activities, the traditional hatred of Jews as the owners of capital has remained. In the struggle between bourgeoisie and proletariat the Jews are bound to suffer doubly. The underprivileged masses hate them as capitalists and the capitalists hate

them as competitors. In the coming duel of classes, the
Jews will be useful as scapegoats. A tragic rôle will fall to
them in the general economic and political reorganization
of peoples.

Heine was convinced as early as 1842 that a world war was
inevitable. In *Lutetia*, he writes that it will be the most
horrible war of destruction ever fought by civilized peoples.
Germany and France will be the chief antagonists. England
and Russia will join the general fray. No matter what the initial outcome may be, England, the great water snake, can
creep back to its watery lair and the Russian bear can find a
safe hiding-place in the immense tundra and steppes. But
Germany and France are likely to emerge from such a war
sick unto death and in danger of complete political collapse.
This world war will, however, be merely the curtain raiser
to a still greater spectacle, merely the first act of a still more
fantastic drama. The second act will be the European or
the world revolution, the colossal struggle between capital
and labor, between the propertied class and the proletariat.
National boundaries will disappear and differences between
religious sects will be of little importance. There will be
only one fatherland: the earth, and only one faith: joy on
earth. The third act is likely to be the conflict between the
new hedonistic faith and the outmoded religious establish-
ments which will unite in all lands for a final desperate
defense of their dogmas and privileges. Perhaps the old
tradition of absolutism will once more appear on the stage,
but in a new costume and with new slogans and catchwords.
A temporary ascendancy of twentieth century European
slogans, such as totalitarianism, fascism, and National-
Socialism dovetails remarkably well with Heine's vision.
The final act of this world spectacle was not wholly clear to

him. Nevertheless, he ventured to prophesy the disintegration of the British Empire, the loss of Russia's border provinces, and the probable rise of a brutal dictatorship to the great injury of European culture. "I do not know, but I think that in the end the great water snake will have its head trodden under foot and the Bear of the North will have its skin pulled over its ears. There will then be perhaps but a single herdsman and a single herd, a free herdsman with an iron staff and an equally shorn, equally bleating human herd. Wild gloomy times are booming anear, and the prophet who undertakes to write a new apocalypse will have to invent new monsters and, indeed, such terrible monsters that the old symbolic beasts of the Apostle John would appear in comparison as mere doves and amoretti. The gods conceal their countenances out of pity for their human charges, their long cherished foster-children, and perhaps also out of fear for their own fate. The future smells of cat-o-nine-tails, blood, godlessness, and very many whippings. I advise our descendants to come into the world with a very thick hide."[2]

Heine expected freedom to be threatened throughout Europe. Soon there would be no place of refuge throughout the Continent, if despotism continued its victorious march. But, fortunately, in the hour of greatest need there would be a haven for free spirits in the New World. "Even if all Europe should become a single prison, there is still another loophole of escape, namely America, and, thank God! the loophole is after all larger than the prison itself."[3]

America, its virgin soil untainted by European political vices, would be the last asylum of liberty-loving individuals. Heine noted that America, the new land of religious freedom, was discovered in the same year that the Jews were expelled

from Spain. America is young. America is sound. America
is resplendent. America is not a romantic graveyard. America is not attached to mouldy symbols and petrified wigs.
America will be the last hope of a dying occident.

The thesis of religious people that problems which are
apparently insoluble in this world will be solved in the
world-to-come finds its parallel in the faith of the irreligious
writers of a century ago, of whom Heine and Börne are
typical, that problems which Europe could not solve satis-
factorily would be solved in America. The duality of East
and West, Jew and German, would cease in the New World,
where ancient animosities are ineffective and man is free to
enter upon a new stage of civilization.

Heine wished to be remembered primarily as a warrior in
man's struggle for liberation. The Germans have, however,
seen him most frequently as the Jew in literature, and their
attitude towards him has been conditioned by their attitude
towards his Hebraic roots. The ebbing and flowing of anti-
Semitic waves coincided with positive and negative ap-
praisals of this poet's qualities. The excommunication from
the German cultural sphere pronounced upon him by the
Federal Diet in 1835 was repeated in 1933 when his books
were banned and his name effaced from German school
texts. But even abroad the attitude towards him can serve
as a barometer of the pressure against Jews. Thus, for example, when Thomas Carlyle referred to him as a "dirty and
blaspheming Jew" and again as a "slimy and greasy Jew —
fit only to eat sausages made of toads," the irascible Scots-
man was merely giving vent to strong anti-Semitic prejudices, which he never sought to conceal. George Eliot,
on the other hand, who adored the biblical people and who

in *Daniel Deronda* painted the most ideal portrait of a Jew in English literature, saw in Heine's Jewishness a badge of honor and, with her apotheosis of the poet in 1856, ushered in the mid-Victorian era of Heine-worship in England and America. Perhaps the *Athenaeum* of January 15, 1876, best summed up current English opinion on Heine's Jewishness. "Jewish he was in his tenderness and, above all, in his hatred; Jewish in his versatility and world-wide sympathy; Jewish in his realistic conception of the ideal, in the fashion in which he conceived the passion of love, which reminded one of the sensuousness of the *Song of Solomon*; Jewish in the proud consciousness of human dignity, in his nervous temperament, his incredible capacity for suffering, his wonderful endurance of sorrow; Jewish in the boldness and recklessness of his scepticism; Jewish, in fine, in never embracing for any length of time a belief which excluded every spiritual element. In his wit and humor also Heine was a true child of the Hebrew race. However original he may have been, he exhibited the characteristics and peculiarities of Hebrew humor, of the wittiest and most light-hearted people of the world, which, in the midst of unparalleled misfortunes and sufferings, has preserved an ineradicable buoyancy and an unconquerable spirit of satire."

The American poetess Emma Lazarus felt that the irreconcilable dualism in Heine's character was not between the German and the Jewish elements but between the Hellenic and the Jewish. He was a Jew with the mind and eyes of a Greek. His was a beauty-loving, myth-creating pagan soul imprisoned in a somber Hebrew frame. His lyrics were unique in Germany and it was necessary to go back to the Hebrew poets of Palestine and Spain to find a parallel in literature for his magnificent imagery and voluptuous

orientalism. After a visit to Heine's grave at the Mont-
martre Cemetery in Paris, the poetess, who was herself of
Sephardic, or Hebrew-Spanish, origin, wrote in 1884 of her
coreligionist: "His was a seed sprung from the golden
branch that flourished in Hebrew-Spain between the years
1000 and 1200. Whoever looks into the poetry of the medieval Spanish Jews will see that Heine, the modern, cynical
German-Parisian, owns a place among these devout and
ardent mystics who preceded him by fully eight centuries.
The *Intermezzo*, so new and individual in German literature,
is but a well-sustained continuation of the *Divan* and *Ga-
zelles* of Judah Halevi, or the thinly veiled sensuousness of
Alcharisi and Ibn Ezra . . . What the world thought dis-
tinctively characteristic of the man was often simply the
mode of expression peculiar to his people at their best."

If English and American writers of Jewish origin, from
Emma Lazarus and Leonard A. Montefiore to Israel Zangwill and Louis Untermeyer, in reclaiming Heine for the
Jews, extolled inordinately the fine traits of their gifted
kinsman, it was not surprising that anti-Semitic publicists,
in agreeing to regard Heine as the Jew rather than the German, should evaluate his character and achievements less
favorably and should scour his prose and verse for possible
fuel for their incendiary agitation. The reactionary forces,
which after 1917 ascribed the Bolshevist revolt to long-
fostered Jewish machinations, saw in Heine not only the
contemporary of Karl Marx and Ferdinand Lassalle but also
the ancestor and inspirer of Leon Trotzky and Russian
Communism. Such views abounded in Germany. They
were not infrequent in France. They were audible even in
England and found their way into dignified English journals.
Thus, the *Quarterly Review* opened its columns, in January

1920, to an article by the Count de Soissons on *The Jews as a Revolutionary Leaven*.

The argument of the aristocratic author ran as follows: Alexander Herzen and Michael Bakunin, forerunners of the Russian Revolution, saw themselves and the intellectuals of their country as outsiders, who stood aloof from the European cultural stream. From their position on the farther bank, they could look upon Europe without love and without hate. They could see Europe's failings more clearly, they could work for the disappearance of western culture without pangs of conscience and without a sense of horror. They could even dream of the dawn of a golden age after the complete destruction of the accumulated treasures of the centuries. While these Russians might have erred in feeling themselves as outsiders, there was no doubt that the able and active Jews, whom they followed and whose doctrines they spread, were indeed aliens, strangers not only to Western Europe but even to Byzantine culture. These Jews were bitter foes of Christianity in all its ramifications. They were without any tie to occidental traditions. They were radicals and nihilists in every department of life. Their approach was best exemplified in their most talented representative, Heinrich Heine.

In the opinion of Count de Soissons, Christianity was a religion of spiritualism, whereas the most striking characteristic of Jews, as evidenced by Heine, was sensualism. There seethed in Heine the hot blood of the Semitic race. His *Book of Songs* continued the tradition of King Solomon, who composed songs in honor of sensual love as the only consolation in life, after having convinced himself that everything else was vanity of vanities. Sensualists have an antipathy to religion. Jews, since they are sensualists, must hate religion. Heine, who was exposed to humiliations on account of his Jewish origin, had to hate Christianity with special vehemence and to plan vengeance. In Germany he had to keep his thoughts of abolishing Christianity to himself, for he could find no sympathizers. In Paris after 1831, however, he discovered allies in the Jewish St. Simonians. Their doctrine of the rehabilitation of the flesh inflamed his imagination and lent confirmation to his sensualism. He became enthusiastic about the new religion of the body, which would replace the Christianity he detested. He found further support for his sensualism in the pantheistic philosophy of the Jew Spinoza, who lived in the epoch of the degeneration of Christianity. Man claimed the place formerly occupied by God. When Heine preached the establishment of the kingdom of heaven on earth, he meant the coming of a regime that would countenance boundless enjoyment of all the physical pleasures the world could furnish. Alexander Herzen, who was allegedly of partly Jewish descent, assigned to Russia a special rôle in the new non-Christian order. The Russians were to bring about this order by revolutionary destructive frenzy. Chaos and annihilation were to be hailed as desirable stages of transition. But even Herzen was morally superior to Heine, perhaps because the Russian was not entirely Jewish. Herzen, the ancestor of anarchism, dreamed of a world of absolute good. Heine, however, found in the overthrow of Christianity his ultimate ideal for mankind — an ideal of pleasures, dances, and feasts of unbridled sensuality. He was prompted by the proneness of the Semite to fleshly pleasures and by the hatred of his people for Christianity, the source of their humiliation. Heine joined hands with his racial brothers, Marx and Lassalle. They foisted socialism upon Europe, because to destroy successfully one must have something to oppose to that which is doomed for annihilation — some clever plan for future building. Wishing to be certain of the destruction of Christianity and prompted by their natural bent for organization, they united revolutionism with socialism and joined in the fight with a plan not only of destruction but also of a future socialistic state in which religion would be a private enterprise, opium for the use of idiots and sluggards. The foundation of socialism was Jewish hatred of Christianity. "Heine had a prophetic vision of the present storm in Russia, during which waves of destruction would rush threateningly towards the West, on the furious billows of which would swim the poet's compatriots, not as paltry herrings but as the companions of whales, carrying with them the watchwords of annihilation and death against the old order . . . Yes, Heine's wish is fulfilled; for in Russia Christian blood is being spilt in abundance, and the followers of Trotzky are carrying to unforeseen but not illogical conclusions the principles of the Jewish revolutionary writers — Spinoza, Heine, Herzen, Marx, and Lassalle."

Thus, a century after Heine's flight from Judaism to nominal Lutheranism and sincere cosmopolitanism, his deeds and misdeeds — real and apocryphal — are accounted for on the basis of his Hebraic ancestry. He is held responsible for alleged Jewish machinations, generations after his death, in lands whose language and ways were unknown to him; and Jews, in turn, are held responsible for his Mephistophelian jests and iconoclastic slogans.

The tragedy of being both German and Jew, illustrated by his life and his afterfame — which is a poet's life after death — was to repeat itself in numerous other sensitive souls and was to give rise to ever new attempts at escape from Teutonism or Judaism, but also to ever subtler efforts at a satisfactory synthesis.

CHAPTER V

BERTHOLD AUERBACH

IN 1836 there appeared at Stuttgart, the capital of Württemberg, a polemic pamphlet by a young writer who was not yet well known. It was entitled *Das Judentum und die neueste Literatur*. It undertook to defend the Jews of Germany against the charge of radicalism hurled against them by Wolfgang Menzel and his allies. It denied that the literary group, known as Young Germany, for which Menzel had suggested the name Young Palestine, contained a majority of Jews. It pointed out that, of the six leaders, four had no personal relation to Jews and Judaism. These four were Karl Gutzkow, Heinrich Laube, Ludolf Wienbarg, and Theodor Mundt. Only Börne and Heine were of Jewish origin, but both had long since abandoned the religion of their ancestors. Furthermore, if they possessed unpleasant traits that might render them obnoxious to many Germans, these traits could not be designated as typically Jewish. In the name of the younger generation of Jews, the author begs of his opponents: "Test us in the fire of danger and you will find us free of the dross of egoism and of all cunning immorality. Give us the fatherland to which we belong by birth, custom, and love, and we will faithfully put our blood and possessions upon its altar. Forget and teach us to forget the dark dividing wall that separated us and spare us the painful effort of taking a stand against you,

BERTHOLD AUERBACH, 1812–1882

because you have so often coupled your patriotism with demonic hatred of Jews."[1]

The author of this pamphlet was Berthold Auerbach, then only twenty-four years of age but soon to blossom forth as an acclaimed novelist, whose realistic tales of peasant life endeared him to his fellow Germans throughout the nineteenth century and whose fame extended to the Russia of Tolstoy, the Scandinavia of Björnson, and the America of post-Civil-War days.

Compared to the venomous satires of Börne and Heine, Auerbach's polemic against Menzel seemed mild, restrained, conciliatory, almost apologetic. The greater part of the pamphlet is devoted to an analysis of the rôle assigned to Jews by German conservatives, liberals, and radicals. The conservatives, in his opinion, are pious, well-meaning individuals, who want to convert all Jews to Christianity but who at the same time believe in the much misunderstood biblical dogma that the Jews are God's chosen people that are ultimately destined to return to Palestine. These conservatives seem to be unaware of the contradiction in this approach. They insist on calling the Jews a people and are vexed when the Jews rightly claim that they ceased to be a people ages ago and are now merely a religious fellowship. The liberals, according to Auerbach, are those Germans who tell a Jew, as soon as they make his acquaintance, that they know many nice Jews; but they never forget that the person they honor with their conversation is, after all, a Jew. As a mark of their liberalism, they like to emphasize their tolerance and expect to be applauded for it. Should a Jew, however, dare to voice a free, bold, and independent opinion, or to take an opposing stand on any vital issue, their suppressed hatred of Jews comes to the surface immedi-

ately. The radicals of the Young German variety, despite
the presence of Jewish proselytes in their midst, direct their
barbed wit against all traditional faiths, Catholicism, Protestantism, Judaism. They want to substitute for the Old
and the New Testaments a Third Testament based on St.
Simonism and on the doctrine of the rehabilitation of the
flesh. They are not the responsible spokesmen for Christianity or Judaism.

Auerbach's first pamphlet, with its mild criticism of all
shades of German political opinion, found little favor with
the contemporary reading public. It was followed by
biographic sketches of famous "Israelites." The best of
these was his sketch of Gabriel Riesser, who soon thereafter became his intimate friend and whose approach to the
problem of German-Jewish duality he shared throughout
many years. Riesser, a lawyer by training, had sought admission to the bar of the Free City of Hamburg and had
been rejected because he refused baptism, a necessary formality in the case of all legal practitioners. He had thereupon begun a life-long struggle for the legal equality of all
Germans, whether they be of Christian or of Mosaic persuasion. A gifted orator and a powerful writer, Riesser won
notable victories. He was elected Vice-President of the
Frankfort Parliament which was convoked during the revolutionary uprising of 1848. Later he became Chief Justice
of the Court at Hamburg, the first Jew to hold such high
office.

Like Riesser, Auerbach regarded himself not as a Jew
resident in Germany but as a German raised in the Mosaic
faith. Like Riesser, he denied the existence of a Jewish
nationality. There had once been a Hebraic nationality,

he held, but it had perished centuries ago. The Jews of Central Europe were Germans, more so than the originally Slavic population of Prussia, for they had imbibed German culture at an earlier date. Hence, their destiny was more closely linked with that of the non-Jewish residents of Germany than with that of the Jews of other lands. Judaism was merely a religion and it might perhaps be desirable to speak of it as Mosaism. Young Auerbach, who had spent several years in an orthodox talmudic school and who was studying theology at the University of Tübingen in preparation for a rabbinical career, wrote in 1832 that it was his highest ambition to effect a synthesis of Hegelian philosophy and purest Mosaism, just as Christian theologians were then attempting a synthesis of Hegelianism and Christianity. Following the example of his teacher, David Friedrich Strauss, who was at work on a humanization of Jesus and a cleansing of the Christian religion of traditionally accepted marvels and miracles, Auerbach desired to make hoary Mosaism conform to the most recent philosophic formulae. "Shall the whole world move about us in a harmony of spheres and we alone remain static as the fixed stars of the ancient world? No, Mosaism is and remains eternally true, but just as Moses revealed his everlasting verities not alone for us, even so did Plato, Leibnitz, Bacon, Kant, and Hegel reveal theirs for us as well. It is the world soul, the spirit of mankind, which manifested itself first in Moses and now in Hegel."[2]

Unlike Börne and Heine, who often mocked at organized religions, Jewish and Christian, but who did not hesitate to accept baptism for economic reasons, Auerbach paid homage to the eternal verities immanent in all religions but remained within the confines of his own ancestral faith.

Purity of conscience restrained him from conversion to an alien religion. His attitude was best expressed by Ephraim Kuh, the Jewish hero of his first novel, *Dichter und Kaufmann* (1836), who explained to his Protestant friends that, just as a person who was born a German could not very well metamorphose himself into a Frenchman or an Englishman, even though these peoples might be more prosperous and more powerful, so likewise he, the Jew, could not change his inner religious configuration. Born a German, he must ever remain a German. Reared in the Jewish faith, his vital roots would be cut from under him, if he became a renegade from Judaism.[3]

Auerbach attended synagogue from time to time in order to document his adherence to the Jewish religious fellowship, but again and again he emphasized that in his eyes Judaism was no more than a religious fellowship. In 1869, at a banquet in honor of the French-Jewish leader, Adolphe Crémieux at Berlin, he spoke of the mission of the Jews to become perfect Frenchmen in France and perfect Germans in Germany. National life must be based not upon blood-relationship but rather upon a community of spirit.

When Benjamin Franklin Peixotto, the New York lawyer of Jewish origin whom President Grant chose as the first American consul-general in Bucharest, sought in 1872 to initiate mass emigration of persecuted Rumanian Jews to the United States, Auerbach was invited to participate in the German committee organized to raise funds for this purpose and to lay the groundwork for an international conference at Brussels, which was to discuss further action. His speech on this occasion illustrates his life-long cautious approach. He had no objection to facilitating the emigration of a few individuals, but he opposed action on a large scale or the holding of a congress limited to Jews. Even when he was informed that the Rumanian government had consented to cooperate in the transference of its Jews to other countries or continents, he still retained dire forebodings. If the expulsion of unwanted Jews from Rumania should be successfully accomplished, he feared that a precedent would then have been established. A year later, the discovery might be made that the Jews of Galicia or elsewhere were unwanted, a new wave of persecutions might sweep Eastern Europe, the necessity of another mass emigration could be urged again, and thus demagogues in many countries would be encouraged to ever new atrocities in order to rid their lands of Jews. It must be made clear to all that Jews were not gypsies, who had no permanent abode, but patriots of their states, rooted in their native soils, attached to the graves of their fathers and the lands of their birth. It was especially dangerous to have a congress devoted exclusively to problems of Jewish refugees. No, the refugee problem must be stripped of its specifically Jewish character. An interfaith council must be organized to help all the oppressed everywhere and to fight against all symptoms of decaying law and order throughout Europe.

When Moses Hess informed Auerbach of his intention to write a study on the Jews as a distinct nationality, the novelist begged him to desist. Such a view, even if sincerely entertained by Hess, must not be made public. Such a view was incendiary. "Who has set you up as lord and judge over us?" Auerbach wrote to Hess, quoting the biblical passage in the original Hebrew. But Hess did not yield to his friend's bitter reproaches. In *Rom und Jerusalem* (1862), the finest masterpiece of pre-Herzlian Zionism in Germany, he propounded his thesis that the Jews were a nation, existing since ancient days as an entity distinct from Germans or Frenchmen, and that their permanent home was Jerusalem and not Berlin or Paris. Hess explained Auerbach's timidity as typical of the entire generation of emancipation. Surrounded by so much hatred, the German Jew was seeking to slough all Jewish characteristics and to deny his origin. No reform of the Jewish cult seemed radical enough for such a person and even baptism failed to free him from the nightmare of German anti-Semitism, because the Germans did not hate the Jewish religion as much as the Jewish race nor the peculiar Jewish customs as much as the Jewish noses. Assimilation in spirit would not change Jewish noses or Jewish tribal reactions. A Jew who, like Auerbach, denied the existence of a Jewish nationality was, in the eyes of Hess, a traitor to his people, his clan, his family. If emancipation could be shown to be incompatible with the survival of a Jewish nationality, then emancipation should be rejected. A Jew must be a Jewish patriot above all and not a German patriot. Scorn should not be visited upon the aged pious Jew, who would sooner have his tongue cut out than use it to deny his nationality. No, the ultra-modern Jew was the one to be despised, the Jew who garbed himself with beautiful phrases of enlightenment and humanitarianism in order to disguise his treason to his people, his fear of solidarity with his unfortunate tribal brethren. All geographic and philosophic alibis will, however, avail naught in the long run. Every insult to the Jewish name will hurt the German of Mosaic faith more deeply than it will the orthodox or ghetto Jew who acknowledged his kinship with his clan.

The views of Hess were anathema to Auerbach, but the prophecy that the cultured German of Jewish origin would be more sensitive to every uncomplimentary reference about Jews was fulfilled in Auerbach's case. There is a story, which was told soon after the novelist's death, that his end was hastened by excessive worry over anti-Jewish agitation, which increased in violence during his later years. Although there is little proof to substantiate this story, the fact that it arose and that it found wide credence is an indication of the common knowledge that the aging author was considerably upset by the unpleasant turn of events taken by German-Jewish relations after the founding of the German Empire. He was especially saddened by the spectacle of his own friends participating in the unworthy agitation. When Heinrich von Treitschke joined the ranks of Jew-haters, Auerbach avoided attending social functions at which he was likely to meet this famous historian, because amicable intercourse or even a tolerable formal relationship was difficult. His friendship with Gutzkow was under a strain because he realized that, in spite of their common struggles in behalf of liberal ideals, Gutzkow never for a moment forgot that Auerbach was a Jew. When Richard Wagner in 1869 launched an invective against the Jews as a people incapable of musical creativeness — an invective which he had first published anonymously in 1850 — Auerbach was tempted to take up the cudgels against this friend of his younger days: "I would I could strike out and let loose my whole anger at this mixture of depravity and insolence. We must control ourselves in order not to despair of the world, if we see that a poison-tree, which we thought cut down once and for all, again grows ever new roots. And that is called Christian love and liberal education and fine humanitarianism! On all sides I am asked to take a hand in this discussion. I feel the urge, but I cannot."[4] When the renowned Viennese surgeon, Theodor Billroth, in 1875 questioned the wisdom of permitting many Jewish students to take up the profession of medicine and frankly confessed that he himself was ever inwardly aware of the gulf between pure German blood and Jewish blood, Auerbach denounced this friend and admirer in a letter to the press. Against Billroth's accusation that Jews were incapable of martyrdom, Auerbach countered that Jewish history was a single martyrology lasting eighteen hundred years and the end was not yet in sight. "Or do you think it is no martyrdom to have to explain in this day and age and to a person of your reputation that we are not Jews who happen to speak German or to be raised in this land, but that we feel ourselves wholly as Germans. You say: the Jews failed to take part in the entire medieval romanticism. In what way did the peasants participate, who were serfs until the beginning of the present century? You ban us into the exile of strangers and claim not to know that the history of the German Jews passed through all phases of German cultural development. The Jews were permeated with German education before your compatriots, the Slavs and Wends, were Germanized."[5]

Auerbach's optimism waned rapidly. His faith in the continual progress of mankind, or at least the European sector of mankind, dwindled from year to year. The Hegelian disciple, who had once resented Heine's sardonic cynicism, came to understand that the poet's extreme embitterment was an inevitable result of his experiences as a Jew in Germany. Auerbach himself began to despair of any improvement in German-Jewish relations for at least another generation. He was hindered in his creative writing by overmuch brooding about this problem. He felt unable to continue with his researches into the hidden mazes of the human heart, or with his speeches on the progress of mankind, while his fellow citizens sanctioned crimes against Jews or at best shrugged their shoulders in absolute indifference. He listened in vain for an outcry of the public conscience when the Jews of Rumania were robbed and plundered by Christian representatives of humanity. He discerned no outbursts of indignation in the daily press when the myth of the Passover blood-ritual was seriously revived in Russia. On the contrary, he learned that a petition, endorsed by prominent men of affairs and signed by a quarter of a million Germans, was to be handed to Bismarck, urging the chancellor to curb the rights of Jews. He spent sleepless days and nights while the petition, submitted in November 1880, was debated in the Chamber of Deputies. Although Bismarck succeeded in sidetracking the anti-Jewish legislation urged by the petitioners, nevertheless the ugly character of the debate produced such a depressing effect upon Auerbach, that at the end he exclaimed: "In vain have I lived and worked! That is the annihilating impression which I have of this two-day debate in the Chamber. And if I say to myself that perhaps things are not so bad, there still remains the horrible fact that such rudeness, such infamy, and such hate are still possible. Day and night I am to think and to devote myself to the task of creating something pure and beautiful, but disgust fills my soul. How shall I overcome, how eradicate this disgust? I have to bear with the disgrace of my fatherland and be patient."[6]

After half a century of devotion to the cause of Germany,

after emphasizing his super-patriotism on every occasion, Auerbach had to confess to himself that the Germans did not want to share their fatherland with his kind and did not feel that he belonged to them. What could he do about it? An epidemic of Jew-hatred had broken out and the tiny plaster he could apply to the symptoms of the disease was woefully inadequate. Perhaps he could appeal to his coreligionists not to yield to disconsolate nihilism, even though he himself found it hard to retain fragments of hope. He ventured such a forlorn plea on the centenary of the death of Lessing, the apostle of tolerance, the representative of the best traits of German character, the author of *Nathan der Weise*. He begged of the Jews: "Hold firm! Do not let your misfortunes and the wickedness of others rob you of your love for mankind! Be too proud to deem yourselves unhappy! Despite all shocks to your spirit, despite all temptation to despair, cry out with me: God exists for a' that, and the spirit of humanity will conquer for a' that."[7]

Auerbach gave similar advice to the Jews of America, when asked to comment on an unfortunate incident in the state of New York. In 1877 the Jewish banker Seligman was refused a room at a hotel in Saratoga Springs because he was a Jew. Auerbach, who learned of this matter from Friedrich Kapp, a German-American editor, was shocked that the virus of anti-Semitism had crossed the Atlantic. In a letter, published in Kapp's newspaper, *Illinois Staats-Zeitung*, he advised America to eradicate the first symptoms of the infection before the moral disease had a chance to spread. The matter should not be treated lightly. "No pastor should mount the pulpit without exclaiming: the

first trace of a horror has dared to show itself among us in
bright daylight, a horror that brands as a lie our religion,
which professes to be a religion of love. Who can say the
Lord's Prayer as long as he denies that all men of all colors
and creeds are God's children . . . As long as a person of
another faith or of another ancestry is looked upon with
hate or even without love, there is no real religion in the
world . . . No doubt, the Jews on both sides of the ocean
have their faults. Above all they often lack quiet poise and
do not content themselves with inner ennoblement and
elevation. There prevails a tendency towards splendor and
ostentation, especially among Jewish women. There is room
for much effort and admonition in order to nourish and to
develop among them simplicity and public modesty. But
is not the same true of Christians of the same class who
have attained to wealth? . . . To the Jews of America there
must finally be directed the reminder not to desist from
the propitiating attempt to disseminate the seeds of goodness in their new fatherland and to show themselves worthy
of being free citizens, above all not to become embittered
if, as is easily possible, Christian fellow citizens do not perform their duty of taking an energetic stand against the
first germ of a moral pest."[8]

Auerbach was saved from complete despair by his faith
in America, the haven of the oppressed, the refuge of the
liberty-loving, the last hope of thwarted European idealists.
As early as 1851, he wrote: "I have always resisted the
idea of pinning all hope on America, but I'm now constantly forced to that conclusion. If we were incapable of
bringing about a condition more worthy of human beings,
then I'm afraid that the next generation will be even more
so."[9] America was in his eyes the land of promise, on

whose soil the seeds of a better future had been planted, the country of great opportunities where man, unfettered by ancient chains, will attain to new supreme goals. Two years before the centenary of the American Declaration of Independence, Auerbach suggested, in his novel *Waldfried* (1874), that, on the occasion of the centenary, a German university be established in the United States, an international academy of the spirit. German students should spend a year in this American Athens and they would as a result have a freer, wider outlook upon all problems. The physical cable, at that time being laid across the Atlantic, needed to be supplemented by this educational link so that an electric stream of the spirit might circulate between the continents, revivifying the Old World and enriching the New World. Perhaps Europe could then imbibe the true religious freedom prevailing in America, where a person could belong to any church or no church or else found a new sect if he so desired. Certainly anti-Jewish prejudice would never flourish there and the tragic duality troubling so many Germans of Jewish faith could not endure in the vast melting-pot of all peoples.

MOSES HESS, 1812–1875

(By courtesy of the *Universal Jewish Encyclopedia*, V, 344)

Chapter VI

MOSES HESS

AUERBACH'S cry of despair that he, the German of Mosaic faith, had vainly lived and vainly worked for Germany came at the end of a long and successful literary career. Moses Hess, who had been his classmate at Bonn, foresaw this final disappointment and urged him to espouse the cause of Jewish national regeneration. Auerbach refused. To affirm the existence of a Jewish nationality would be to undo the work of emancipation and to play into the hands of anti-Jewish agitators. But Hess persisted in his "incendiary" views.

Hess too had for decades been led astray by the will-o'-the-wisp of assimilation. Indeed, so great was his early longing to escape from Judaism that in his first literary venture, *Die Heilige Geschichte der Menschheit* (1837), he clothed his philosophic views in Christian symbols and grouped his divisions of human history under the headings: God the Father, God the Son, God the Holy Ghost. He had moreover included in his second book, *Die europäische Triarchie* (1841), a fervent plea for the right of Jews, unbaptized as well as baptized, to marry Christians and protested against difficulties imposed by the Archbishop of Cologne in the way of such marriages. He himself sought a wife of Christian descent in order to facilitate his part in the process of merging Jews and Christians in a higher synthesis. He even went further and documented his will to be

accepted as a pure German by participating in the battle
of the Rhine, which was fought in 1840. This battle, which
broke out soon after Frederick William IV ascended the
throne of Prussia, resulted in no physical casualties. It was
a battle of poets and it had its repercussions in Germany,
in France, and among Jews.

Its initial impulse came from one of those perennial duels
between French and German journalists as to the French
or German character of the Rhineland. Into the fray rushed
Nikolaus Becker, a German law-clerk of the Prussian Rhine
Province, with a stirring battle-song entitled *Der deutsche
Rhein*. It was addressed to the French poet Alphonse de
Lamartine. The opening stanza told the French that they
could not have the free German Rhine, even if like avaricious ravens they shouted themselves hoarse for it. The
concluding stanza re-emphasized that not until the Rhine's
waters covered the last man would it cease to be free and
German.

To this defiant song Alfred de Musset gave a poetic
reply that was no less defiant: *Le Rhin allemand: Réponse
à la chanson de Becker*. He taunted his German adversary
with the reminder that the so-called German Rhine had
more than once been in the hands of the French.

The battle was joined. On the German side the most
talented participants were Georg Herwegh with his *Rhein-
weinlied* and Max Schneckenburger with his *Wacht am
Rhein*. Hoffmann von Fallersleben, who is chiefly remembered as the author of *Deutschland, Deutschland über alles*,
took a hand. Ernst Moritz Arndt, the aged poet who had
once stirred the Germans to war against Napoleon, again
raised his militant voice in a battle hymn. Even the Prince
of Prussia, later Emperor William I, felt it a patriotic duty

to give vent to his sentiments in song and called attention
to the fact that the German city of Strasbourg and the
road to Burgundy were still in French hands.

The best French answer was Lamartine's *La Marseillaise
de la paix: Réponse à Msr. Becker.* The Rhine was in his
eyes the Nile of the Occident. Its common possession by
the French and the Germans was a symbol of the fraternity
of nations and of a longed-for world peace.

From Parisian exile, Heine entered the fray with a few
sardonic verses put in the mouth of Father Rhine, who
complained that he was fed up with the song of Becker and
that he hated to be depicted as a pure virgin after he had
so often been through French hands.

Hess, who was a native of the Rhineland and who in his
youth felt more Prussian than the Prussians, wrote a mel-
ody for Becker's song and sent it to the poet as a patriotic
contribution. The musical composition was returned to
him by Becker with the words: *Du bist ein Jud* — "You are
a Jew!"

This was but one of many instances in which the wooing
of Germany by the young Jewish idealist met with an insulting rebuff. Later on, he recognized that Becker's reply
was not necessarily insulting but rather a statement of
fact. The Jew *was not* of German nationality and should
not therefore fight Germany's battles. In his twenties, however, Hess was bewildered by such experiences. He had
stated in his first published work that Judaism was merely
the preliminary stage for Christianity, that the people of
the Old Testament had perished beyond hope of resurrection in order that the higher life of Christianity might
sprout and flourish. He sincerely believed that the Jews

committed a great error when they had refused to accept
Jesus upon his appearance and that this error had resulted
in their gradual mummification while other peoples pro-
gressed. But all his advances towards his Christian countrymen met with coldness and disfavor.

Hess was wounded in his pride. Still more was he shocked
by the Damascus Affair of 1840, when the official consular
representative of France, the most advanced of western
democracies, vouched for the truth of the accusation that
Jews required Christian blood for the baking of Passover
bread. Hess tried to drown the stirring of his Jewish consciousness by flight to abstract cosmopolitan theories. He
collaborated with Karl Marx and helped to shape the doctrines of early socialism. *Die europäische Triarchie*, which
appeared in 1841, pleaded for a reconstruction of the social
and political order by an alliance or federation of the three
powerful states: Prussia, France, and England. In this new
Pan-Europa the individual Jew might still play an important rôle. For, although the ancient holy Jewish state had
long since perished, its spirit lived on to some extent in its
dispersed offspring. The Mosaic state, based on justice,
freedom, and equality, contained the germ of the coming
world order. In the dim past it mirrored the social structure
of the remote future. The individual descendant of the
once existent Mosaic state should therefore be permitted to
make his patriotic contribution to the socialistic Pan-
Europa of the morrow.

If the reasoning of young Hess on the Jewish question
lacked complete clarity and was not entirely logical, the
fact must be ascribed to the confusion of motives that impelled his occupation with this problem. On the one hand,
he was not able to emancipate himself completely from the

orthodox memories into which he was born and from the
religious training which he received in his boyhood. On
the other hand, he was in revolt against parental tyranny
based upon unaltering Jewish family traditions. Hence, he
loved and hated his Jewish background, and in his shifting
moods he idealized and deprecated Jewish traits and the
Jewish way of life. Flight to German patriotism was rendered impossible by the anti-Semitic Teutomaniacs. Flight
to cosmopolitanism offered a possible solution for his spiritual distress and homelessness. But here too he met with
disappointments. His very allies in the struggle for a better
order conferred upon him the nickname of "communistic
rabbi" and were no less conscious of his Jewish origin than
his adversaries. Friends and foes seemed to be in agreement
that the messianic flights of his apparently scientific doctrines had not been uninfluenced by his Jewish roots.

Hess began to feel that perhaps both were right. Perhaps
a person's doctrines, a person's psychic structure, no less
than his physical appearance, were conditioned by his
nationality, his race, the historic experience of his ancestors.
Perhaps the merging of the individual with humanity at
large was not a single simple process. Perhaps the ascent
to ultimate unity of mankind must be made by means of
several steps or gradations, the individuals growing into
families, the families into nationalities, and these into a
federation of nations. Perhaps in the organism of mankind,
each organ or nationality had a function of its own. Each
people had its own peculiar contribution, its own way of
life, resulting from its past experiences and foreshadowing
its future rôle. Races and nations were necessary, the
numerically weaker no less than the numerically stronger.
Certainly racial superiority was a myth and national superi-

ority an absurdity. Racial conceit merely masked lust for
dominion. National arrogance led inevitably to hatred and
oppression of less fortunate ethnic groups. It never led to
social progress or to the creation of higher ethical values.
All nationalities must first be liberated as nationalities, if
they were to make their best contributions to the common
advancement of civilization. The eighteenth century took
the first step when it proclaimed the equality of all persons.
The French Revolution of 1789 succeeded in bringing about
the emancipation of the individual human being. The
nineteenth century must take the second step. It must
proclaim the equality of all peoples, great and small, and
must bring about the liberation of all nationalities and
races. Already a beginning was being made. Greece was
re-arisen after centuries of twilight. Poland was breathing
anew. Hungary was preparing for a final effort at resurrection. Rome was reawakened. The hour seemed to be
at hand for the Jewish people to take its legitimate place
among the world's free nations.

In his fiftieth year Hess proclaimed this new insight in
his book *Rom und Jerusalem*, published in 1862. He con-
fesses that he has been estranged from his people for twenty
years but that now he is returning to his own fold, prepared
to participate in its joys and sorrows, its memories and
hopes, its internal and external struggles. On the basis of
personal experiences and after considerable study, he has
arrived at the conclusion that Jews can never become an
organic part of the cultures among which they have lived
for two thousand years and that all contemporary efforts
at amalgamation must end in failure. For, the Jews are a
separate nationality, linked by unbreakable spiritual bonds

to the heritage of their fathers and to the holy land which
first fashioned them. In Eastern Europe millions of Jews
still pray night and day for the restoration of their nation
and a return to their ancient abode. Were Judaism merely
a religion, solely a confession of faith, it would long since
have ossified and been swept away together with other
dogmas, Catholic and Protestant, when confronted with the
enlightened conclusions of modern science. But Judaism is
not a passive philosophy. It is an active mode of living. It
is the cult of a nationality. It is the organic expression of
a nation. This nation once made an important contribution
to humanity. It is again ready to resume its function, for
it still has a function to perform in the coming rejuvenation of all historic and cultural groups. It must still battle
for the doctrine of the divine unity of all life. When others
stress salvation for the individual and the attainment of
personal immortality, it must continue to stress its teaching that the individual is inseparable from the family, the
family from the nation, the nation from humanity, humanity
from all organic and cosmic creation, and all creation from
the Creator. The messianic realm desired by Judaism is the
realm of unity on earth and not a kingdom somewhere in
heaven. It is a realm in which all beings shall participate
at the end of the historic process. This end may still be
distant — the era when the holy spirit of Judaism will be
the common possession of mankind, the era of social cooperation when the earth will be a temple wherein shall
dwell the spirit of God.

A beginning must, however, be made in the transformation
of our egoistic or individualistic system into that socialistic
or messianic system envisaged by Jewish sages and prophets.
It can be made with the return of the Jews to their ancient

land and the founding of a Jewish cooperative commonwealth in Palestine. The creative genius, which once infused
Jewish life and Jewish doctrine, departed from Israel when
Israel began to be ashamed of its nationality. But as soon
as the Jews will get rid of their inferiority complex and
resume a normal existence on their ancestral soil, then the
holy spirit will return to them and they will create values,
such as we hardly even dream of today.

The immediate task facing world Jewry is, therefore,
agitation for the revival of the dormant national forces,
constant political awareness and increasing financial pre-
paredness, so that the moment a favorable opportunity
presents itself, practical colonization may be begun and a
network of colonies established north of the projected Suez
Canal and throughout the area between the Mediterranean
and the Jordan. France, interested in Suez and in safeguard-
ing for the western nations the road to India and China, will
gladly lend a helping hand.

The Jewish intellectuals must first be roused from their
vague cosmopolitanism. A patriotic spirit must be awakened
in their hearts and they must then assume the leadership in
liberating the Jewish masses from deadening formalism. If
this first step is successful, the resurgent national genius of
the people will find the proper solutions for the many practical difficulties arising during the actual process of building
a new state. These difficulties need not be minimized, but
it must be remembered that no great historic change ever
comes about without heroic efforts or mighty struggles. The
Jews are gifted with a lot of common sense, with a healthy
conception of realities, and they can draw upon a vast fund of
past experience. The time is at hand when even the enlightened liberals and radicals, who often regard their Jewish

origin as a misfortune, will at last realize that they can under
no circumstances escape this misfortune, neither through
baptism nor through their vague humanitarianism. They,
too, will then want to save their people from sinking to the
level of parasitism. They, too, will clamor for a Jewish
homeland and for national independence, so that they might
develop on their own soil progressive political and social
institutions.

Capitalism, with its exploitation of man by man and
class by class, is coming to an end. Imperialism, with its
exploitation of weaker nations by stronger ones, cannot
endure much longer. The Jews have become aware that the
key to progress and the only stable basis for the future
world order must be sought in productive labor and they
are therefore making strenuous efforts to train the younger
generation for useful work in agriculture and handicraft.
But so long as the Jews are in exile, the vast majority
will never become laborers, for they are ever aware that the
soil they till cannot be theirs and the factories they build
cannot belong to them. Differences in national cults will
always prevent their merging successfully with their neighbors. Exile can never be home.

Judaism cannot be regenerated in the Diaspora. Its revival
can take place only in Palestine. If, under the protection of
the great powers, the seed of a Jewish state is once planted
along the future highway to India and China, a new tree of
life will grow up and bear nourishing fruit. A revitalized
nation will have its creative forces unleashed and will bring
a blessing to all peoples.

Perhaps a majority of Jews will not return to the Holy
Land after this second exile that has lasted two thousand
years. Probably less will return from Western Europe than

from other parts of the world. However, the moral and political condition of the Jews everywhere will be immensely strengthened by the existence of a Palestinian state. The concessions of freedom and equality, which the individual Jew cannot wrest from his unwilling contemporaries, the Jewish nation will be able to obtain from its sister nations. For, these nations would be committing moral suicide if they granted citizenship to all other inhabitants of various racial origins, who happened to be born in their territory or who happened to reside there for a number of years, and at the same time refused citizenship and the rights accompanying citizenship to the Jews who have dwelt in their midst for centuries.

Until the Jewish state shall have been restored and a territorial basis for the Jewish nationality assured, all tampering with the Jewish religion by so-called reformers must be frowned upon and all time-honored customs must be retained. The ancient Hebrew prayers must not be discarded, mutilated, or camouflaged, for the spirit of the race lives on in them and, despite their apparent irrationality, they are valuable in preserving the unity of the Jews. The religious longing for Zion should not be minimized but must rather be expanded into political action, so that Israel, or at least the remnant of Israel that is not seduced by the Golden Calf, may soon begin to betake itself to the land of its glorious past and resume its long interrupted creative activity.

The ideas of Hess have been taken over by a large sector of contemporary Jewry, and the solitary thinker of a century ago is today revered as the chief forerunner of Theodor Herzl, the assimilated Viennese who became the founder of political Zionism.

PART III

THE TURN OF THE CENTURY

THEODOR HERZL, 1860–1904

Chapter VII

THEODOR HERZL

THEODOR HERZL was thirty-five years of age, a luxury-loving aesthete, an elegant dramatist, a successful essayist, a well-mannered dandy, a witty salon hero, when in 1895 the Jewish problem seized hold of his imagination, tore at his heart, and whirled him from his safe and sheltered existence into the maelstrom of public life. Before a decade had passed, he was dead, but his spiritual restlessness had set ideas fermenting and had called into being a popular movement whose repercussions have been felt for half a century in many lands.

The first reaction of readers of the influential Viennese *Neue Freie Presse* to the news that its feuilletonist and Parisian correspondent, Theodor Herzl, had turned his attention to the Jewish problem was that either he was engaged in a new type of jesting or that he was becoming insane. The first friend, to whom he confided his belief that he had found a solution of the Jewish question and to whom he outlined the main principles upon which he based his belief, burst into tears: alas! that so gifted a writer should go mad at so early an age. And yet, though Herzl's Jewish vision burst forth in 1895 with the elemental force of a volcanic eruption, it had been smouldering within him from boyhood. He was ever aware, painfully aware of his Jewish roots. His sensitiveness cropped out at school, when he resented the derisive allusions of an anti-Semitic teacher and, as a consequence, transferred to another school. This sensitiveness led him later to resign from his student fraternity at the University of Vienna, when this German nationalistic organization in 1883 participated in anti-Jewish demonstrations. A year earlier, he had reacted violently to Eugen Dühring's diatribes against Jews. The twenty-two-year-old law student recorded in his notebook, under the date of February 9, 1882, that he had just read Dühring's well-written but infamous book, which advocated the end of Jewish emancipation and the restoration of the ghetto. He did not see how one could expect decent behavior on the part of the uneducated, uncritical masses, if a learned professor of Dühring's rank did not scruple to dip his pen in poison and to heap vile calumny upon an entire people. Herzl afterwards confessed that since his acquaintance with Dühring's essays, the Jewish question gnawed at his vitals and caused him untold torments. At first he was angry at his origin and embittered at his Jewish background. Gladly would he have escaped, if escape had been possible. But the way of baptism did not appeal to his sense of honor. From the beer-hall the cry "Hep Hep" resounded in his ears and from the gutter the appellation "Jewish swine" pursued him. All apologetic pamphlets, all literary appeals for tolerance and decency would never reach these anonymous shouters. Indeed, all rational pleas that could be made for the Jews had already been made and, while they were not without beneficial influence upon choice spirits, such as Lessing, they never succeeded in seeping down into the masses, whose approach was still reminiscent of the Middle Ages.

Herzl arrived at the conclusion that, wherever there are Jews in perceptible numbers, anti-Semitism exists and even the most liberal governments are unable to eradicate this evil.

Enlightened states made their finest contribution and displayed utmost magnanimity when they emancipated the Jews in their midst; yet emancipation merely aggravated existing difficulties. The failure of a country to persecute Jews adequately attracts them to its soil in ever increasing numbers, with the result that their immigration on a large scale rouses resentment among the native population and gives birth to anti-Semitism where none may have existed previously. Why is this reaction inevitable? Why is it often justified as a form of self-defense? Because the Jews are a people, a distinct people with common ethnic characteristics, and their immigration into any country is experienced by the inhabitants of that country as an invasion by an alien people. Nations do not, as a rule, object to infiltration by individual foreigners, who can be assimilated, but no nation will stand for the entry into its land of another dynamic nationality, which seeks to continue on the new soil its own peculiar way of living. Jews may plead that they are only a religious federation. The neighbors, among whom they dwell or seek to dwell, are of a different opinion. Jews may assert their willingness to merge with the dominant nationality or racial strain. They may prove themselves loyal patriots. They may sacrifice their blood and their wealth. They may further arts and sciences, commerce and industry, glory and power of their so-called fatherlands. All in vain! They will continue to be regarded as strangers by all other groups, even by those whose forefathers may have come into the land long after their own. Why? Because the majority alone determines who is a stranger and who is a native.

Jews are, however, a minority in every land and are hence at home nowhere. They can cease to be strangers only in a land in which they will form a majority. Such a land will be the Jewish State.

The restoration of the Jewish State was the solution offered by Herzl in his pamphlet *Der Judenstaat,* which was written in 1895 and which has since become the basic text of Zionism. The Jewish State is not a Utopia, it is a necessity — this thought Herzl sought to hammer into the souls of his contemporaries, Jews and non-Jews. All other solutions have been tried and have proved unsuccessful. It is folly to experiment with them again.

Persecution has failed. No people has ever been subjected to greater pressure or for longer periods of time. From parliaments, assemblies, press, pulpits, street corners, hotel lobbies, Jews are constantly being attacked. In Russia, entire Jewish villages go up in flames; in Rumania, a few Jews are killed here and there; in Germany, they are merely beaten up now and then; in Austria, one type of terror is applied and in Algeria another; in France, social ostracism is the method used, and elsewhere other nuances are applied in order to rid the land of Jews or to make their lot unbearable. Nevertheless, the Jews have shown themselves to be indestructible as a people. Individuals have fallen by the wayside. Weaklings have become renegades. The overwhelming majority, however, has stubbornly retained its ancient affiliation in the midst of all efforts at extermination. Israel is a stiff-necked people.

Intermarriage has been suggested by some well-meaning souls as the most attractive solution. If, however, the ancient prejudices lodged deep within the heart of the

Christian peoples are to be so far eradicated as to make mixed marriages the norm instead of the exception, then this could come about only because the Jews have first obtained such tremendous economic power that mating with them is deemed desirable, despite long prevailing social objections. Impoverished aristocrats have often married the daughters of Jewish bankers. Indeed, the proportion of Jewish blood in German, Austrian, and Hungarian noble families is extraordinarily large. But it must be remembered that, before the Central European bourgeoisie can be induced to forego ancient aversions and to favor intermarriage with the Jewish bourgeoisie, the latter would have to possess economic power to the point of supremacy. Herzl believes that such a point cannot be reached, however, since the majority population with an army, navy, and political apparatus at its disposal will never submit to economic dominance by a scorned minority. The wealthier the Jews become, the stronger will the waves of anti-Semitism surge about them.

The establishment of Jewish settlements in various parts of the globe is seen by some as a possible solution. Baron de Hirsch experimented with such colonies, by transporting a few thousand Jews to Argentina at a cost of many millions of dollars. Herzl is sceptical of the results obtained or to be expected. He predicts that, if these colonies prosper and increase in wealth, they will further the rise of anti-Semitism in the new territory; but if, on the other hand, they collapse, they will rouse doubts as to the productive ability of the Jewish people.

Socialism will bring about the desired solution, in the opinion of some followers of the Marxian philosophy. Herzl does not agree. He states that the Jews, because of their historic position as the possessors of liquid capital, have

become primarily a bourgeois people. Deprived of the right
to own land and long excluded from workers' guilds, they
are not to any appreciable extent landowners or proletarians.
They rather exercise in the main the functions of middlemen
and entrepreneurs. They have in addition produced a dis-
proportionate number of intellectuals, who in many countries
are driven into the arms of extreme radicalism, since they
cannot be absorbed in the economic process. The Jews,
therefore, occupy the most exposed positions, both on the
capitalistic and on the socialistic fronts. In any class struggle,
the Jews will be the victims, no matter which side wins.

Gradual assimilation is advocated by those who have
faith in the inherent goodness of human beings. Treat the
Jews kindly, exercise tolerance towards them, permit them
to prosper for a few generations, and they will be so weakened by luxury and western culture that they will voluntarily
give up their tribal ways and ultimately disappear without
a trace. Herzl questions whether the complete effacement
of a historic group that undeniably has certain fine qualities
can be acclaimed as a desirable solution. But even if it were
desirable, it is not a practical possibility to which one can
look forward in the immediate future. The Jews will not be
let alone for as many generations as is necessary for them
to lose their consciousness of kinship and historic solidarity.
Both Jewish sociologists of the present day, such as Arthur
Ruppin, and German anthropologists, whose conclusions
are embodied in the Nuremberg racial laws of 1935, agree
with Herzl's statement of forty years ago. They insist that
at least four generations must elapse before the average
Jewish family can bridge the gulf from the ghetto to complete effacement of Jewish consciousness. The process generally involves an ascent in the economic status. But Jewish

prosperity somehow provokes antagonism. The masses, accustomed to despise the Jews as the most contemptible of the poor, do not let them enjoy wealth and luxury in peace. The process of assimilation is arrested before it is completed. Pressure hurls the Jews back to the ghetto; hate forces them to return to their tribal bonds; distress forges them into a community of fate; prejudice impels them to continue their historic existence.

If the Jews are a people and if they must remain so, whether they will it or not, then the only sensible solution, said Herzl, seems to be the restoration of a Jewish State. Throughout the long night of their history, Jews have not ceased to dream the royal dream of a Jewish State; indeed, they begin each New Year with a prayer for their return to Jerusalem during the coming year.

Can this dream become a reality? Yes, answered Herzl, if the Jews desire it and if the other nations are convinced that it is the only feasible way of getting rid of their unwanted Jews. These other nations, afflicted with anti-Semitism, merely have to agree to give the Jews a bit of undeveloped territory wherein to exercise complete sovereignty, and the Jews will do the rest. What land shall the Jews take? Whatever they can get. Argentina, which has immense virgin territory, is a possibility. Palestine, their historic home, is of course to be preferred. Herzl felt that for Palestine Jews would be ready to make greater sacrifices. What can they offer in return for such a land? To the European powers, who act as guarantors of the projected state, they offer the removal of an unwanted alien population; to Turkey, the owner of Palestine, they offer the regulation and sanitation of the pressing Ottoman debt; to the world at large, they offer a healthy bridge between Europe and Asia, a guard-of-honor for the holy cradle of three great religions.

The exodus of the Jews will not be a migration from Western Civilization to a more primitive life. "We shall not revert to a lower stage; we shall rise to a higher one. We shall not dwell in mud huts; we shall build new and more beautiful and modern houses, and possess them in safety. We shall not lose our acquired possessions; we shall realize them. We shall surrender our well-earned rights, but only for better ones. We shall not sacrifice our beloved customs; we shall find them again. We shall not leave our own home before the new one is prepared for us. Those only will depart who are sure thereby to improve their position: those who are now desperate will go first; after them the poor; next the prosperous, and, last of all, the wealthy. Those who go in advance will raise themselves to a higher grade, equal to that whose representatives will shortly follow. Thus the exodus will be at the same time an ascent of the classes. The departure of the Jews will involve no economic disturbances, no crises, no persecutions; in fact, the countries they abandon will revive to a new period of prosperity. There will be an inner migration of Christian citizens into the positions evacuated by Jews. The outgoing current will be gradual, without any disturbance, and its initial movement will put an end to anti-Semitism. The Jews will leave as honored friends, and if some of them return, they will receive the same favorable welcome and treatment at the hands of civilized nations as is accorded to all foreign visitors. Their exodus will have no resemblance to a flight, for it will be a well-regulated movement under control of public opinion. The movement will not only be inaugurated with absolute conformity to law, but it cannot even be carried out without the friendly cooperation of interested governments, who would derive considerable benefits from it."[1]

The Zionist movement is to be the organization of the Jewish people on the march, and Herzl sees in Zionism neither a party nor a religious sect but the stage of transition from the Diaspora to the Jewish Commonwealth. Whosoever does not wish to identify himself with the Jewish nation, need not do so. Whosoever wants to assimilate to another people, let him participate wholeheartedly in that other people's affairs, but let him refrain from interfering with internal Jewish matters. The Zionists alone are to be the public body responsible for the Jewish people. In order that this body might be formally established on a world-wide basis, a congress of Zionists is the first essential step, and this step must be taken at the earliest possible moment. Jewry must have an influential voice in the determination of its future. It must have a political agency that can confer authoritatively with other political powers. Herzl, therefore, decides to issue a call for such a congress, to meet in the summer of 1897. He notes that his agitation is arousing considerable interest throughout Europe; Zionist cells are being formed in various countries; diplomats are lending a serious ear to his plans; emissaries of the Sultan of Turkey are conferring with him; a successful congress would inaugurate the practical realization of his "royal" thought.

Herzl's plan to make Munich the seat of the Congress was frustrated by the protest of the local Jewish community, which feared that its German patriotism might be called into question. Influential rabbis in other German cities issued a condemnation of Zionist aspirations, branding them

as contrary to the spirit of the Jewish religion and to the
feeling of the loyal German inhabitants of Mosaic persuasion.
Herzl replied with a withering satire on the religious leaders
who stood in the way of Jewish salvation. He dubbed them
Protestrabbiner and likened them to the persons who sit in a
secure boat and strike out with their oars against the drown-
ing, who try to hold on to its edge. He transferred the seat
of the congress from Germany to Switzerland. On August
29, 1897, the memorable First Congress was opened at
Basel. One hundred and ninety-seven delegates from important Jewish centers of population attended the three-day
sessions. Herzl's introductory remarks defined Zionism as
a return to Jewry even before the return to Judea. A common bond was to be forged, linking the most modern sectors
of Western Jewry with the most conservative sectors of
Eastern Jewry. All were part of one nation, the Jewish
nation. The animated discussions culminated in the formu-
lation of a common aim for the movement: the establishment
in Palestine of a publicly guaranteed and legally sanctioned
national home for those Jews who are unable or unwilling
to assimilate elsewhere. The acceptance of this aim was
thenceforth to constitute the basis for all Zionist activity.
Amidst tremendous enthusiasm, Herzl's "royal" thought
became the property of the Jewish people and the delegates
dispersed to carry on Zionist propaganda in all the corners
of the earth.

The launching of the Zionist movement was Herzl's solution of the tragic duality which troubled German-Jewish
writers. Whosoever accepts the Zionist approach must
henceforth, according to Herzl, deem himself a member of
the Jewish people and, though he sojourn temporarily in the
German Diaspora, his permanent homeland is Palestine.

Since he is a German or an Austrian citizen, it is his duty to fulfill all the obligations and to insist upon all the rights of citizenship. But he definitely renounces all claim to German ethnic kinship. A new nobility is born in his soul. He does not feel himself inferior to his German neighbors, nor does he have to compensate for inner humility by outward arrogance. He has acquired mental poise, emotional equilibrium, moral dignity. He can now work for the improvement of humanity not as an indefinable cosmopolitan individual but as a part of the Jewish people. His achievement will henceforth redound to their credit, and their increased prestige will heighten his self-respect.

Herzl's thought revolutionized all speculation on Jewish matters. Ever since the turn of the century, all discussions of the tragic duality, in which German Jews found themselves, have centered about Zionism. During successive congresses of Herzl's disciples, the national idea was deepened, interpreted, rendered more practical, and transformed into concrete achievements. Meanwhile, men of letters, whose task it is to burrow into the recesses of the human heart, have undertaken a searching analysis of the spiritual implications of this apparent panacea, an analysis which reveals difficulties and weaknesses, but which also elucidates and enriches Zionist thought.

Chapter VIII

ARTHUR SCHNITZLER

THE Zionist movement, launched by Theodor Herzl at the First Basel Congress in 1897, found an instantaneous, enthusiastic response among the poverty-stricken, unassimilated Jewish masses of Eastern Europe. These were ready to follow the new messiah to Palestine as soon as the signal for departure was given. They were willing to suffer privations and hardships in the rebuilding of a homeland long envisaged in their prayers and dreams. Among the well-to-do, assimilated, Western Jews, however, Herzl's idea met with scepticism, indifference, fear, and derision. Only a few prominent individuals rallied to his standard. The first writers of repute to endorse his cause wholeheartedly were Max Nordau and Israel Zangwill. But, as the dynamic Viennese journalist continued his agitation, convoking one congress of his disciples after another, presenting his plan to the chancelleries of Europe, winning the attention of Kaiser and Czar and Sultan, repercussions of the Zionist approach to the Jewish problem became noticeable in German fiction, drama, and poetry. Though writers at the turn of the century did not generally agree with Herzl's solution, nevertheless they included a criticism of its fundamental tenets in their discussion of the German-Jewish duality. To these writers belong Arthur Schnitzler, the mellowest dramatist of the Danubian dual-monarchy, and Jakob Wassermann, the most popular novelist of Franconia.

ARTHUR SCHNITZLER, 1862–1931

Arthur Schnitzler, who was born in 1862 and who began his career as a physician, attained triumphs with his plays in the 1890's far beyond the moderate theater-successes of Herzl. The correspondence between the two during the years 1892 and 1893, part of which has been published and part of which still reposes in the Schnitzler-Archive, reveals a similarity of literary interests. Herzl, in his very first letter, praised the talent of the younger poet: "When I see a talent such as yours blossom, I am happy as if I had never been a literary practitioner, which means, a narrow, intolerant, envious, malicious fool; I am as happy as when I see the carnations awaken below in the garden."[1] Schnitzler, in his reply, gave his first impressions of Herzl as an elegant aesthete and adored dandy, a Beau Brummel and the envied idol of Viennese polite society.

The following years saw the metamorphosis of Herzl into a fiery crusader. Schnitzler continued to write oversophisticated tales, disillusioned dramas, witty epigrams. He always kept aloof from religious, racial, or political parties. As a keen interpreter of the European scene, however, he could not remain wholly silent about a problem which troubled his generation and which at times subjected him to unpleasant and even dangerous experiences. His views on the place of the Jew in modern life can be gleaned largely from his autobiographical novel, *Der Weg ins Freie*, begun in 1902 and completed in 1907, and from his play, *Professor Bernhardi*, upon which he worked from 1899 until 1912.

As a German writer of Jewish origin, Schnitzler was often the target for anti-Semitic attacks. Once, while on a visit to Prague, he barely escaped physical injury at the hands of Jew-baiting youths. The wrath of Teutomaniacs pursued him even after his death and brought about the burning of his books in 1933. Nevertheless, in his literary treatment of the Jewish question, Schnitzler managed to retain his wonted philosophic calm. He pleaded the cause of no single party. He advocated no royal road to salvation. He merely brought to bear upon a very complex problem the light of a kind and critical temperament. His views on the Jew in Germany are wise and well worth careful study.

In grappling with the Jewish problem, Schnitzler did not minimize its difficulties. He did not not mask its ugliness. He made no predictions as to its future trend. He merely laid bare a moral and social condition that brought suffering and bewilderment to millions of people.

The Jewish problem has its origin, he believed, in the existence of the Jews as a minority in each nation. Therein he was in complete agreement with Herzl. Schnitzler, too, held that any human group, which lives in the midst of a numerically larger group and which retains its own peculiarities, must inevitably arouse in the majority a consciousness of difference. This consciousness usually gives birth to dislike, resentment, contempt, and hate. It should not, but it does. It may manifest itself in mild forms of injustice and slander, or in the more brutal forms of murder and pogroms. This anthropological law applies to all peoples, irrespective of their specific characteristics. Thus, if Aryans should happen to be in a minority in any country, anti-Aryanism would immediately develop. Attention would be focused upon all the faults of the Aryans from the dawn of history to the present time. Examples of cruelty, cowardice, cunning, avarice, and baseness would be collected from all periods to justify dislike for Aryans and to refute any Aryan champion who might complain that his people deserved better treatment at the hands of the majority. Similarly, anti-Semitism

is the natural outcome of the historic position in which the
Jews, as a minority group, find themselves in every land; and
no amount of Jewish or Christian sentimentality will eradicate this feeling. Perhaps in a thousand years the whole
Jewish question will have ceased to exist; but in our generation, in our century, and as long as the sense of difference is
deep-rooted in Jews and in their neighbors, no solution need
be expected — at least, no general solution that will be
applicable to all Jewish people. It will rather be up to each
individual to adjust himself as best he may. Schnitzler discussed possible types of adjustments, and subjected to close
scrutiny the two most important tendencies in Jewish life at
the turn of the century, namely, Zionism and Assimilation.

In the figure of Leo Golowsky, in *Der Weg ins Freie*,
Schnitzler pays stirring tribute to Herzl and the philosophy
of Zionism. The novelist himself remains a heretic, but a
heretic with considerable sympathy for those who have
found a refuge in the new gospel. He agrees that, in spite
of so-called political equality, Jews are everywhere regarded
as citizens of the second rank; and he can appreciate the
feelings of those who are tired of being perpetual objects of
well-meaning tolerance, and who would rather look upon
themselves as strangers sojourning in a foreign land —
strangers with a real home in some country that takes a
genuine interest in their welfare. He can also justify Zionism
as a philanthropic venture that offers a secure resting place
for millions of his coreligionists who suffer from physical or
spiritual persecution and who would gladly exchange their
ghetto quarters for some fruitful land, where they would
form a majority and where they would be governed by
their own kin. He does not, however, accept the fundamental
assumption of political Zionism that this land must be Pales-

tine. He does not believe that Jews everywhere are animated
by a longing for a land of which they know little more than
that their ancestors, according to tradition, lived there in
some remote past. He feels that the enthusiasm for Palestine
has been artificially created, and is directly traceable to the
spread of anti-Semitism in Europe. Not even Herzl, the
father of political Zionism, ever thought of Palestine as his
fatherland until the Dreyfus affair in Paris made him aware
of the strong undercurrent of anti-Jewish sentiment in
most European countries. If an American, whose ancestors
emigrated from England, or France, or Germany a century
ago, never regards these mother countries as his home, why
should one expect a Jew, whose ancestors left Palestine two
thousand years ago, still to cherish within his blood longings
for this remote land? Palestine is not, according to Schnitzler,
the home of all the Jews. For the concept of home denotes
not the abode of one's ancestors, nor even the place of one's
own birth; but rather it is the center of a person's activity,
the circle in which he grew up, the culture to which he owes
his development and in which he is most comfortable. The
Viennese physician and author feels most strongly that
Vienna is his home, and he loves this home more deeply
than the loud-mouthed patriots who would exile him from
this city, if they had the power to do so. "Though all who
dwell in this land from time immemorial were to shout in my
face the epithet 'stranger,' and though they were even to
erect the stake for me, neither their threats nor their hate
could ever destroy this feeling. You, Earth, know that I
have grown out of you; and you, Heaven, know that it is *my*
home on which you are throwing your brilliant light. It is
not as an outcast that I breathe among you."[2]

German, not Hebrew, is the language of his literary

masterpieces — the language he thrills to. The psyche of Central Europe is more intelligible to him than the psyche of the Orient. He sees no justification for Zionism in the reputed longing of the Jews for the Holy Land. He finds it natural for Jews to be enraged at injustices committed against them or their kin because of racial origin, and for them to experience in such moments a desire to go off and settle elsewhere. He depicts in Salomon Ehrenberg, in *Der Weg ins Freie*, a Jew whose anger and chagrin lead him to Palestine, but who returns in a chastened mood ready to continue the struggle against his foes in Vienna itself, the city which is, after all, home to him. Schnitzler maintains that it is as incorrect to speak of the Jews as homeless as it would be to speak of those people as sleepless who are not allowed to fall asleep, whose pillows are snatched from under their heads, whose quilts are pulled away from them, whose toes are tickled, and whose noses are constantly twitted. The Jews have their homes in every country. What they lack are fellow citizens.

Heinrich Bermann, who, in *Der Weg ins Freie*, often voices Schnitzler's sincerest beliefs, gives vent to his chagrin at this state of affairs. He asks the Catholic Baron Georg von Wergenthin: "Do you think that there is in this world a single Christian — even assuming that he is the noblest, fairest, and most trustworthy of men — a single Christian who, in some moment of disappointment and anger at his best friend, sweetheart, or wife, would not throw up their Jewishness to them, if they happened to be Jews, or of Jewish descent? He may not do it in so many words, but certainly he will think it in his heart of hearts. As a proof, pick up the letters of any famous person who is, in every other respect, intelligent and admirable. Read carefully the passages con-

taining hostile and ironic comments about his contemporaries. In ninety-nine cases out of a hundred, these concern
individuals whose race and religion are not taken into
account. In the hundredth case, where the attacked human
being has the misfortune to be a Jew, the author certainly
does not fail to mention this fact."[3] Against the Baron's
criticism that Heinrich must be suffering from "persecution-
mania," the latter counters with the assertion that Jews are
more likely to suffer from a "security-mania," in other words,
that they are more likely to regard themselves as safe in the
house of friends, simply because they are for a time left in
peace. What the Baron regards as "persecution-mania" is
really nothing more than an acute awareness of the true,
unstable condition in which the Jews find themselves. Every
Jew, though he may have little in common with his coreligionists, feels that, somehow, in the eyes of others, he is
held responsible for every fault and every error committed
by a fellow Jew. Hence, his extreme sensitiveness towards
any tactlessness, or any wrongdoing, of which a member of
his race may be guilty. From childhood he learns through
contact with his neighbors that Jewish traits are especially
funny or disagreeable. If he, then, sees a Jew misbehaving,
he is overcome by a feeling of shame similar to that which a
brother would experience if his sister were to undress before
him. Jews are, therefore, their own severest critics; they are
the least tolerant of all people with members of their own
group.

In *Der Weg ins Freie*, Schnitzler lets Leo Golowsky, tne
Zionist, and Heinrich Bermann, the tortured sceptic, air
their contradictory views on the Jewish question before the
sympathetic Georg von Wergenthin. Georg, who tries to be
objective, finds himself agreeing at one moment with Leo,

who is too proud to force himself upon fellow citizens that will not accept him as their equal and who, therefore, wants to go off with his fellow Jews to a land of their own. The following moment, however, Georg feels himself more nearly in accord with Heinrich, who speaks of Zionism as a fantastic and short-sighted policy, and who sees no particular gain in gathering from all ends of the world and in sending off to a strange land the members of a people, most of whom are participating to the best of their ability in the culture of their various countries, and almost all of whom have no particular homesickness for any other abode. For the first time, Georg begins to suspect the difficult position in which the best Jews find themselves, those Jews who, on the one hand, do not want to impose themselves where they are not welcome, and who, on the other hand, are embittered by the demand that they become assimilated to the insolent majority. "For the first time, the word 'Jew,' which he had himself so often uttered thoughtlessly and even scornfully, appeared to him from a new and gloomy angle. An insight was granted him into this people's mysterious lot — an insight which affected all who sprang from its ranks: those who sought to escape from their origin as from a disgrace, pain, or fairy tale that did not concern them, as well as those others who stubbornly harped upon their origin as upon a fate, an honor, or an unalterable historic fact."[4]

The hopelessness of all immediate solutions of this complicated problem is brought home to Georg even further when, in answer to his supposition that gradual assimilation might be the best remedy, he is disillusioned by Heinrich's painful remarks: "Assimilation . . . a word . . . yes, it will come, some day . . . in the far, far distant future. It will not come in the way some wish and others fear. It will not be exactly assimilation . . . but, perhaps, something essentially similar. Do you know what the final conclusion will probably prove? That we, we Jews I mean, were, in a sense, a ferment of humanity — yes, that will, perhaps, be realized in a thousand or two thousand years."[5]

Until then the solution is hopeless. Schnitzler expressed the pessimistic view that Jews and non-Jews are separated by a gulf which cannot be wholly bridged, and that all efforts at eradicating their differences must fail. There is no reason, however, why an understanding of these differences should not take the place of mutual distrust. Understanding will efface bitterness. Understanding will prevent persecution and injustice. Understanding will further tolerance, and make life easier for all concerned.

To Schnitzler it seemed absurd for people to wrangle over questions of faith and to abuse each other because of their beliefs, or even lack of belief. What is faith, or belief? he once asked. When we say we believe, are we not merely asserting that a certain explanation appeals to us as the most plausible one for a certain phenomenon? When we say we believe in God, do we not merely state that we do not accept finite explanations as the most plausible ones for certain phenomena? In this sense, the difference between human beings is really very slight, for even so-called atheists merely substitute an equivalent concept for that which others call God — a different name, another guess. Disputes between religious creeds are waged over the acceptance or rejection of this or that mythology. These disputes could be avoided if Christianity, Judaism, and other creeds of today were studied more often in the same scientific spirit as are the creeds of ancient Assyria, Greece, or Rome; or if

the facts, theories, and assumptions of religion were regarded
in the same light as are those of music, biology, or astronomy.
Why should the person who ridicules Darwin, Goethe,
Beethoven, or Michael Angelo be tolerated as a respectable
member of society; and the one who mocks at Jesus or St.
Francis of Assisi be looked at askance? Surely, that mysterious divine element, whatever it may turn out to be,
manifested itself in Goethe and Copernicus no less than in
Jesus and his apostles. But no artistic or scientific genius is
ever worshipped in the manner in which saints are.

Were the differences between Jews and their neighbors
purely religious, reconciliation might, in that case, not be so
hopeless; for there are millions of people today in whose lives
organized religion plays no important rôle. These differences
lie much deeper, however, and cannot be easily grasped in
words. Georg von Wergenthin, who associates much with
Jews, feels that, in spite of all sympathy toward them, he
will never attain the same unembarrassing intimacy with
them that he feels for his other friends. He asks himself
whether, perhaps, racial antagonism accounts for this mutual
strangeness; but he must reply in the negative. In the depth
of his heart there are stronger bonds uniting him with the
Jews Heinrich Bermann and Leo Golowsky than with his
non-Jewish companions, or even with his own brother. Yet,
if this is so, why is he ill at ease when he listens to Heinrich
and Leo discussing the Jewish question? To his own sur-
prise, he discovers that he himself had been guilty of un-
justified animosity toward the members of this people, an
animosity that he could not explain on the basis of personal
experience. He, too, had lightheartedly contributed his
share towards swelling the distrust and defiance which he
encountered among Jews. "This thought aroused in him a

growing discomfort, which he could not quite interpret, and which was nothing else than a vague recognition that pure relations could not flourish, even between individually pure characters, in an atmosphere of folly, injustice, and insincerity."[6] Until this atmosphere is completely dissipated, many centuries will pass. Meanwhile, each Jew will have to find his own way out of despair and disgust, his own way to a freedom that will permit him to breathe unmolested. "Perhaps there are really some who will have to go to Jerusalem," says Schnitzler, through the mask of Heinrich Bermann. "I fear, however, that, on reaching this illusory goal, they will find themselves in a still greater mess. I do not believe at all that such wanderings on to freedom can be undertaken *en masse* . . . . for the roads to freedom do not run through the lands out yonder, but rather through our inner selves. It is up to each person to find his inner path. To do so, it is, of course, necessary for him to attain clarity within himself, to light up the most hidden corners of his soul, to have the courage of following his own nature, and not to let himself be led astray. Yes, the daily prayer of every decent person ought to be: no straying from the inner path!"[7]

Schnitzler did not believe that apologetic works in behalf of the Jews or polemics against the ever rising tide of anti-Semitism are of any value. He distrusted political agitation by Jews. In critical hours the Jews will be unable to rely upon any political party. "Who called into being the liberal movement in Austria? . . . The Jews! By whom were the Jews betrayed and deserted? By the Liberals. Who created the Pan-German movement in Austria? The Jews! By whom were the Jews left in the lurch? . . . nay more, spat on like dogs? . . . By the Germans! And the same thing will

happen to them at the hands of the Socialists and Communists. When the soup is served at the table, you will be
chased away. This was always so and will always remain
so."[8]

Schnitzler's aversion to politics as a method of amelio-
rating Jewish spiritual distress is treated in great detail in
his drama, *Professor Bernhardi*. When the title hero is subjected to unjust persecution and condemned to imprisonment, his friends want to call mass meetings to arouse public
opinion. But Bernhardi refuses to be made the plaything
of politicians. He is first and foremost a scientist. His
profession is to cure people. This calling he intends to continue, for it is productive of human happiness. But the
calling of a politician is not a desirable one, especially for a
Jew. Bernhardi's stand resembles that of old Dr. Stauber,
in *Der Weg ins Freie*. When the latter's son, Berthold, outraged at unfair anti-Semitic attacks, gives up his political
career in order to resume his study of bacteriology, the
father heartily endorses the young man's decision. When
Berthold, however, a year later accepts nomination to the
Austrian Parliament and thereby again turns his back upon
medicine, his father wisely points out the futility of engaging
in such activity. One cannot serve two masters. If the choice
lies between science and politics, the older physician insists
that it is absurd to give up the positive task of healing for
the doubtful privilege of haranguing people whose minds are
mostly made up in advance, or of combating opponents who
generally do not themselves believe the tenets they pretend
to defend. Especially is it absurd for a Jew to interfere in
his country's political squabbles. In the field of science even
a Jew may hope to earn his laurels and to contribute to
human welfare. In the field of politics, however, he will be

made to feel at every turn that he is an unwelcome stranger,
though his ancestors may have sojourned in the land close
to two thousand years.

Schnitzler died in 1931. For half a century he noted the
ebb and flow of anti-Jewish agitation in his native land and
always retained his attitude of patience, serenity, dignified
indifference, mild scepticism, tolerant understanding, and
superhuman forgiveness.

Among his literary remains there came to light, in 1942,
an undated letter in which he summarized his final conclusions on the German-Jewish duality, as he experienced it in
the depths of his soul. Replying to an appeal addressed to
him as a Jewish poet, he insisted that he never saw himself
in that category. He was a German poet, in so far as such
a label could be applied to anyone of Jewish ancestry. It was
true that many Hebraic characteristics were discoverable
in his writings. But any literary historian could also discover
Hellenic and Romanic traits in his style and subject-matter.
He owed a great deal to the cultural wealth of the Hebrews,
Greeks, Romans, and French. The determining factors were,
however, his writing in the German language, his living in a
predominantly German cultural sphere, his being chiefly
indebted to the German spirit, past and present. "Neither
Jewish-Zionist *ressentiment* nor the stupidity and impudence
of German Nationalists will make me doubt in the least that
I am a German poet; not even the suspicion that I would
like to worm my way into Teutonism and its wretched
circles will hinder me from feeling what I do feel, from
knowing what I do know, and from expressing what I feel
and know. I would not want Zionism eliminated from the
world's political scene of today or from the soul-economy of

contemporary Jewry. As a spiritual element to elevate one's self-consciousness, as a possibility for reacting against all sorts of dark hatreds, and especially as a philanthropic action of the highest rank, Zionism will always retain its importance, even if it should some day prove to have been merely a historic episode. — I find it proper that authors whose language is Hebrew should call themselves Hebrew writers or Jewish writers. Neither could I object if poets of Jewish background, who have hitherto written in another language, became outraged at the stupidity and vulgarity of anti-Semitism, which would deny them membership in a nation on whose territory they were born, in whose speech they were reared and which they even helped to shape; and if, as a result, these poets abjured the beloved language hitherto employed by them and turned to Hebrew as the medium for their creative works. Such poets would thereby have obtained the right to designate themselves as Jewish poets. But as long as they continue to write in German, they must call themselves German poets — even though their sympathy may have considerably decreased for this people in whose midst they live, because of the slanders and other vileness suffered at the hands of certain representatives of this people. They are German poets as surely as Heine, Börne, Gundolf, and a hundred others of Jewish origin are German; as surely as Brandes is a Danish writer and Proust a French writer. Just ask any genuine living German poet, ask Heinrich Mann, Thomas Mann, Gerhart Hauptmann, Hesse, Unruh, whom they feel to be more German: Wolzogen, Dinter, and that crowd, or Wassermann, Werfel, Beer-Hofmann, and a dozen others of Jewish origin that I could name."[9]

Schnitzler sang the swan-song of old Vienna. He caught in his gentle hand the last golden glow of its setting glory and converted it into art. The peculiar culture and aroma of the Danubian metropolis are present in his works, even as in the songs of Franz Schubert and in the waltzes of Johann Strauss. Yet, a little over a year after his death, his books were banned in Germany and a few years later in the Vienna that he loved. His words of wisdom found no echo among his countrymen. Hitler's intolerant dynamism triumphed over Schnitzler's tolerant passivism.

ARTHUR SCHNITZLER, 1862–1931

CHAPTER IX

WALTER RATHENAU

IN 1897, the year in which Theodor Herzl issued his call for the First Zionist Congress, Maximilian Harden, the Jewish ally of the aged Bismarck and the feared editor of the influential *Zukunft*, opened the columns of his periodical to an anonymous but sensational essay entitled *Hear, O Israel*.[1] Five years later, when this article was reprinted in the first collection of essays by Walter Rathenau, the identity of the writer was revealed.

Rathenau, an economist and industrialist, had until then been known to a small circle because of his scientific studies, but now for the first time he entered upon a controversial field. Within a few years he was to attain prominence as a master of prose, as a philosopher and aesthete, as a statesman and financier. Before a quarter of a century elapsed, he was to become Foreign Minister of republican Germany and to be murdered by fanatical extremists, who could not reconcile themselves to his Jewish origin.

This origin was never denied by Rathenau — his first essay opens with the words: "I will confess at the outset that I am a Jew"— but it was a source of great pain to him. In the year in which Herzl initiated the homecoming of the Jewish people, their return to Palestine, Rathenau called upon them to discard all their ethnic characteristics, the good and the bad, which might seem repugnant to their fellow Germans, and to replace them with other traits less objectionable to their neighbors. While Herzl defined the Jews of the next generation as a people on the march, as exiles retracing their steps from the Diaspora to their homeland Zion, Rathenau asked the Jews to participate in an event without historical precedent: the conscious effort of a historical group to commit national suicide. This group was to efface voluntarily all its peculiarities, the inferior and the superior, and to adapt itself to alien conditions. The young philosopher understood adaptation not in the sense of Darwin's theory of mimicry, according to which certain insects have the power of assuming the color of their environment, but in the sense of complete assimilation, so that Jews would ultimately emerge not as imitative Germans but as genuine Germans, bred and educated in accordance with the traditions of the majority population.

Rathenau, in his essay, did not set out to defend his co-religionists. As a person who, in outward appearance and in inner craving, resembled the ethnic Germans more than the ethnic Jews, he was determined not to resort to philo-Semitic apologetics but rather to agree in part with the anti-Semitic guardians of pure Germanism in the hope of reaching a common understanding. He was sincerely convinced that the Jews — or at least a majority of them — formed an alien enclave within the heart of Germany, an Asiatic horde on the sandy plains of Prussia. He described them as a foreign and isolated race of human beings, strutting in the midst of cultured Europeans, loud and self-conscious in dress, hot-blooded and restless in manner, an object of old, insatiable hate. The closing nineteenth century, which held in fetters all natural forces, succeeded in protecting the Jews from the violence which their ancestors had always suffered; but the fetters might give way one day. The Jews sensed the tenseness of their relations to the outer world; for they kept largely to themselves, lived in an invisible ghetto, and reacted not as a living limb of a magnificent people but rather as an alien organism in its body. Many an explanation could be offered for this unhappy condition. The question as to the historic responsibility for this deplorable state of affairs might be debated at great length. But there was no doubt that even the best Germans had an aversion — rightly or wrongly — towards Jewish being and Jewish characteristics. An intelligent German might be silent about this aversion, or he might make an exception in favor of a few individuals, rare freaks of nature, but he would never completely overcome his dislike of the group. This dislike was everywhere in evidence. It interpenetrated schools and colleges, streets and stores, factories and offices, railroad compartments and beer-halls, army barracks and courtrooms. The German had no reason to brood over his instinctive dislike. He was content to keep the undesirables at a distance. He had enough trouble assimilating Poles and Danes. Why should he bother about assimilating Jews? This was Israel's task. Yet Israel remained strangely inactive, apparently waiting for God and the Messiah to solve his problems. But the God of wrath and of victory, who once loved his nation of warriors, has turned his face from a people of shopkeepers and brokers. The Lord, who throned on Horeb and on Zion, has lost interest in His worshippers who dwelt in Berlin. Hence, the best Jews, in their desire to become good Germans, have chosen the path of conversion. There were, however, other fine Jews who, on the one hand, did not want to be branded as renegades, but who, on the other hand, were pained and shamed by being strangers and

half-citizens of the land and who therefore longed to escape
from the sultriness of the ghetto into the pure air of the
German woods and hills. These must become the pioneers
of assimilation, the vanguard of the Orientals who wished
to perish as Jews and to be reborn as Germans. Their baptism was a private matter; for, in Rathenau's opinion, there
was no important distinction between the deism of a liberal
Protestant pastor and that of an enlightened rabbi. Furthermore, Christian morality was so obviously the morality of
educated Jews that the former even tried to find its roots in
the Old Testament. Conversion did not, therefore, do
violence to the conscience of a modern Jew. Indeed, the
oldest and richest Jewish families had recognized the desirability of conversion decades ago and the procession to the
Church had proceeded undiminished ever since the emancipation. But conversion was not enough! If half of Israel
were converted, the probable result would be a passionate
hatred directed against the baptized half of Jewry and at the
same time a degeneration of the unbaptized half, caused by
the loss of leaders and intellectuals. Despite this likely development, the Jews, since they were a minority, had to
persist in wooing the majority, in neutralizing its aversion,
and in hoping for complete effacement of differences within
a few generations. The German state, recognizing the sin-
cerity of the Jewish effort to overcome Jewishness, should
encourage it by abandoning the slogan "once a Jew — always a Jew," and by opening to a few worthy individuals
the careers of army officer and government official.

In a letter to Herzl, Rathenau took account of the fact
that readers of his essay *Höre Israel* accused him of furthering anti-Semitism. He assured the Zionist leader that this
was not his intention. Since he was himself a Jew, he did

not feel justified in strengthening anti-Jewish agitation. Nevertheless, despite his admirable motives, his essay did have a harmful effect. The warning he intended for his co-religionists contained too much negation and accusation. The bitterness of his attack could not possibly persuade his Jewish readers to undertake a reform of their habits. When he afterwards became aware of the injurious implications of his caricature of the German Jew, he withdrew from circulation the volume in which his essay was reprinted. Nor did he include it in his collected works, which appeared at the end of the First World War. The National Socialists, however, gave it wide circulation when they attained power in 1933. They suggested that it be read by the school youth and that it be discussed in German classrooms as a Jewish avowal of Jewish parasitism and degeneracy. They commended the author for his frankness, agreed with his satiric references, and censured him solely for his insufficient emphasis upon racial incompatibility of Jews and Aryans.[2]

Unlike the theorists of National Socialism, Rathenau opposed strict segregation of the two groups. He, too, was of the opinion that the Jewish stock, whatever its ancient qualities might have been, had deteriorated as a result of many centuries of debasement. But he felt that this stock could still be ennobled, if it were grafted on to the superior Germanic stem. Jewish disappearance would not be tragic, but Aryan disappearance would be a catastrophe for civilization. The progress of humanity was linked with the welfare of the blond and marvelous people which arose in the north. In the past this people, in overflowing fertility, sent wave upon wave into the southern world. Each migration became a conquest, each conquest a source of character and civilization. But, as the population of the world increased, the

waves of the dark people made inroads upon the Aryan
territory. At last the south attained its first important
victory, when it forced its oriental religion, Christianity,
upon the northern lands. The Germans continued to defend
themselves by preserving their ancient code of ethics, their
Viking courage. But the worst danger of all loomed when
industrial civilization gained control of the world. Brains
and cunning, embodied in democracy and capitalism, were
pitted against the heroic Nordic soul. Rathenau wished to
identify himself unreservedly with this soul. "I have and I
know no other blood than German, no other stem, no other
people. If I am driven from my German soil, I shall remain
German and nothing will be altered . . . I share nothing with
the Jews save what every German shares with them: the
Bible, the memory and the figures of the Old and the New
Testaments. My ancestors and I myself have been nourished
by German soil and German spirit, and have given to the
German people whatever lay within our power. My father
and I have had no thought which was not German and for
Germany; as far as I can trace back my family, this has been
so."[3] "My people are the Germans and no other. For me the
Jews are a German tribe like the Saxons, the Bavarians, or
the Wends . . . For me the factors that decide whether one
belongs to a people or a nation are those of heart, mind, character, and soul. From this point of view, I place the Jews
somewhere between the Saxons and the Swabians. They are
less near to me than Brandenburgers or Holsteiners and perhaps somewhat nearer than Silesians or Lorrainers. I am
speaking, of course, only of German Jews. Eastern Jews, I
regard as Russians, Poles, or Galicians, just as every other
German does; Western Jews, I regard as Spaniards or
Frenchmen. Anti-Semitism and local nationalism are for me

on an equal plane; if I examine myself closely I find that I am
hurt more if a Bavarian declaims against the Prussians than
if he does so against the Jews."[4]

A month before the Balfour Declaration, which promised
"the establishment in Palestine of a national home for the
Jewish people," Rathenau wrote that the only nationality
which a moral and educated Jew in Central Europe could
claim was the German nationality, that all racial theories
about the different composition of Jewish blood were nonsense, and that peoples were fused into nations and nations
into states primarily by common soil, common experiences,
and common attitudes. Jewish solidarity was, in his opinion,
a myth propagated by ill-wishers. German Jews were not
responsible for Jewish crimes, policies, or achievements elsewhere any more than German Saxons were responsible for
the behavior of the Anglo-Saxons.

As the antipode of Herzl, Rathenau vigorously opposed
Zionist aspirations. Palestine might be preferable to Argentina as a territory for Jewish colonists from Eastern Europe,
and from a business or from a philanthropic viewpoint, he
was willing to consider lending his moral and financial support to the project. Indeed, he looked forward to the day
when he could visit the Holy Land and survey its resources.
But he and the German Jews of his physical and spiritual
make-up were not attracted to Asia as their future home.
They wished to live and to die for the Reich, as did their
fathers before them. They expected the solution of the
Jewish problem to come from a general increase in the
moral sense of the world and not from a return to a Jewish
state, an anachronism of two thousand years.

But why must the solution be delayed until some day in

the vague future? Would not conversion to Christianity
effect an instantaneous improvement in German-Jewish relations? What was there in liberal Christianity which an
enlightened Jew like Rathenau could not accept? These
were the questions asked of him by Curt von Trutzschler-
Falkenstein, the author of a pamphlet entitled *Die Lösung
der Judenfrage im Deutschen Reich*. A copy of the pamphlet
was sent to Rathenau on March 26, 1917, with the request
that he formulate his attitude towards the proposed solution.
A similar appeal had been made a century and a half earlier
to Moses Mendelssohn by Lavater. In his thirtieth year,
Rathenau himself had expressed doubts as to the desirability
of patriotic German inhabitants adhering to a religion which
was not that of the German state. Now in his fiftieth year,
two decades after the appearance of his essay, *Höre Israel*,
he was asked either to accept Christianity or else to explain
what supreme value adhered to the Jewish faith that for
its sake a modern humanitarian was still willing to make
sacrifices.

Rathenau, in his reply, published under the title *Eine
Streitschrift vom Glauben*, does not deny that religions, like
all other forms of spiritual life, undergo constant change
from century to century. Judaism was first a tribal faith,
then a state religion, then subjected to scholastic dogmatism
during the Middle Ages, to the influence of rationalistic
deism in the eighteenth century and to that of scientific
criticism in the nineteenth century. Beyond all transformations, however, Judaism retained certain permanent features.
What were these?

In the first place, Judaism differs from Christianity in
that it is not a Church. Its synagogues are merely schools
or halls of prayer, in which certain cult ceremonies can be

performed. No law requires any Jew to attend these halls.
The officials, who administer the religious rites, are not
priests but teachers of the community. They are employed
and can be dismissed. They cannot prescribe binding interpretations of the faith, much less the content of the faith.
Not even a conclave of all rabbis or teachers has this power.
The spiritual leaders of Israel cannot bind or loosen, they
cannot grant or deny eternal salvation. They cannot compel
obedience to faith. They cannot supervise. They cannot
discipline. They cannot expel. A Jew may participate in
religious observances, if he wishes; but he loses no rights if
he fails to participate. Indeed, there are a great many
educated persons who lead a Jewish religious life without
ever having performed any cult action or ever having entered
a synagogue. They are not admonished or censured.

In the second place, this religion without a Church is also
a religion without dogmas. It unites its adherents by means
of a single article of faith, which in its original Hebrew contains merely four words and which may be translated into
English: the Lord is our God, the Lord is One. The canonical
books of the Old Testament, assembled in the age of Ezra
and Nehemiah, were binding upon the Palestinian commonwealth. They do not possess this authority today, and no
religious body can restore the theocratic regime of the
Persian era, with all the social, juridical, and sanitary
prescriptions. The prophetic, historic, and poetic books of
the Old Testament, as well as the talmudic literature of the
scholastics and the modern collections of religious tracts and
rabbinical decisions, are likewise without binding force.
They have inspired comfort, happiness, and hope; sorrow,
fear, and despair. They are human products. The Jew is
no more bound by these texts than the educated person of

the twentieth century is bound by the opinions of the philosophers of bygone ages. Belief neither in a Messiah nor
in the sanctity of the Sabbath nor in the separation of clean
and unclean is an essential component of Judaism.

For a Jew to accept Christianity means not only that he
must accept the teachings of Jesus and the gospels — for
these were, after all, creations of the Jewish spirit and worthy
of admiration — but also that he must leave a free community of believers and enter into an organized Church, a
mechanized form of faith, with priests, dogmas, sacraments,
images, liturgies. It means further that he must submit to
compulsion and supervision. This is undesirable. The Jews
should be urged to include Jesus among their spiritual
leaders, even as they should include Spinoza. They should
pay the same homage to the New Testament as to the Old
Testament. But they should not join a Church — Catholic,
Protestant, or Byzantine. The German people, as a mature
and educated group, ought not to insist on absolute uniform-
ity in religious matters. Though the German realm would
never put up with anarchy or license, it does, after all,
treasure increasing growth in freedom, and it therefore must
exercise tolerance towards all religious forms that are not
repugnant to reason and morality.

Such opinions did not, however, save Rathenau from
the increasingly virulent anti-Jewish agitation of post-war
Germany. To many he was the symbol of the Jewish influence in politics and industry. He was accused of being
the leader of the so-called Elders of Zion and of having
worked for the defeat of Germany throughout the war
years. Rathenau rarely replied to the many slanders in the
press and continued his constructive work for the young

republic. When asked in 1920 to participate in the fight against anti-Semitism, he refused on the grounds that it was undignified and unnecessary. An immoral movement, based on appeals to vulgar passions, might do considerable temporary harm but was bound to collapse of its own inner viciousness without outside interference. Only once during the post-war years did he undertake a refutation of the racial theories, which afterwards became the stock-in-trade of the Third Reich. In a letter to a friend, who was a believer in these theories and whom he wished to win over to a saner view, he patiently explained his opposition on the following logical grounds:[5]

1. Modern Europeans cannot be divided on the basis of race differences, for these differences — assuming that they are capable of definition — are relatively unimportant compared to the differences between classes. A Pommeranian Junker resembles an English or French aristocrat more than he does a Silesian peasant or a Berlin proletarian. A Jewish storekeeper is physically and mentally more sharply differentiated from a Jewish patrician than from a Christian storekeeper. The inhabitants of metropolises, such as New York, London, Paris, Berlin, are hardly distinguishable from each other. The pure Nordic type is a rarity in Germany and, where it survives, as in Iceland, it is further removed from the average German than is the latter from the average Jew.

2. Differences in the spiritual structure of the most cultured individuals cannot be traced back to race. Confucius could just as well have been a Frenchman. Laotse borders on German mysticism. Plato, Augustine, Spinoza would have understood each other perfectly. Goethe felt himself attached to Spinoza more than to any other thinker. This holds true of Lessing as well. Schopenhauer and

Buddha are related spirits. The Western soul is deeply rooted in Jesus, Paul, and John. The human spirit in its finest representatives attaches no importance to hypothetical blood differences.

3. Racial pride is an absurdity. But, if Aryan fanatics insist on claiming superiority for themselves and denying creativeness to Jews, then let them not forget that no other group of such small numbers as the Jewish group influenced humanity so decisively. Moses, Isaiah, Jesus, Paul, and, more recently, Spinoza and Marx were beacons in the spiritual history of mankind.

4. The color of eyes, skin, or hair is no criterion of superiority. If anyone, however, insists on claiming superiority for the blond, let him be reminded that the five world figures that arose on Germanic territory were all dark. Their names are Luther, Goethe, Beethoven, Rembrandt, and Shakespeare.

Rathenau's logical arguments proved powerless against the inflamed oratory of the ultra-nationalists, who pilloried him as the Jew responsible for Germany's mishaps and who in song and speech called for his death as an arch-traitor. When Rathenau, who had reluctantly accepted the office of Foreign Minister, returned at the end of May 1922 from an international conference at Genoa, a conspiracy of young nationalists was formed for the purpose of assassinating him. On June 24, 1922, the conspirators attained their objective. With hand grenade and machine gun they riddled the body of the German-Jewish patriot who, only a few days before his death, wrote that it was his destiny to be ever ready to lift from others the burden which oppressed them, while he himself remained without desire.

The assassination had dire consequences for Germany.

It was followed by the French invasion of the Ruhr, a catastrophe which Rathenau might have prevented through his well-known policy of reconciliation and treaty fulfillment. It was followed by the collapse of the mark-currency and the ruin of the middle class. It brought Germany to the verge of despair and furthered the rise of the subversive forces that ultimately destroyed the Republic. The last supreme attempt of a German Jew to serve the cause of his beloved fatherland in its hour of great need bared the tragedy inherent in the German-Jewish duality.

CHAPTER X

THEODOR LESSING

ALTHOUGH Jews comprised less than one per cent of the population of Germany throughout the nineteenth and twentieth centuries, nevertheless they exercised an unabating fascination upon the mind of the entire population, a fascination which gave rise to varying reactions ranging from admiration to horror. Not even German philosophers, despite their pose of world-aloofness, were immune to this fascination. German thinkers, ever since Fichte and Hegel, Bruno Bauer and Karl Marx, in seeking to encompass the multiplicity of phenomena within a unified logical system, deemed it necessary to include an analysis of Jewish life, historic and contemporary, within the orbit of their speculation. Especially was this true in the decades following Nietzsche's attempted transvaluation of values. Houston Stewart Chamberlain and Oswald Spengler, among cultural historians of non-Jewish origin, and Theodor Lessing and Otto Weininger, among those of Jewish origin, continued the grand manner of philosophic generalizations on Jewish questions initiated by Nietzsche, and thus opened the door wide for the still more startling pseudo-philosophic and pseudo-scientific conclusions of the propagandists of the Third Reich. It is true that the approach of the thinkers who followed in the wake of Nietzsche was not always unfriendly to Jews. The chief danger of their

THEODOR LESSING, 1872–1933
(By courtesy of the *Universal Jewish Encyclopedia*, VI, 613)

method, however, lay in their representing their insights, which were often accurate, and their prejudices, which were generally less in accord with factual evidence, as profound logical deductions and as scholarly historic verdicts.

Nietzsche's impress upon German mentality was especially important after 1933 when he was reinterpreted by the Nazi regime as the chief pioneer of their *Weltanschauung* and misinterpreted in his remarks on Jews. Nietzsche's views on Judaism were colored by his aversion to Christianity, an aversion later shared by Adolf Hitler, Alfred Rosenberg, and the Nazi élite. He held Judaism responsible for the birth of Christianity and hence for the Christian inversion of all moral values, the Christian substitution of the slave-morality of the poor and the feeble for the master-morality of the strong and the mighty. The Jew Jesus was, in his opinion, the political criminal chiefly responsible for the successful uprising of the servile souls and their assumption of dominance in the field of morals. The Jew Jesus, though himself the noblest of individuals, was a saintly anarchist who had a false philosophy of history and who incited the rabble, the pariahs, and the sinners to revolt against the ruling order. Jesus was a Hebraic Gandhi whose seditious utterances would have brought about his exile and imprisonment even in our century and who in his day was justifiably nailed to the cross. Despite the suppression of this trouble-maker, however, the master-race of Romans ultimately had to give the palm of victory to the little priestly people of Judea. If proof were necessary, one had but to consider before whom all bent the knee ever since as the personification of the highest values — not alone in Rome but over half the globe, wherever man had become tame or wanted to become tame — before three Jews and a Jewess: before Jesus of Nazareth, the fisherman Peter, the carpet-weaver Paul, and the Virgin Mary.[1]

While disliking the historic rôle of ancient Jewry, Nietzsche's attitude towards medieval and modern Jewry was far from hostile. He credited medieval Jewry with the preservation of Hellenic rationalism for the Occident. "In the darkest periods of the Middle Ages, when the Asiatic cloud camped above Europe, Jewish freethinkers, scholars, and physicians held firm the banner of enlightenment and of spiritual independence under the hardest personal strain and defended Europe against Asia. We owe it in no small measure to their efforts that a natural, more rational, and at any rate less mystical interpretation of the world could finally emerge victorious and that the ring of culture which now unites us with the enlightenment of Graeco-Roman antiquity remains unbroken. If Christianity has done everything to orientalize the Occident, then Judaism has helped in many essentials in the re-occidentalizing process, namely in making Europe's mission and history a continuation of the mission and history of the Greeks.[2]

Far from agreeing with his Nazi followers, who brand all mating of Jews and Germans as racial defilement, Nietzsche advocated the mating of Prussian nobility and Jewish intelligence as a desirable step to hasten the evolution of a superior type of humanity. He rejected every invitation of anti-Semitic groups to join their ranks. His closest friends included Jews. From one of them, Paul Rée, he derived much stimulus during his most productive years. Another, Georg Brandes, became the earliest trumpeter of his fame. This Jewish scholar of Copenhagen published in 1889 the first comprehensive book on the iconoclastic, lonely philosopher. Other Jews, such as Karl Joel and

Stefan Zweig, later helped to unravel Nietzsche's obscure utterances and to arouse sympathy for his pugnacious personality. The fact that the composer Jacques Offenbach was of Jewish origin did not prevent Nietzsche from being his life-long admirer. Nor did Nietzsche hesitate to call Heine, the Jewish poet, the sole literary genius of Goethe's caliber produced by Germany. To those contemporaries who stressed the unpleasant characteristics of Jews, Nietzsche replied that every nation and every person had unpleasant and even dangerous characteristics, and that it was cruel to insist that the Jews should form an exception. If a balance were struck, one would have to place to the credit of the Jews the fact that they had a most tragic history, for which non-Jews were not entirely blameless, and the further fact that they gave to mankind its noblest personality — Jesus, its purest sage —Spinoza, and its most influential ethical code. Persecution of the Jews stemmed not from their wicked, but rather from their superior traits. Such traits were their dynamic energy, their higher intelligence, their rich reserves of spirit and will accumulated from generation to generation in the long school of suffering, their reverence for father and mother, and their devotion to the family. These traits, which made them mighty and eternal, also evoked envy and hatred among their neighbors, and, as a result, all nations became addicted to the bad habit of leading the Jews to the slaughter-pen as scapegoats for all sorts of public and private misfortunes.

In *Beyond Good and Evil*, Nietzsche posed the question: what does Europe owe to the Jews? His reply was: "Many things, good and bad, and above all one thing of the nature both of the best and the worst: the grand style in morality, the fearfulness and majesty of infinite demands, of infinite

significations, the whole Romanticism and sublimity of
moral questionableness — and consequently just the most
attractive, ensnaring, and exquisite element in those iri-
descences and allurements to life, in the aftersheen of which
the sky of our European culture, its evening sky, now
glows — perhaps glows out. For this, we artists among
the spectators and philosophers are grateful to the Jews."[3]

R. M. Lonsbach, in his study *Friedrich Nietzsche und
die Juden*, sets up an interesting theory to explain why
Nietzsche, the philosophic exponent of Aryanism, bitterly
fought the rising tide of anti-Semitism. He holds that
Nietzsche recognized the revolutionary character of this
movement, whose ideology and cultural aims were dia-
metrically opposed to his own. A new revolt of the slave-
man was brewing in Europe and Nietzsche foresaw that this
revolt would go far beyond all former uprisings of the
rabble. Such uprisings had resulted in Christianity, the
Reformation, and the French Revolution, all three of which
stressed the rights of the weak and the untalented, the common man and the underdog, at the expense of the strong
and the gifted, the aristocrat and the patrician. The anti-
Semitic threat was even more dangerous. Anti-Semitism
was the philosophy not of a people or of a class but of those
vile and worthless individuals among all peoples and all
classes who had been worsted in the struggle for existence.
Nietzsche coined a new word to designate them: *die Schlecht-
weggekommenen*. They were the adventurers and unsuccessful factory-owners, the unscrupulous go-getters and the
bankrupt journalists, the hysterical women of both sexes,
the illiterate and the misanthropic. All were gathered
under the banner of anti-Semitism and incited against Jewish
wealth and Jewish richness of spirit. Anti-Semitism was the

revolt of the herd, poor in spiritual values, against culture
and spirit. It was evidence of an envious and cowardly
personality, of a rabble-soul. And so Nietzsche noted in
one of his last fragments: "I want all anti-Semites shot."[4]

Nietzsche often pondered on the probable future of the
Jews in the midst of a hostile German population and won-
dered what steps could be taken to lessen the long prevalent
dislike. He recorded some of his observations and conclusions
in the following statement: "I have never yet met a German
who was favorably inclined to the Jews; and however de-
cided the repudiation of actual anti-Semitism may be on
the part of all prudent and political men, this prudence and
policy is not perhaps directed against the nature of the
sentiment itself, but only against its dangerous excess, and
especially against the distasteful and infamous expression
of this excess of sentiment; — on this point we must not
deceive ourselves. That Germany has amply sufficient Jews,
that the German stomach, the German blood, has difficulty
(and will long have difficulty) in disposing only of this
quantity of *Jew* — as the Italian, the Frenchman, and the
Englishman have done by means of a stronger digestion: —
that is the unmistakable declaration and language of a general instinct, to which one must listen and according to which
one must act. 'Let no more Jews come in! And shut the
doors, especially towards the East (also towards Austria)!'—
thus commands the instinct of a people whose nature is
still feeble and uncertain, so that it could be easily wiped
out, easily extinguished by a stronger race. The Jews,
however, are beyond all doubt the strongest, toughest, and
purest race at present living in Europe; they know how to
succeed even under the worst conditions (in fact better than
under favorable ones) by means of virtues of some sort,

which one would like nowadays to label as vices — owing
above all to a resolute faith which does not need to be
ashamed before 'modern ideas'. . . It is certain that the
Jews, if they desired — or if they were driven to it, as the
anti-Semites seem to wish — could now have the ascendancy, nay, literally the supremacy, over Europe; that they
are not working and planning for that end is equally certain.
Meanwhile, they rather wish and desire, even somewhat
importunely, to be inscribed and absorbed by Europe; they
long to be finally settled, authorized, and respected somewhere, and wish to put an end to the nomadic life, to the
'wandering Jew' — and one should certainly take account
of this impulse and tendency and make advances to it (it
possibly betokens a mitigation of the Jewish instincts): for
which purpose it would perhaps be useful and fair to banish
the anti-Semitic bawlers out of the country. One should
make advances with all prudency and with selection: pretty
much as the English nobility do. It stands to reason that
the more powerful and strongly marked types of new Germanism could enter into relation with the Jews with the
least hesitation, for instance, the nobleman officer from the
Prussian border: it would be interesting in many ways to
see whether the genius for money and patience (and especially some intellect and intellectuality — sadly lacking in
the place referred to) could not in addition be annexed and
trained to the hereditary art of commanding and obey-
ing — for both of which the country in question has now a
classic reputation."[5]

At a time when German philosophers of Jewish origin
often lacked either the courage or the desire to break a
lance in behalf of their coreligionists and when escape from
minority status through baptism or intermarriage was

sought by a large sector of liberal intellectuals, Nietzsche, the son of a Lutheran pastor, let loose a panegyric upon the coming renaissance of Judaism in the twentieth century which left his readers overwhelmed, a bit sceptical, and not entirely pleased. In an intoxicating vision, he welcomed a possible world hegemony of Jewry and, though his prophecy seems all awry from the vantage point of the mid-twentieth century, it is nevertheless not without interest as the speculation of an unusual mind. It is to be found among the aphorisms of his *Morgenröte:*

"One of the spectacles which the next century will invite us to witness is the decision regarding the fate of the European Jews. It is quite obvious now that they have cast their die and crossed their Rubicon: the only thing that remains for them is either to become masters of Europe or to lose Europe, as they once centuries ago lost Egypt where they were confronted with similar alternatives. In Europe, however, they have gone through a schooling of eighteen centuries such as no other nation has ever undergone, and the experiences of this dreadful time of probation have benefited not only the Jewish community but, even to a greater extent, the individual. As a consequence of this, the resourcefulness of the modern Jews, both in mind and soul, is extraordinary. Amongst all the inhabitants of Europe it is the Jews least of all who try to escape from any deep distress by recourse to drink or to suicide, as other, less gifted, people are so prone to do. Every Jew can find in the history of his own family and his ancestors a long record of instances of the greatest coolness and perseverance amid difficulties and dreadful situations, an artful cunning in fighting with misfortune and hazard.

"And above all it is their bravery under the cloak of

wretched submission, their heroic *spernere se sperni* that surpasses the virtues of all the saints. — People wished to make them contemptible by treating them contemptibly for nearly twenty centuries, and refusing them access to all honorable positions and dignities, and by pushing them further down into the meaner trades — and under this process indeed they have not become any cleaner. But contemptible? They have never ceased for a moment from believing themselves qualified for the very highest functions, nor have the virtues of the suffering ever ceased to adorn them. Their manner of honoring their parents and children, the rationality of their marriages and marriage customs, distinguishes them amongst all Europeans. Besides this, they have been able to create for themselves a sense of power and eternal vengeance from the very trades that were left to them (or to which they were abandoned). Even in palliation of their usury we cannot help saying that, without this occasional pleasant and useful torture inflicted on their scorners, they would have experienced difficulty in preserving their self-respect for so long. For our self-respect depends upon our ability to make reprisals in both good and evil things. Nevertheless, their revenge never urges them on too far, for they all have that liberty of mind, and even of soul, produced in men by frequent changes of place, climate, and customs of neighbors and oppressors; they possess by far the greatest experience in all human intercourse, and even in their passions they exercise the caution which this experience has developed in them. They are so certain of their intellectual versatility and shrewdness that they never, even when reduced to the direst straits, have to earn their bread by manual labor as common workmen, porters, or farm hands. In their manners we can still see that they have never been inspired by chivalric and noble feelings, or that their bodies have ever been girt with fine weapons: a certain obtrusiveness alternates with a submissiveness which is often tender and almost always painful.

"Now, however, that they unavoidably intermarry more and more year after year with the noblest blood of Europe, they will soon have a considerable heritage of good intellectual and physical manners, so that in another hundred years they will have a sufficiently noble aspect not to render themselves, as masters, ridiculous to those whom they will have subdued. And this is important! and therefore a settlement of the question is still premature. They themselves know very well that the conquest of Europe or any act of violence is not to be thought of; but they also know that some day or other Europe may, like a ripe fruit, fall into their hands, if they do not clutch at it too eagerly. In the meantime, it is necessary for them to distinguish themselves in all departments of European distinction and to stand in the front rank: until they shall have advanced so far as to determine themselves what distinction shall mean. Then they will be called the pioneers and guides of the Europeans whose modesty they will no longer offend.

"And then where shall an outlet be found for this abundant wealth of great impressions accumulated during such an extended period and representing Jewish history for every Jewish family, this wealth of passions, virtues, resolutions, resignations, struggles, and conquests of all kinds — where can it find an outlet but in great intellectual men and works! On the day when the Jews will be able to exhibit to us as their own work such jewels and golden vessels as no European nation, with its shorter and less profound experience, can or could produce, when Israel shall have changed its eternal vengeance into an eternal benediction for Europe, then that seventh day will once more appear when old Jehovah may rejoice in Himself, in His creation, in His chosen people — and all, all of us, will rejoice with Him!"[6]

If Nietzsche, operating with unproved generalizations, predicted and welcomed a rise to dominance of European Jewry, his disciples among the cultural historians, operating with equally unproved generalizations, predicted and welcomed a disappearance of this ancient communal group. The most brilliant and influential of these cultural historians was Oswald Spengler, whose monumental work, *Der Untergang des Abendlandes*, or, as it was better known to English readers, *The Decline of the West*, provoked sensational controversies and endless discussions on both sides of the Atlantic in the interval between the two World Wars.

Spengler held that Judaism, having performed its historic function, was at last on the verge of disappearing. It had lost every kind of inward cohesion and what remained was simply a cohesion for practical questions. The lead it enjoyed in former centuries because of its long habituation to thinking in business terms had become ever less and less important. As soon as the cosmopolitan civilization of the Occident shall have arrived at full maturity, the destiny of Jewry, or at least of Western Jewry, shall have been accomplished and it would vanish from the stage of history.

Spengler traced the antagonism between the Jews and the Occidental peoples to differences in their cultural level or historic age. He maintained that mutual hate and contempt existed between the two groups ever since the Middle Ages, caused not by any race distinction but by an inevitable lack of understanding between a primitive, young culture and a

senile, overripe civilization. The *Judengasse* was a thousand
years in advance of the Gothic town. "The Jew could not
comprehend the Gothic inwardness, the castle, the Cathe-
dral; nor the Christian the Jew's superior, almost cynical,
intelligence and his finished expertness in money-thinking."[7]
Furthermore, to the young nations, bound up with the soil
and the idea of a fatherland, the landless, roaming Jews appeared uncanny and incomprehensible, and these nations
recorded their impression in the legend of the Wandering
Jew. "It meant a good deal for a Scottish monk to visit a
Lombard monastery, and nostalgia soon took him home
again; but when a rabbi of Mainz — in 1000 the seat of the
most important talmudic seminary of the West — or of
Salerno betook himself to Cairo or Merv or Basra, he was
at home in every ghetto."[8] For the Jews, state and church
and people were all synonymous. They had their own juris-
prudence and their own public life, and despised the sur-
rounding world of the host-peoples as a sort of alien land.
When Western culture began to catch up with the Jews and
when the discrepancy of historic age, expressed in the way
of life and in the increasing primacy of reason, became
smaller, hatred between the two groups grew in intensity.

The Jewish and the Western human types, though living
side by side, were far from identical in their reactions, and
both knew it. "This feeling of being different is more potent
on both sides, the more breed the individual possesses. It is
want of race, and nothing else, that makes intellectuals —
philosophers, doctrinaires, Utopists — incapable of understanding the depth of this metaphysical hatred, which is
the beat-difference of two currents of being manifested as
an unbearable dissonance, a hatred that may become tragic
for both. . . During the Gothic age this difference is deep

and religious, and the object of hatred is the Consensus as religion; only with the beginning of Western Civilization does it become materialist and begin to attack Jewry on its intellectual and business sides, on which the West suddenly finds itself confronted by an even challenger."[9]

But the deepest cause of separation and bitterness, according to Spengler, must be seen in Jewish aloofness from the historic currents that surged about them. The historic mission of the Jews was at an end. "The Jewish Consensus ceased to have a history at all. Its problems were solved, its inner form was complete, conclusive, and unalterable. .. Epochs succeeded to epochs, every century witnessed fundamental human changes, but in the ghetto and in the souls of its denizens all stood still. And even when a Jew regarded himself as a member of the people amongst whom he sojourned and took part in their good and evil fortune — as happened in so many countries in 1914 — he lived these experiences, not really as something *his own*, but as a partisan, a supporter; he judged them as an interested spectator, and hence it is just the deepest meanings of the struggle that must ever remain hidden from him. A Jewish cavalry-general fought in the Thirty Years' War — he lies buried in the old Jewish cemetery at Prague — but what did the ideas of Luther or Loyola mean to him?"[10]

Eduard Meyer, the famed historian who had devoted decades to the study of the origin and progress of ancient Israel, hailed Spengler's unflattering comments on modern Jewry as among the profoundest utterances on this theme.[11] Spengler's vaunted objectivity and Meyer's endorsement lent scientific authority to otherwise unproved statements and supplied National Socialists with additional ammunition for their anti-Jewish campaign.

These agitators did not, however, have to turn to philosophers and historians of non-Jewish origin for arguments to justify their negative appraisal of Jewish traits. In the work of Otto Weininger they could point to a Jewish philosopher who undertook to prove scientifically the myth of Aryan superiority and the worthlessness of Semitic traits. In the early essays of Theodor Lessing, they could point to a Jewish cultural historian who was no less harsh in his condemnation of his coreligionists, especially of those whose habitat lay east of Berlin, Breslau, and Vienna.

Lessing, a disciple of Nietzsche and a contemporary of Spengler, was professor of philosophy at Hanover and a publicist of note, famed for his bold paradoxes, pungent anecdotes, and vitriolic satires. In his early years, when he strutted about as a German super-patriot and as an associate of the mighty and influential Maximilian Harden, he exercised his wit and scholarship in furthering anti-Jewish feeling. Later, when he underwent a complete change of heart and trumpeted forth his faith in the Jewish renaissance, he made a public confession that his former views resulted from self-hatred, a psychological phenomenon to which German Jews of assimilationist background easily fell a prey. It was self-hatred that led him to ridicule and defame the Eastern Jews after a tour of several weeks in Galicia. It was self-hatred that led him to pillory the literary and critical contributions of Jews in such unfair and extravagant language that Thomas Mann, a non-Jew, had to take him to task and had to castigate him for his anti-Semitic approach to intellectual problems. This extreme self-hatred, which he himself afterwards best described in his book *Jüdischer Selbsthass*, changed under the impact of the First World War to an equally extreme overestimation of Judaism, so that by 1933 the Nazis rightfully saw in him a most violent champion of the non-Aryans and found it necessary to send assassins to Prague in order to put an end to his dangerous pen.

During the First World War, when Spengler prepared his cultural history, *Der Untergang des Abendlandes*, for publication, Lessing was at work on a similar grandiose project, which finally appeared under the title *Untergang der Erde am Geist*. In this book, Lessing assigned various historic functions to the diverse peoples of Europe and Asia and, in the manner of Nietzsche and Spengler, foretold the likely course of events in the generations to come.

In the Jews he saw an Asiatic people hurled upon the European scene and hence foreordained to occupy an intermediate position between the two cultural continents. Transvaluating accepted values, he discovered the strength of the Jews in a direction which others failed to perceive, in a closeness to life's elemental roots, in a proximity to the warm bosom of nature, in a preservation of pagan, pre-Christian opposition to all logical and ethical obscurantism, in an awareness of the relative unimportance of the individual soul in comparison with the eternally immutable absolute, in a fearless facing of fate, and in a consciousness of the responsibility of each being towards every other being. Despite the strong earth-bound instincts with which fate endowed the Jews, a tragic history cut them off from all contact with the soil and subjected them, ever since the dim and distant past, to thousands of years of torture amidst artificial surroundings, until their divorce from nature was complete and until this people of peasants became over-spiritualized and decadent. To appreciate what happened to this group, Lessing compared it to a beautiful body subjected to tortures, infected with poisons, and then exhibited with all its sores and wounds to prove it contaminated and unworthy of brotherhood. Judaism was made a victim of the economy of exploitation during the centuries of Christianity and, in the end, it was held responsible for the exploitation practiced by those centuries. As the oldest and most closely knit group on this planet, the Jews could by now have supplied the world with its most ancient nobility, if it had been allowed a normal development. The Jewish group could have surpassed the more fortunate peoples because of its long accumulated psychic energy. Unfortunately, this fettered energy was liberated too suddenly in the nineteenth century and used up with reckless abandon in all the occidental centers. Far too quickly there went up in flames the faith, the dreams, the suffering, and the discipline of thousands of years. For the sake of a few decades of cheap European fame, a talented people exhausted its vitality. Its brief moment of brilliant fireworks aroused envy among the rabble, righteous indignation among the wise, and shudders of awe among those who had forebodings of the aftermath. A small minority — Lessing called them the élite of contemporary Jewry — found its way back to the horribly abused and exploited Asiatic soil and, beginning with the afforestation of the ruined Palestinian land, paved the way for others to follow. A people, dying and almost dead, started to trek back to its historic soil, which was also apparently beyond recovery; and in the union of this people with this particular land, both were being revived and restored to health. While all the nations of the earth were busy killing each other, the Jews set out to fertilize, with their blood and sweat, the holy soil, once the cradle of historic man and now again the seed of a spiritual renascence.

Lessing's intoxicating tribute to the Palestinian ideal was penned by this ex-anti-Semite and sudden convert to Zionism soon after the Balfour Declaration. A new wave of pessimism overcame him, however, when another decade passed without any apparent improvement of the Jewish position in Palestine and with a constant deterioration of the Jewish position in Europe. The Arab massacres of 1929 and the growth in strength of National Socialism in Germany caused Lessing to cry out in despair: what does the world want of us? "We were told: you are parasites on the land of others — and so we tore ourselves loose. We were told: you are the middlemen among the peoples — and so we raised our children to be farmers and peasants. We were told: you are decaying and becoming cowardly weaklings — and so we went into battles and produced the best soldiers. We were told: everywhere you are only tolerated — and we answered: our greatest longing is to be an object of tolerance no more. But when we insisted on maintaining ourselves as a distinct people, we were told: have you not yet learned that your preserving your distinctiveness is treason against all international, pan-human values? And so we replied by quietly disbanding the Jewish Legion, by giving up our self-defense, and by placing our just cause under the protection of the European conscience. And what is the result?" — Massacres in Palestine and agitation for pogroms in the Diaspora. From nowhere can help be expected. Hereafter each Jew must plan his own salvation. He must grope his way to some kind of spiritual equanimity. He is most likely to find this equanimity by learning to love his fate, by learning to will what he must. Fate and necessity have made him part of a people — as strange as any, as heroic and as decadent as others on the present scene. Let him learn to love this people and to help in its resurgence. He is not only the son of some peddling tradesman and some insignificant woman, but also the offspring of Judas Maccabaeus and Queen Esther. He is a link in a chain that reaches back to Saul and David and Moses. By regenerating himself and by assuming his share of the suffering and struggle that fall to the lot of Jews, let him pave the way for a brighter heaven for his children and the children of his people.[12]

This miracle of regeneration, which Lessing preached to others, he experienced in his own soul. The ultra-German philosopher of the early twentieth century, with his scorn of Jews and hatred of Judaism, ended as an ultra-Jewish patriot, atoning for his former aberration by his death in 1933 at the hands of Gestapo agents sent abroad from the Reich with instructions to silence the renegade to the cause of anti-Semitism and the fearless foe of Hitlerism.

PART IV

THE END OF EMANCIPATION

JAKOB WASSERMANN, 1873–1933

Chapter XI

JAKOB WASSERMANN

HUMAN beings experience years of calm and years of unrest. Jakob Wassermann is the chronicler of the restless years. Families know decades of undisturbed peace and interludes of turbulent stress. Jakob Wassermann is the novelist of the turbulent interludes. Nations go through periods of productive progress and suddenly are whirled into war and destruction. Jakob Wassermann is the painter of the fateful hours that are surcharged with foreboding of national conflagrations. Social systems evolve slowly and laboriously until they reach their zenith and seem to head downward toward decay and revolution. Jakob Wassermann is the narrator of a decadent society that sensed the onrush of its doom. Civilizations require centuries to blossom and to unfold their cultural contributions, yet they, too, ultimately pass away and are supplanted. Jakob Wassermann is the apocalyptic prophet of occidental civilization.

Gifted with extraordinary talent as a storyteller, Wassermann was tempted to assume the rôle of a German Dostoyevsky. He sought to be both the prophet of a world collapse and the herald of the reawakened human soul, cleansed by pain and conscious of a new dignity. He projected, in his long prose epics, characters of all social strata who had somehow lost their anchor in life; creatures set adrift on uncharted psychic streams and whirling past abysmal horrors; men, women, and children, tortured by

173

gruesome experiences, seeking God throughout their distress, and finding him only after extreme exhaustion at the end of their perilous adventures.

Wassermann brought to his heroes and heroines the realization that everything they had planned, fought for, and accomplished up to a certain moment was vanity of vanities, a mistaken goal, a waste of time, a loss of precious values. He called upon them to remove the dross from their souls, to rid themselves of pleasant illusions, to steel themselves against hardships and loneliness, and to follow without compromises or deviations the law of their inner being, though this law be at variance with common notions of good and evil and though it lead to the verge of ruin and death. In unraveling the tangled skein of human relations, the novelist undertook to discover, amidst the multiplicity of confused events, the single all-directing inner motive, to lay bare the unchanging type or *Gestalt* behind the ever shifting daily masks.

Wassermann was born in 1873 at Fürth, an industrial center of Franconia, or Northern Bavaria, and the seat of an ancient Jewish community. He began his literary career as early as 1897 with his novel, *Die Juden von Zirndorf*, which has been translated into English under the title, *The Dark Pilgrimage*. In this novel he utilized personal experiences as well as myths and legends of his Jewish ancestors in order to unfold a vivid portrait of changing Jewish life in his native province. The Jewish religion, as depicted by him, was something lifeless, ghostlike, ossified, incapable of resurrection. Irreligious Jews, on the other hand, were in his eyes wrecks of a great tradition, who had been cast adrift on the ocean of life. Jewish fate claimed him; but it was utterly devoid of desirable content. He hated the Jewish types, with whom he was constantly brought into contact, the scorned beggars and the mighty bankers, the bloodless intellectuals and the ascetic idealists, but nevertheless he felt himself bound to them by inexorable ties.

Wassermann first won wide recognition in 1908, with the appearance of *Caspar Hauser*, a narrative of a mysterious foundling, whom some regarded as a prince and others as a charlatan and who perished tragically because his purity of heart was no match for the turbid influences about him.

The climax of Wassermann's creative activity was reached in *Christian Wahnschaffe*, which appeared in 1919 and which was read by hundreds of thousands in America under the title, *The World's Illusion*. This grandiose epic of European civilization during the pre-war decade is reminiscent of Tolstoy and Dostoyevsky. Like the Russian masters, the German novelist addressed himself to the conscience of his readers; he wanted to be an ethical teacher, pointing the way to the good life. He selected as his main character an elegant sportsman and dandy, who had been blessed with all the gifts that human beings normally aspire to: wealth reaching into millions, social prestige and the power that flows from money, physical strength, health, attractiveness, youth, friendship, love; and then the question is put to this magnificent personality: what will you do with your life? Shadows from the lower depths flit across Christian's horizon and begin to trouble him. The more insight he gains into the souls and activities of the men and women at the base of the social pyramid, the more lonely, useless, and guilty he feels in his position at the apex. His lightheartedness gives way to a growing discomfort. As the scion of an industrial baron, he recognizes himself as one of the pillars of an unjust system.

His continued existence as a beneficiary of this system seems to him to be criminal and impossible. In the end, he renounces his flirtations and amusements, disposes of his estates and his millions, turns his back upon his parasitical past, descends to the slums, nurses a harlot, fraternizes with a murderer, and serves his fellowmen as the humblest among the humble. In addition to Christian Wahnschaffe's spiritual crisis, the novel also deals with the transformations that swept over dozens of other typical representatives of the pre-war generation, Jews and non-Jews. The nervous clash of temperaments, the hasty sipping of pleasures, the hysterical unrest gripping everyone foreboded the onrush of a cleansing hurricane, a deluge to wash away the weakened social structure, rich in glamor but undermined by injustice.

Wassermann's later novels continued his intimate portraits of the German bourgeoisie between 1870 and 1920, the half century which saw the rise, efflorescence, and collapse of a mighty industrial and political empire reared by this class and the expression of its will to power, its unbounded confidence, its overweaning ambition, its arrogance and soullessness. The novelist had no faith in the future of European civilization and after his trip to America he was without faith in the New World. His pessimism was most pronounced in his last years, and especially in his treatment of the Jewish problem.

Wassermann was the implacable foe of all Jewish separatist movements. He denied the fundamental assumptions of Zionism. He negated the thesis of Herzl that the Jews are a people, one people, even if scattered over all continents, and that therefore a national homeland is a necessity if this people is ever to regain health, equilibrium, and universal good will. Wassermann characterized this thesis as erroneous, criminal, suicidal. In his opinion, the Jews are not a people and can never again be a people. They are a sum of individuals. This fact accounts for their peculiar fate. It gives meaning to their past on the European scene. It foreshadows their future rôle in coming world events. It is the key to their ultimate happiness or doom.

In 1897, the year of the First Zionist Congress at Basel, he asserted, in *Die Juden von Zirndorf*, that the surest way of annihilating the Jews is to buy a land for them and establish a state for them. As a nation, they would then be a mockery for the entire world. Jews are strong only as individuals, as priests, as prophets, as servants of the spirit, as missionaries among other peoples; but they are not fit for common action and have no talent for political deeds.

As late as 1923, when Jewish national aspirations were already recognized by the League of Nations, Wassermann still reiterated this view: "Even if the Jews now succeed in establishing a state, they may perhaps be acknowledged as a nation or as a people; but they will in that case have ceased to be Jews. They may possibly attain prosperity, national unity, external success, a position among the other numerous national entities of this rationalistic age; but their historic world-mission is then at an end. . . Let the Jews be killed or exiled, let them be made the bugaboo of children and an object of scorn: all this would be less fatal for the culture of mankind than if the Jews themselves were to give up the rôle which they have hitherto played in the world arena, in accordance with their mission and destiny."[1]

Wassermann could not, however, shut his eyes to the fact that in the twentieth century the Western Jews did not seem to be aware of any special world-mission and that the East-

ern Jews were flocking to the Zionist standard. He therefore
arrived at the pessimistic prophecy that the Western Jews,
because of their inner emptiness and lack of real faith, will
perish before long, and that the Eastern Jews, by becoming
nationalists and Zionists, will cease to be Jews. To the
reminder that Palestine, whose settlement by Jews he opposed, had, after all, once been the land of his forefathers,
he replied angrily that every European village meant more
to him than the soil of a so-called Holy Land. He granted
that he might be driven forth from his German home by
insane anti-Semitic agitation, but even in exile he would
remain a German and could never conceive of himself as a
Palestinian. In his opinion, it was the height of madness to
persuade Jews to immigrate into the artificial state in Asia
Minor, which had been called into existence by the exigencies
of English imperialism and where settlers would be exposed
to repeated massacres at the hands of Turks, Arabs, Greeks,
and Persians. And even if this state managed to survive
somehow, what would be gained for mankind at large? Instead of two dozen wrangling, jealous, little nations, there
would be two dozen and one. Furthermore, how could one
expect German Jews, who had for centuries imbibed the
culture of German earth and air, to form a happy union with
other Jews on foreign soil, with whom they have had little
in common for at least half a thousand years!

Wassermann confessed that he himself felt no sense of
brotherhood or kinship with non-German Jews. These were
completely alien to him, alien in their idiom, alien in their
every breath. He could bring himself to sympathize with
some of them as individuals; but as a group they were re-
pulsive to him. He spoke of the Austrian Jews, who came
to Germany during and after the World War, as Galician

moles whom the European cataclysm had driven out of their filthy holes. He spoke of the Polish and Russian Jews as a misfortune let loose upon Germany, and again, as hosts of semi-barbarians lusting for life and booty after generations of imprisonment in a ghetto jungle by a savage autocracy. He exclaimed wrathfully: "What have I to do with them, I, whose ancestors on my father's and on my mother's side have for six hundred years lived and worked in the heart of Germany?"[2]

Wassermann frankly stated that he saw in the Eastern Jew and in the German Jew two distinct species, two distinct races, or at least two distinct modes of life and thought. He was filled with joy when he succeeded in convincing an anti-Semitic friend that he, the novelist, had forged into a unity the duality of German and Jew and had thus proved the possibility of complete immersion of a non-Aryan in German culture. Though he may have been the first person to effect this synthesis, he had nevertheless succeeded in showing that it was not beyond attainment. "I am only seemingly an exception. I represent all. I am the expression of a definite will inherent in our age, our generation, our fate. In me are all, even the resisting, I clear the path for all, I sweep away the lie for all."[3]

Wassermann did not wish to accept the alternatives: German or Jew. He began by holding that his literary work proved him to be both German *and* Jew, one as much and as fully as the other, both simultaneously and irrevocably. He therefore entitled his autobiography, published in 1921, *My Life as German and Jew*. His difficulty lay in convincing others of the reality of this unique harmony. He was constantly forced into a defensive position. Subconsciously, he always laid the stress on the German rather than on the Jew. All others, even those who expressed agreement with him, reversed the stress.

He explained that he was not a believer in the Jewish faith, any more than many of his neighbors were believing Christians. He received the reply that Jewishness was not a matter of faith but of blood. But how was one to judge blood? he asked. Had not German blood been mixed with that of French Huguenots, Slavs, Norsemen, Spaniards, Italians, even with that of Huns and Mongols, when these hordes invaded German territory? Furthermore, had not Jewish blood been modified by two thousand years of sojourning in the West? Assuming that Jewish blood had once been alien and inferior, has it not been improved and purified by German air and soil and water, by some actual interbreeding, by a common history and a common destiny in the heart of Europe? Wassermann's questions met with vague answers. Finally, the hopelessness of his efforts to be accepted by Germans on terms of equality overcame him and filled him with fury and despair. His disgust and horror then found vent in bitter accusations:

"Vain to adjure the nation of poets and thinkers in the name of its poets and thinkers. Every prejudice one thinks disposed of breeds a thousand others, as carrion breeds maggots. — Vain to present the right cheek after the left has been struck. It does not move them to the slightest thoughtfulness; it neither touches nor disarms them; they strike the right cheek too.— Vain to interject words of reason into their crazy shrieking. They say: He dares to open his mouth? Gag him! — Vain to act in exemplary fashion. They say: We know nothing, we have seen nothing, we have heard nothing.— Vain to seek obscurity. They say: The coward!

He is creeping into hiding, driven by his evil conscience.—
Vain to go among them and offer them one's hand. They
say: Why does he take such liberties, with his Jewish obtrusiveness? — Vain to keep faith with them, as a comrade-
in-arms or a fellow citizen. They say: He is Proteus, he can
assume any shape or form.— Vain to help them strip off
the chains of slavery. They say: No doubt he found it
profitable.— Vain to counteract the poison. They brew
fresh venom.— Vain to live for them and die for them. They
say: He is a Jew."⁴

What then can the person of Jewish origin do to win the
affection of his fellow Germans? Nothing. As an illustration,
Wassermann recalled the case of Walter Rathenau, the
Minister of Foreign Affairs, who rushed to the aid of his
country in Germany's hour of defeat and who was murdered
by anti-Semitic youths. Wassermann felt a spiritual affinity
with Rathenau. "Serve us, he was told, sacrifice yourself
for us, breathe the hot breath of life into that which under
our touch is neither body nor spirit, open new roads, dig
deep vaults, burst gates, strike water from rocks and light
up the dark firmament, be a man, be a genius, be a God; in
our mind you don't count, in our eyes you don't exist, we
don't accept you, we don't welcome you; for you are of alien
blood and therefore harmful, our foe and destroyer: Jew."⁵

Wassermann's intense suffering because of the strained
German-Jewish relations led his friends to warn him against
succumbing to persecution-mania. They felt that, after all,
he personally should have no cause for complaint, since he
was read and respected by so-called Aryans and non-Aryans
alike. His novels were best sellers in both hemispheres; a
talented Jewish man of letters could reckon with an inter-

national audience to the same extent as a non-Jewish writer. Thomas Mann expressed this view as late as 1921 in a letter in which he pointed out the recognition accorded Jews throughout Europe, and then asked Wassermann whether he could name a single country that in the twentieth century, and especially after the World War, still sought to exclude Jews from its national life. As for Germany, Mann assured his fellow novelist that it was the land least suited for the growth of anti-Semitism. "Germany, at any rate, cosmopolitan in essence, receptive to all influences, ready to assimilate all forces, a nationality in which Northern heathendom and Southern longing are ever in conflict and in which the Western bourgeois approach and Eastern mysticism mingle — is this the soil in which the plant of anti-Semitism could ever take root?"[6]

Wassermann, in his reply, reminded Thomas Mann that the success of the Jews, their apparent dominance in contemporary European movements, was always accompanied by the inextinguishable hatred of the masses and the distrust and misgivings even of the elect individuals. He asked Mann to reflect what enormous energy, what tremendous self-restraint, what immense overcoming of obstacles were necessary to attain this level of excellence. Besides, it was only a thin upper layer which has succeeded in attaining it, while eight or nine million other Jews continued to suffer in *Galut*. How should Thomas Mann, the offspring of Lübeck patricians, who had never experienced exile, disgrace, or scorn, fathom all the pain which is contained in this single expression *Galut*? The success of a Jew was not a natural phenomenon but the result of a demonic upsurge of forces born of despair. It was therefore not a healthy consequence of achievement, but a morbid consequence of defiance.

Wassermann never escaped the consciousness that he was branded by his origin. Apostasy was obnoxious to him. He reveled in the dream that he could set an example of complete assimilation and that his precedent would be generally followed. The victory of National Socialism doomed his hopes. The burning of his books in the public squares of the German cities in May 1933 and the banning of all his works, past and future, throughout the territory of the Third Reich hurled him back to the spiritual ghetto from which he had always fled. Injustice welded him to those who suffered wrong. In the last months of his life he began an epic narrative of Jewish fate down the ages. The outlines bear the title *Ahasver*. But the novel was to remain a fragment. The author could not survive the collapse of his world. In the last hours of the catastrophic year 1933, death tore from his grasp the pen that pleaded for a cultural fusion of Jew and German. The beautiful dream of assimilation had turned into a nightmare. Its ablest exponent found refuge in the grave.

CHAPTER XII

JEWISH ARYANS

WASSERMANN was not happy as a Jew. Neverthe-less, he sought to convince the Germans that his Jewish origin did not constitute a blemish of sufficient magnitude to make him unworthy of participating in Central European culture on terms of equality with his fellow citizens of so-called Aryan origin. Although he did not hesitate to join the anti-Semites in the chorus of abuse levelled at non-German Jewry, he was hurt whenever German Jews were attacked and he always rushed to their defense. Although he was willing to accept the principle of inferiority for *Ostjuden*, he insisted on equality of rights for those of his coreligionists who were born and bred in Germany.

Rudolph Borchardt and Otto Weininger went beyond Wassermann in their endorsement of the myth of Aryan superiority. Borchardt, a master of prose and verse but an unoriginal thinker, was so captivated by German race doctrines that he could not reconcile himself to his Jewish origin and sought to transform himself into an apostle of Aryanism and Pan-Germanism. Weininger escaped what seemed to him a cursed origin by firing a bullet into his breast.

According to Oswald Spengler, Judaism produced three saints in recent centuries. These were Spinoza, the philosopher, Israel Ba'al-Shem-Tov, the founder of Hasidism,

OTTO WEININGER, 1880–1903

and Otto Weininger. The death of Weininger on October 4, 1903, at the age of twenty-three, caused a sensation and served to call attention to his only published work, which had appeared a few months earlier and which had at first provoked angry comment. This book, *Geschlecht und Charakter*, was an extension of a thesis which he had submitted to the University of Vienna for the degree of Doctor of Philosophy. It may be divided into three sections: a scientific, a philosophic, and an anti-Semitic.

The scientific part deals with the effect of sex on character. Weininger starts with the assumption that there are no men or women, but only male and female substances, and that every individual is a mixture of these two substances. The pure male and the pure female are ideal types that do not actually exist but that can be theoretically constructed. All existing human beings are intermediate forms between the two extremes. All are bisexual and differ only in the varying proportions in which the two substances are combined. From this basic assumption, Weininger derives his laws of sexual attraction and his interpretations of human character.

The philosophic part of Weininger's book postulates Maleness and Femaleness as Platonic ideas. Masculinity and Femininity are opposite poles, positive and negative. Masculinity is Being, and Femininity is non-Being. All the qualities of woman depend on her non-existence, on her want of character or individuality. Woman is nothing but man's expression and projection of his own sexuality. Every man creates for himself a woman, in whom he embodies himself and his own guilt. Woman is guilt, man's lower self, negation; and yet no less eternal than existence itself.

The anti-Semitic part comprises the last two chapters.

Under the influence of Houston Stewart Chamberlain's theories, which he quotes as his source and inspiration, Weininger arrives at the conclusion that Judaism is hateful and loathsome. He is impressed by Chamberlain's argument that a person of Semitic origin should no longer be branded as a Jew if he succeeds in throwing off the fetters of Ezra and Nehemiah and severing himself from the code of Moses. In the summer of 1900, Weininger expressed his desire to leave the Jewish fold, but was dissuaded by his father. On July 21, 1902, the day on which he received his doctoral degree, he was baptized as a Protestant. His baptism was not the result of economic pressure, but of genuine conviction. It was not due to his indifference to Judaism but rather to his fierce hatred of its practitioners and his desire to escape from all association with it.

Weininger did not wish to be merely a baptized Jew. He wanted to be a non-Jew. He therefore had to find a definition of Judaism which would make such a transformation possible. He could not define Judaism as a racial doctrine, since escape from one's racial origin is impossible. Nor could he define it as a creed, since the Viennese Jews were on the whole no more religious than he himself. Nor could he define the Jews as a people, since the Jews of his acquaintance claimed to be part of the German people. He, therefore, resorted to the novel definition of Judaism as a Platonic idea, as a tendency of the mind, as a psychological structure to which all mankind may be subject. It found its most grandiose realization among the Jews and its least frequent embodiment among the Aryans.

This definition enabled Weininger, despite his background, to exclude himself from the exponents of Judaism, for there could thus exist persons of Jewish birth who were more Aryan than some Aryans, and also native Aryans who were more Jewish than many Jews. This definition also enabled him to identify Aryanism with Masculinity and Judaism with Femininity. Aryanism is Being; Judaism is non-Being. The Aryan possesses individuality; but the Jew has none. The Aryan believes in some Absolute; the Jew is ever the unbeliever. The Aryan strives for eternal being and therefore is something; the Jew, utterly without faith, is Nothing. The Aryan, like Man, knows extremes of good and evil, of brilliance and stupidity. The Jew, like Woman, is utterly devoid of genius, and hence always mediocre and imitative.

Weininger held that the bitterest anti-Semites are to be found among the Jews themselves; and their anti-Semitism bears witness to the fact that not even they themselves consider their kind lovable.

Zionism is, in Weininger's philosophy, the negation of Judaism, for it seeks to ennoble this guilty condition of the soul. It seeks to bring the concept of a state to beings in whose psychic structure this concept has never existed and can never exist. Judaism stands for world-wide dispersion. It is formless, unaristocratic, undignified, worthless. Before Zionism is possible, the Jew must first conquer Judaism. He must first war against his inner nature. A beginning has already been made, since the Jew has learned to respect the Aryan more than himself. His will to free himself from Jewishness must be strengthened. If a Jew demonstrates this will and asks for baptism, then he should be accepted by non-Jews as an Aryan and should not be condemned for his past affiliation with a race above which his moral efforts have elevated him.

Of all Germanic races, the English resemble the Jews most closely. England is like Israel and like Woman.

In biblical times there were two possibilities dormant in Israel: Being and non-Being, affirmation and negation. Jesus gave reality to one of these possibilities. He founded Christianity, the strongest affirmation. Those who refused to accept Jesus remained with negation. Since the founding of the present era, Israel divided into Christians and Jews. The opposite of Jesus is the Jew. Jesus was the greatest personality because he conquered the greatest enemy; he was in historic times the only Jew to overcome Judaism. But perhaps Judaism may still produce another Christ; perhaps the new savior, the founder of the next religion, will also pass through Jewry; perhaps the time is no longer distant when the eagerly awaited Messiah will redeem the Jews from Judaism.

Weininger saw himself as this messiah, as the liberator of civilization from the guilt of womanhood and the sin of Judaism. In his opinion, our age is the most feminine and the most Jewish of all ages. It is an age of superficiality and injustice, of anarchism and communism, of the most foolish of all historical interpretations — the materialistic interpretation of history. It is a time when genius is looked upon as a form of insanity, when life and science are mechanized, when great artists and great philosophers do not flourish, when the cult of the Virgin has yielded to that of the *demivierge*. But a new Christianity is arising, a new Redeemer is at hand. As in the year One, the struggle is entering upon a decisive phase and the choice must be made between Judaism or Christianity, business or culture, Woman or Man, matter or spirit, negation or divinity. These are the two poles. There is no Third Reich.

A few months after publishing these startling conclusions, Weininger, the would-be Messiah of the dawning twentieth century, rented a room in the house in which Beethoven had died, and, without a word of farewell, fired a bullet into his heart.

This suicide found numerous interpretations among his followers. One of his most devoted disciples, Arthur Trebitsch, attributed it to the fact that Weininger, who had overcome the negative force of Jewishness within himself and had by his nobility of soul attained to the positive pole of Aryanism, could not convince anyone else of this miraculous inner transformation and in his abysmal loneliness succumbed to hopelessness and despair. A genius, like Weininger, might have gotten along without public applause and press approval, but he yearned for the warm love of the Aryan world. Had an Aryan received him in his home as his friend and equal, he might not have sought death. This liberated personality was, however, condemned to live in the atmosphere and environment of the slavish non-Aryans, unable to make the slightest impression upon the splendid, free Aryans. The latter distrusted his overtures and rejected his gifts, while the former dubbed him renegade and traitor, hated him because of his truthfulness, and persecuted him because of his revelations of their iniquities. He thus knew neither health-bringing peace nor emotional equilibrium. Shunned and distraught, joyless and aimless, he had to choose self-destruction.

Arthur Trebitsch saw in Weininger's martyrdom a prefiguration of his own struggle to escape from ancestral bondage to pure Aryanism. But, while Weininger lacked the strength to weather the racial storm and resorted to suicide as the only means of destroying the Ahasverus-heritage in his personality, Trebitsch hoped to endure and to carry on to victory the battle for liberation from Semitism.

Born in 1879, Arthur Trebitsch was the son of a Jewish silk merchant of Vienna and the brother of Siegfried Trebitsch, the German translator of George Bernard Shaw. His family had resided in Vienna for several generations. Upon this fact Trebitsch based his claim to Aryanism. "I am no Jew," he repeatedly exclaimed, "I never was a Jew, and never will be one! And I gladly confess that my great-grandfather belonged to that race!"[1]

German anti-Semitism, Trebitsch felt, did not get very far because it alternated between religious hatred and race hatred, without making a final choice between either. Had the healthy instinct of the masses been consulted, the decision would have been for race hatred, since what distinguished human beings from another was race and not religion. In fact, both Judaism and Christianity were afflicted with the same slave-morality. Both were mouldy ruins, useless and senseless. Mankind would have to learn to get along without them and would have to look about for a newer, better, more heroic faith. Danger threatened not from the Jewish religion but from the Jewish race. This race was the bearer of the poisonous germs infecting Europe's body. Only a few individuals, such as Weininger and Trebitsch himself, succeeded, after generations of effort, in evolving into pure Aryans, despite ancestral impurity. In them alone had Ahasverus, the Wandering Jew, found the death and stability he ever desired and hardly hoped to achieve any longer. But as for the millions of other Jews, especially the turbid human stream from the East, iron severity must be exercised towards them by the master race.

Europe, if it wished to regain its health, must not tolerate any of the destructive seed of the accursed brood. It must expel all except those few families whose sons were willing to bind themselves to compulsory physical work in labor battalions. After three generations of fertilizing the German earth with the sweat of their forced labor, these selected individuals will have rid their bodies and souls of the poison of Judaism. They could then be received as pure, honorable Aryans, whose roots reached deep into German soil.

Trebitsch insisted that Judaism and Germanism cannot exist in harmony side by side, because they are opposite poles. One or the other must perish. The doom of noble Germany can be predicted, unless it succeeds in quarantining all who were infected with *morbus Judaicus*.

This theoretical analysis of the German-Jewish duality was written by Trebitsch during the First World War and published in 1919 under the title *Geist und Judentum*. At the end of that war, Trebitsch arrived at the conclusion that Germany was defeated because of Jewish machinations. The collapse of the Hohenzollern and Hapsburg monarchies must be attributed to Jewish revolutionary efforts. Just as the Jews in past centuries put an end to the realms of Canaan, Persia, Egypt, Greece, and Rome, so they now threatened the engulfment of the Reich, the last strong bulwark of Aryanism. England was Israel's stronghold and under the English mask the Jews were seeking world hegemony. The decline of the West was inevitable, unless the Occident finally awakened from its sleep or paralysis, its blindness or hypnotic trance; unless it recognized its implacable destroyer and quickly developed an antitoxin against the poisonous foreign body. Since antitoxins were often best derived from toxins, salvation from the Semitic poison could best come from individuals like himself, who had recovered from their Jewishness. It could also come from the half-Aryans and three-quarters-Aryans, who were aware of their biological function as antitoxins and who were more sensitive to the Jewish peril than were the full-blooded Aryans. Though the Jews pursued these few elect individuals with mortal hate and though the Germans distrusted them, they would nevertheless proceed with their historic mission to save their beloved fatherland from Judean enslavement.

To critical-minded people, who doubted the existence of a Jewish conspiracy to dominate and to debauch the world, Trebitsch replied with documentary evidence based upon the tract *Die Weisen von Zion* ("The Protocols of the Elders of Zion"). This infamous forgery, whose genuineness Trebitsch did not question, formed the backbone of his volume, *Deutscher Geist — oder Judentum*, published in 1921. To those readers who doubted the ability of a small Jewish minority to overcome the resistance of a vast German majority, Trebitsch countered with "proof" of an alliance between Zion and Rome. The Catholic Church, despairing of sole dominion, had agreed to join World Jewry in a common assault upon the Nordic Protestants. Victory was to be followed by a common division of spoils. Bolshevism, the deadliest weapon hitherto forged by the Elders of Zion, was to be called upon to deal the Reich its death-blow. Thereafter, Rome was to inherit Catholic Austria and Catholic South Germany, while the Northland was to fall into the hands of Zion. But Rome would not long enjoy its booty, according to the prediction of Trebitsch, for, after the bulwark of Northern Germany shall have been removed, all of

Europe would fall an easy prey to the Jews. It was even absurd to hope that distant America would stem the tide of destruction, since America was already in the hands of financial magnates and was therefore the ideal state of international Jewry. Should Europe ever sink to the level of America, then the bright Aryan glance would be dulled, love would perish, and the whole of life would degenerate to a senseless mechanism. The decisive hour had struck. "Thou, my beloved, trusting, guileless, unsuspecting, childlike, pure German people, awaken to manly perception, drive away the diabolical misleaders as well as the erring, incapable leaders, and save for yourself and for all other peoples of the earth the proper world order compatible with your vital essence."[2]

Trebitsch offered his services as propagandist and awakener of the New Germany. Until his death, in 1927, he wrote and lectured on the Jewish menace. Like Weininger, he was an admirer of Houston Stewart Chamberlain, whose philosophy he praised as "the transition from Kant to Trebitsch," and whose racial theories he expanded to a pathological extreme. The intensity of his faith in his Aryan mission is said to have moved listeners, especially women and youths, to tears and to ecstasy. In the birth-years of Austrian National Socialism, he was for a time the *Führer*, but managed to quarrel with his few disciples. These deserted him and followed the rising star of Adolf Hitler. Trebitsch's fixed idea of the Jewish menace became an integral part of Nazi ideology and his pathological rantings about a world-wide conspiracy of the Elders of Zion became an article of faith that dared not be questioned in the Third Reich.

The seed sown by Houston Stewart Chamberlain and by

the Jewish Aryans, Otto Weininger and Arthur Trebitsch, came to fruition in the 1930's. Popularized by Adolf Hitler and Julius Streicher, racial anti-Semitism was incorporated by the totalitarian Reich in its legislative code, and inhuman restrictions were applied to all inhabitants of non-Aryan or only partly-Aryan blood.

ERNST TOLLER, 1893–1939

Chapter XIII

MARGINAL JEWS

THE affection of the Jewish Aryans for Germany borders on the pathological. Their hatred of the ancestral roots within their personality leads them to self-destruction or psychic disintegration. They are tragic because they are homeless. They reject all affinity with the Jewish community and are, at the same time, unwelcome among their non-Jewish contemporaries.

An equal tragedy befalls those intellectuals of Germany who leave the Jewish fold in order to embrace a vague cosmopolitanism or the panaceas of socialism and communism. These also find themselves homeless and devoid of influence on the European scene. These also ultimately end in suicide or in the solitude of exile. The life and death of Ernst Toller, the gifted Expressionist poet and dramatist, is so typical of the entire group of German-Jewish radicals as to merit careful and detailed analysis.

The suicide of Toller on May 22, 1939, created a sensation in literary circles throughout the Western World. The German writer's nay-saying to life was immediately sensed to be symbolic of a growing mood of despair among the finest spirits of the present generation. For all recognized in him the pure soul who believed in certain holy ideals and who refused to survive the apparent twilight of his ideals.

Though only forty-five years old, Toller had already lived three lives and he did not desire a fourth.

His first life had been filled with battles and had ended in
Bavarian prison-entombment. Barely twenty when the First
World War broke out, and animated by purest patriotism,
he had abandoned his studies at a French university and
returned to the Fatherland on the last train before the border
was closed. He enlisted for service at the front and fought
like a hero. During thirteen months in the trenches his eyes
were opened to the futility of mass murder as a means of
settling political disputes and, when he was sent home as an
invalid, he agitated against war, participated in strikes,
suffered arrest, was kept in a military prison, and on his
release resumed his revolutionary activities. As a leader of
the Bavarian Soviet Republic of 1919, he was hounded by
the victors after the suppression of the proletarian uprising
and a price of 10,000 Marks was set on his head. He was
captured and condemned to imprisonment in the fortress
of Niederschoenfeld, and there he remained for five full
years.

His second life began with his release from prison at the
age of thirty and ended with his exile at the age of forty. He
was received by his admirers in Berlin amidst tremendous
ovations and immediately plunged into the thick of the
battle for the emancipation of the workers. His dramas—
Masse Mensch, Maschinenstürmer, Hinkemann — written
while in prison, were known to tens of thousands of theater-
goers throughout the length and breadth of Germany and
widely beyond its borders. He dipped his pen in fire and
hurled flaming darts against the bourgeoisie. He fashioned
of his wrath literary bullets against the rising reactionary
forces during that decade when socialists, communists, and
democrats were battling Hitler's cohorts. But in 1933 the
whirlwind swept over Germany, tore to shreds the work of

his mature years, and left him stranded and alone upon a foreign shore.

A third time Toller rose from the dead. Once more he entered the arena of political and social conflicts and again his voice was heard pleading for the rights of man made in the image of God. As a person who believed in the sanctity of the individual human life and who saw in the state primarily a union of free persons engaged in common enterprises to further each other's welfare, he watched with increasing dismay the retreat of the democratic tradition in state and society. As an internationalist who espoused a world brotherhood and refused to acknowledge as desirable the boundaries that separated one people from another, he had to look on helplessly while nationalism was everywhere resurgent and defiant shouts of hatred were being hurled across boundaries of steel and concrete. As a pacifist who had written that no man had a right to kill others to further any cause, he had to arrive at the contrary conclusion that his ideal of non-resistance had been an error and a crime, that it had merely needlessly sapped the virility of the Weimar Republic, and that it had made more easy the victory of the National Socialist regime, founded on the opposite principle of brute force and unsentimental ruthlessness. On the battlefields of Spain early in 1939 he saw the fate of Europe in the balance. He realized: Germany was one vast concentration camp; Italy was another; Austria was engulfed; the Peace of Munich was a desecration of the tender word Peace. Spain was his last hope. The final months of his life found him engaged in unremitting efforts to help the cause of Spanish democracy. His eloquent appeals in behalf of the starving civilians of Madrid were acted upon by statesmen and governments at the beginning of 1939; but before food-ships could sail or food-trucks cross the border, Fascism triumphed in that country. The fall of Madrid opened his heart to the inroads of despair. He felt that soon men would again murder each other in a second World War. He recalled the final vision of his hero Hinkemann: "And there are people who don't see it. And there are people who have forgotten it. They suffered in war and hated their masters and obeyed and murdered. . . All forgotten. . . They will again suffer and again hate their masters and again . . . obey and again . . . murder. That's how human beings are . . . And could be otherwise, if they wished. But they don't wish. They stone the spirit, they mock it; they disgrace life, they crucify it . . . again and ever again . . . How senseless all! Impoverish themselves, when they could be rich and would not need a heavenly savior . . . the blind fools! As if they had to do this in the blind whirl of millennia! As if they could not act otherwise! As if they had to! Like ships caught in the maelstrom and compelled to annihilate each other."[1]

On May 22, 1939, Ernst Toller sought peace in the grave, peace that he never knew while he roamed among the living, peace that might have come to him had he succeeded in finding his way back to his ancestral roots. His tragedy was his homelessness. He had torn himself loose from the Jewish community and had been ousted by the German.

A reading of his autobiography, which appeared after the accession of Hitler to power and which bears in the English translation the sad title *I was a German*, reveals how much sounder and saner was the existence of his unmodern forefathers. He relates that his great-grandparents came from Spain and from Poland. They found a new home in Prussia under Frederick the Great and they retained their Orthodox way of life, untempted by German Enlightenment. Toller's grandfather still studied the Talmud by day and by night, poring over gigantic Hebrew folios yellow with age, and unaffected by the ebb and flow of German Romantic and Nationalistic tides. Toller's father received his education in a German *Gymnasium* and felt himself to be a pioneer of imperial German culture in a district with a large Polish population. His bonds with the Jewish community were less firm, but it never occurred to him to sever them entirely. Complete separation from the Jewish community was first undertaken by Ernst Toller. His childhood dreams already centered about escape from Judaism. As a boy he felt himself a member of the superior German group and looked down with contempt upon the Slavic inhabitants. He thought of them as offspring of Cain, branded by God as inferior creatures. This young German patriot could not, however, avoid noticing that his classmates had equal scorn for Jews, pursued these on the streets with cries of "Hep-Hep," and constantly hurled unflattering epithets at them. He heard his friends tell of Jews slaughtering Christian boys in order to bake unleavened bread with their blood. He did not, of course, believe the wicked slanders about Jews, but he wanted to escape from his humiliating position as a member of an inferior group. He did not fancy growing up to be chased by catcalling children. Once he found his way to a Christian group and experienced shudders of ecstasy when told that he was on the path towards true salvation and when permitted to participate in a Christmas celebration. Toller's flight from Judaism led him at first to ultra-nationalism and super-patriotism and then to socialism and cosmopolitanism. But, at the end of his days, in the loneliness of exile, he brooded over his past illusions and attempted a revaluation of his position as a German and as a Jew. In his autobiography, Toller summarized his life-long reactions towards the German-Jewish duality, as follows:

"I think of my early youth, of my pain as a boy, when the other boys hurled the word 'Jew' at me, of my overwhelming joy when I was not recognized as a Jew, of the early war-days, when I was filled with the passionate desire to prove at the risk of my life that I was a German, nothing but a German. From the front I wrote to the court to erase my name from the Jewish rolls. Was all in vain? Or was I mistaken? Do I not love this land? Did I not long for its barren forests and its hidden seas, even amidst the rich landscape of the Mediterranean? Did not the verses of Goethe and Hölderlin, which I read as a wide-awake youngster, stir me to intense gratitude? Is not the German language my language, the language in which I feel and think, speak and act, a part of my being, home that nourished me, hearth in which I grew up?

"But am I not also a Jew? Do I not belong to that people which for thousands of years is being persecuted, hunted, tortured, murdered, whose prophets hurled into this world the cry for justice, a cry which the wretched and oppressed took up and handed down the ages, whose boldest souls never bowed and preferred to die rather than to be unfaithful? I wanted to repudiate my mother; I am ashamed of myself. That a child was compelled to resort to such lies, what a horrible indictment against all who drove him to it.

"But am I, therefore, a stranger in Germany? Does the fiction of blood alone have validity? Is no importance to be attached to my growing up in the land of my birth, whose air I breathe, whose language I live, whose spirit formed me? Do I not as a German author wrestle for the pure expression, the pure image? If you were to ask me: Toller, where are your German roots and where your Jewish, I would remain silent.

"Blind nationalism and racial conceit are stirring in every land. Must I, too, participate in the madness of this age, in the patriotism of this epoch? Am I not also for this reason a socialist, because I believe that socialism will do away with the hatred of nations as well as with the hatred of classes?

"The words: I am proud to be a German, or: I am proud to be a Jew, sound as foolish to me as if a person were to say: I am proud to have brown eyes.

"Must I succumb to the madness of my persecutors and accept Jewish instead of German arrogance? Arrogance and love are not synonymous, and, if anyone asked me where I belonged, my answer would be: a Jewish mother brought me into this world, Germany has nourished me, Europe has educated me, my home is this earth, and the world my fatherland."[2]

Toller's escape to cosmopolitanism and Utopian socialism finds a parallel in the escape of Franz Werfel to an idealized Catholicism, which is to be a synthesis of pure Judaism and pure Christianity.

The brilliant Austrian poet, dramatist, and novelist, who thinks in images and argues by means of visions, was early fascinated by the symbolism of Jesus' life and death. Before he passed his twenties, he published his confession of faith in an essay entitled *Die christliche Sendung* (1917). He speaks from the viewpoint of a person who has just discovered Christianity, after wandering about as an exile far from its shores, and he undertakes to defend his new discovery against all unbelievers and misinterpreters. Yet, his re-definition of Christianity sounds strangely like a definition of Judaism. "All talk of the negation of the world, which is supposedly contained in Christianity, is pure nonsense. Christianity does not exercise compulsion. Christianity is the only spiritual attitude which does not need laws but only insight. Christian justice is the only human justice which is identical with human happiness, because Christianity is directed against the — 'just.' The Christian doctrine of salvation is the only ethical pronouncement which makes joy, the highest form of joy, the goal of its activity. Christianity is wholly devoid of any preaching and asceticism and, if it turns against the brutal excremental pleasures, it does so in order to pave the way for the winged, diversified, sublime pleasures . . . Above all, Christian philosophy is the most rational of all philosophies."[3]

Though Werfel often repeats his conviction that Jesus first opened the way for man to God and though his yearning for this mystic savior often finds expression in prose and verse, he yet hesitates to accept baptism and in certain circles he is even regarded as a spokesman for contemporary Jewry. Thus, his biblical play, *The Eternal Road*, set to synagogal music by Kurt Weill and magnificently staged in New York in 1936 by Max Reinhardt, was hailed by some as the artistic embodiment of the Jewish fate. It impressed tens of thousands of spectators as a genuine portrayal of personalities, motivation, beliefs, and aspirations, current among Jews. This very spectacle, however, clearly reveals Werfel's spiritual homelessness, his tragic position between two religions and two peoples.

The framework of the drama is comparatively simple. A Jewish community seeks refuge in the synagogue during a night of terror, while an angry mob rages through the streets demanding that the town be rid of all the members of the accursed race. The king has not yet spoken the final word, but his decision is expected by dawn. At best the Jewish community can hope for exile; at worst it must fear physical annihilation. The Rabbi asks that the Torah be taken from the ark, and during the dreadful night of suspense he reads to the assembled congregation portions of the Torah and of the Prophets in order to remind his listeners of the glorious Jewish past and to steel them for the future. The portions read by the Rabbi are enacted on a symbolic stage and are commented on by various members of the congregation.

The biblical scenes enable Werfel to sketch a panorama of the Jewish past and the realistic interludes enable him to give a cross-section of the Jewish present. For, it must be remembered that the drama was conceived in 1933 upon Hitler's accession to power and it is therefore filled with numerous allusions to Germany and the fate of contemporary Jewry.

The Jewish past is depicted in the simple immortal words of the Bible and here Werfel's contribution consists primarily in the selection of the biblical scenes and passages which he regards as most symbolic of the Jewish fate. The Jewish present is reproduced in Werfel's own words, as spoken by characters of his own creation.

Now what sort of characters are those that listen to the Rabbi and that Werfel assumes to be typical of all Jewry? On the whole, they may be classified as either rogues or simpletons. There is the cynical adversary who has contributed his bit to the solution of the Jewish problem by not marrying and not having any children. He constantly asks questions that attack Judaism and that are never answered.

There is the timid soul who wants the watchman to make
sure to issue a warning when the mob or the soldiers will
arrive to begin the slaughtering. There is the rich man who
brings along to the synagogue his chests of gold and who is
constantly bewailing the loss of his immovable property, his
five houses. There are the pious men, fanatical, intolerant,
experienced prayer-dervishes. The sympathetic characters
are: the alien girl — a non-Jewess, who like Ruth of Moab
is ready to follow her beloved to death or exile; the thirteen-
year-old boy, who was reared in ignorance of his origin and
hence was not yet subjected to the "degrading" influence of
a Jewish environment; and the Estranged Person, who
wanted to escape his Jewishness and who has been hurled
back into it by the mob's actions much against his own will.
In this person, one recognizes the portrait of the author
himself.

The following defense can, of course, be set up for Werfel:
it may have been his purpose to show that contemporary
Jewry, as he envisaged it — a degenerate stock, sunk in
ignorance, depravity, arrogance, and superstition — can
still be rehabilitated by contact with its glorious past, by a
return to its biblical heritage, now that the blessed road to
assimilation and to baptism has been closed to its members.
However, if we survey the biblical scenes which the dramatist selected, supposedly as object-lessons for the regeneration of Jewry, we must marvel at his consistent bad taste in
emphasizing the most disagreeable episodes of the Old Testament, the very episodes that have supplied mockers, from
Voltaire to the contemporary neo-pagans, with ammunition
to undermine all faith.

The following illustrations, all chosen from the first act,

will serve as proof of this conclusion: Abraham is shown haggling with God for the preservation of Sodom until he reduces the price for God's mercy from fifty righteous souls to ten, God hesitating ever more and more as Abraham tries to drive a hard bargain. Sarah is shown laughing incredulously when she overhears the prophecy of the angels that a son is to be born to her; whereupon she denies that she laughed and thus compounds her disbelief with lying. Abraham does not fail to address Sarah as "my wife" and "my sister," thereby unnecessarily reminding us that the sacred relationship was also an incestuous one. Abraham is then displayed covering the eyes of Isaac with his left hand and wielding the slaughtering knife with his right, all for the greater glory of God. And what a God! Jacob is shown in a sentimental scene with Rachel, recalling the dastardly treachery on that night when he was given the wrong girl to wife and also his own harshness towards the right girl because she bore him no children. Jacob is then shown as a doting father and Joseph as an insolent youngster. Joseph's brothers are ready to commit fratricide but cannot resist the temptation to earn silver coins by selling Joseph. The haggling with all ten fingers and the weighing of the silver are especially emphasized. Of Joseph's stay in Egypt, the stress is placed on the trickery of the stolen cup.

What sardonic irony that Werfel, who ever sought estrangement from his coreligionists, should be held up by the unknowing as the ideal interpreter of the Jewish soul! And that a play, which was perhaps born of Werfel's dislike of certain Jewish traits and which may help to explain and even justify to his own conscience his aloofness from the Jewish tragedy of the nineteen-thirties, should be blazoned forth as a genuine expression of the Jewish renaissance!

In 1940 Werfel published *Embezzled Heaven*, a novel that affords once more an interesting insight into his troubled soul. In the epilogue to this work he laments that he stands *extra muros*, but he makes it clear that his greatest sympathy is with Roman Catholicism. In Catholicism he envisages the unity of mankind. "The unity was real, even though incomplete. It was more universal than anything else on earth, for it cut across all races and classes. It was also the only form of unity in this world which did not see its purpose in hostility to something."[4] Werfel attributes our modern ills to our revolt against metaphysics and the supernatural. He would restore faith and ban logic as a guide to life. In *Embezzled Heaven* he therefore selects as his heroine a humble cook who performs her appointed tasks on earth to the best of her ability and whose commonplace existence is irradiated by her faith in immortality.

The cook, Teta Linek, uses her life earnings to educate her nephew for the clergy and hopes thereby to earn admission to heaven. Although her nephew turns out to be a fraud, she nevertheless does attain to a blissful end because of her naive religious aspirations.

Werfel sheds the warmth of compassion over his Austrian plebeians and aristocrats, but has only words of scorn and dislike for the Jews in his few references to them. It is true that the strictures against Jews, put in the mouth of Herr Bichler, a communist turned Nazi, can be explained as artistically necessary. But it is questionable whether the plea of poetic necessity can also be made for Werfel's insistence on presenting, as the leader of a Catholic pilgrimage, a converted Jew, Josef Eusebius Kompert. One wonders whether Werfel, who in 1943 and 1944 was to attain the height of fame with his magnificent glorification of Catholicism in *The Song of Bernadette*, did not subconsciously uncover too much of his own soul when he introduced this character as follows: "He devoted himself with even greater ardor to ecclesiastical affairs than he did to mundane matters. As his name and visage indicated, he had not always belonged to the Roman Catholic Church, but new brooms sweep clean and the zeal of converts generally exceeds that of those who were born in the faith. They did not inherit their religion, so they cannot afford to take it passively, to say nothing of neglecting it. For them the various ceremonies are never hackneyed or tedious, everything has an atmosphere of freshness, their hold is still insecure, and their vain hearts spur them on to excel in activities which for the majority are all too often merely a matter of dull habit."[5]

Despite Werfel's oft-expressed love for the Old and the New Testaments, he cannot find space for a single generous reference to Jews in this religious novel written in one of the darkest years in Jewish history. He does, however, go into great detail in showing how a guileful ex-Jew manages to get the sick Pope Pius to grant an audience to the former's tourist clients. "Though he had fallen away from the faith of his fathers, he still retained in his blood the inherited readiness to face up fervently to any difficulty and never regard the impossible as being in fact impossible. The persuading at the last minute of a mortally sick Pope to hold an audience that had been as good as cancelled was an inspiring task which not only the convert but also the original soul deep down within Herr Kompert felt to be supremely tempting."[6] Kompert's success in winning over the Pope earns him the applause of the pious pilgrims. "An infernally

cunning fellow, this Jew. He managed to get onto the right
side in good time. And you can always rely on that type
being able to arrange things when there's any difficulty."

What a contrast between the depreciation of Jewish traits
by the marginal Jew, Franz Werfel, and the supreme evaluation of such traits by the non-Jewish literary masters of his
own Expressionistic generation! Two examples may serve
to illustrate the latter approach.

When Heinrich Mann, brother of Thomas Mann and himself a novelist of international repute, was asked whether he
would endorse either mass-baptism of Jews or their forced
emigration to Palestine, in order to relieve the host-people
of the unassimilated guests, he replied with the outcry: "But
what is to become of the so-called host-people, already suffering from spiritual undernourishment, if the Jews were
now also to fail them? — if no Jew were to infiltrate public
life with a little more spirit and no Jewess were to make love
a little more soulful? The consequences of complete assimilation and those of separation would be equally horrible."[7]

When Frank Wedekind, the most prominent dramatist
among the Expressionists, was asked for his solution of the
apparent conflict between Jews and non-Jews, he replied
that he did not want the conflict solved: Jew and non-Jew
were two souls in the breast of mankind, eternal opposites,
yet both eternally indispensable to the human species — a
dualism comparable to that of man and woman, each destined to influence the other for the greater good of the whole.[8]
According to Wedekind, the Diaspora did not commence in
the year 70 A. D. It existed as early as the first Jews, who
were already strangers in the land of Egypt. The independent
Jewish states were but a brief interlude. The dispersal of the

Jews would probably continue indefinitely. Why must this be so? Because the Jews were politically unproductive. They have in the past been politically dependent upon others and will ever remain in this condition. Europeans, on the other hand, were morally unproductive. They have in the past depended upon the Jews for standards of morality and will continue to look upon them as the conscience of the world. Lacking political talent, the Jewish people lived as a political guest among other peoples. Whenever these were on a lower level of culture, it had no difficulty in maintaining its separate identity and its own way of life. If, on the other hand, these occupied a higher cultural level, it was not profitable for the Jewish people to form a state of its own and to carry on separatist politics. As proof of the unpolitical character of Jewry, Wedekind pointed out that in hundreds of cities Jews were herded together in ghettos throughout the Middle Ages and that not a single ghetto ever took over control of a city. The dramatist dismissed the tales of Jewish oppression down the ages as gross exaggerations, certainly not to be compared in cruelty with the oppression inflicted upon the landed populace in former centuries. He observed that the medieval Jews were able to purchase from Popes and Emperors special privileges and immunities, which were denied to other commoners, and that Jewish emancipation, which was brought about by the victory of the French revolutionary slogans, was not as spectacular a cultural achievement or as important for mankind as the simultaneous emancipation of the European serf-population. When the disparity in numbers between Jews and non-Jews was brought to Wedekind's attention in order to refute his theory of a basic dualism within mankind, he countered with the argument that numerical inferiority had been compensated

for in various ways: the Jews had been at the hub of civilization for three thousand years; they had imposed their
Judaeo-Christian morality upon all Christendom; they had
ever held stubbornly to their racial configuration; they
managed to keep their distinctiveness in all political melting-
pots; they were not circumscribed by national boundaries.
He therefore felt that in the long run the Jews were more
likely to assimilate the non-Jews than vice versa, in other
words, they would ultimately win the others over to their
unpolitical, purely moral order.

The insights of the "Aryan" Expressionists Frank Wedekind and Heinrich Mann may be more picturesque than
accurate, but their conclusions stem from a genuine love for
the biblical people and a high regard for its historic achievements and its contemporary qualities. This love and this
regard are lacking in the published works of the "non-Aryan"
Expressionists Ernst Toller and Franz Werfel. Both of these
writers, in their tortured efforts to escape from the stigma-
tized Jewish community and in their final inability to make
good this escape, are symbolic of many marginal Jews of
Central Europe on the eve of Hitlerism and even thereafter.
Homeless and unhappy they wander about on the world's
highways, unaware of the call of the Jewish renaissance.

STEFAN ZWEIG, 1881–1942

CHAPTER XIV

STEFAN ZWEIG

O N FEBRUARY 23, 1942, Stefan Zweig, citizen of the world, voluntarily departed from it, after having reached the age of sixty and after having been sated with a wealth of experiences, joyous and bitter, personal, cosmopolitan, and Jewish. As the youngest disciple of the literary group known as *Young Vienna*, Zweig lived until his mid-thirties the life of an Austrian aesthete, dabbling in verse, playing with prose essays, experimenting with subtle short stories. The First World War shocked him out of his complacent dreams and hurled him into dynamic creative activity. It brought him wisdom and maturity and, before long, his fame extended to the ends of the globe. From the collapse of the Danubian Dual-Monarchy in 1918 — a collapse he prophetically predicted in his pacifistic tragedy *Jeremias* — until the burial of the Austrian Republic by the Nazi avalanche in 1938, he knew two full decades of intensive and prolific literary labor in behalf of European solidarity and international good will. During this period, he, like his hero Erasmus of Rotterdam, strove for the humanistic ideal and sought, beyond the wrangling of chauvinistic politicians, a unity of peoples in a Europe in which hatred and distrust between neighboring nations and between Jews and Gentiles within each nation would be wholly eradicated. The nightmare that descended upon his native land and upon his entire continent after 1938 finally sapped his strength and undermined his courage. When the shadows of cultural barbarism began to creep on to other continents, he lost all faith in any immediate better future for mankind. The defeats of 1941 and of 1942, suffered by the warring democracies, drove him beyond deepest despair to the extreme step of self-annihilation. Overtired, he penned his last message: "After I saw the country of my own language fall, and my spiritual land — Europe — destroying itself, and I have reached the age of sixty, it would require immense strength to reconstruct my life, and my energy is exhausted by long years of peregrination as one without a country. Therefore, I believe it is time to end a life that was dedicated only to spiritual work, considering human liberty and my own as the greatest wealth in the world. I leave an affectionate good-bye to all my friends."

Thus ended in Petropolis, Brazil's summer capital, the talented Jew-Austrian-European, and his tragic death confirmed the failure of another attempted synthesis of Germanic and Hebraic culture.

Zweig's intellectual life was rooted in *Young Vienna,* a circle of patricians, dandies, thinkers, and scoffers, who at the turn of the century dominated the literary, theatrical, and journalistic activities of the bustling Danubian metropolis. The Jewish members of this circle included Arthur Schnitzler and Richard Beer-Hofmann, Theodor Herzl and Felix Salten, Peter Altenberg and Felix Dörmann. Jakob Wassermann narrated in his autobiography that, when he first visited pre-War Vienna, he was amazed to discover that its intellectual life seemed to be dominated by Jews. Press, theater, literature, social organizations, all lay in their hands. The explanation which he offered for this unusual phenomenon was the following: "The aristocracy would have nothing to do with such things; with the exception of a few nonconformists who had been ejected from the fold, a few who saw things in a different light, they not only maintained a respectful distance from intellectual and artistic life but feared and condemned it. The small number of untitled patrician families imitated the aristocracy; the original upper middle class had disappeared, leaving a gap now occupied by government functionaries, army officers, and professors; then came the closed circle of the lower middle class. The court, the lower middle class, and the Jews gave the city its stamp. And that the Jews, as the most mobile group, kept all the others in continuous motion is, on the whole, not surprising. Yet I was amazed at the hosts of Jewish physicians, attorneys, clubmen, snobs, dandies, proletarians, actors, newspapermen, and poets."[1]

Out of this soil sprang Sigmund Freud, the founder of psychoanalysis and an inspirer of Stefan Zweig. Out of this soil there also sprang such antithetical personalities as Theodor Herzl, the prophet of Jewish rebirth, and Otto Weininger, the Jewish high priest of anti-Semitism. But Zweig's earliest and closest affiliation was with the literary masters of *Young Vienna*: Hermann Bahr, Arthur Schnitzler, Hugo von Hofmannsthal, and Richard Beer-Hofmann.

In lyrics of sweet weariness, in tales of sad disillusionment, in playlets overladen with the fruit of contemplation, these aesthetes wrote of pleasures that palled, of comedies that ended tragically, of reality that bordered on dreamland, of love with its ecstasy and sorrow, of age with its loneliness and silence, and of Death — the ever-present guest at the banquet of life. Their longing for gaiety, frivolity, and irresponsibility alternated with their desire to serve, to suffer,

and to shoulder responsibilities. Though they nipped at
every passing pleasure, they sensed in their heart of hearts
that pleasure was no goal but rather led deeper into slavery.
Though they worshipped beauty and adored art, they were
painfully aware that a life of beauty impoverished, and that
too much devotion to art sapped all vital energy. As a result,
a heavy haze of melancholy overhung their lightest verses
and a hypersensitive conscience gave the lie to their amoral
pretensions.

Their works circled about eternal problems, yet nowhere
did they make the pompous claim that they had found a
single solution to a single important problem. It is true that
they were incapable of embracing enthusiastically any slogan
or of devoting their all to any party. On the other hand, they
were equally incapable of condemning, hating or liquidating
opponents and foes. They knew too much. Their insight
into life's labyrinthian depths made them hesitate constantly and robbed them of quick decisions and dynamic
action. Their awareness that all human beings are but
super-marionettes, impelled by the inscrutable supreme
puppet-player of the universe, rendered them far too tolerant. They had no joy in vengeance, no endurance in anger,
no desire for martyrdom. They bowed their heads before
every passing storm. They accepted wars and revolutions
as natural cataclysms against which resistance is vain. They
did not mock the sinner nor praise the noble spirit, for in
their eyes all judgments were folly and all punishments
absurd. Human delusions and superstitions, emotions and
relations, visions and ideals ebb and flow, have their moments of triumph and pass away.

As thinkers they were determinists, but as poets they were

believers in free will. They held that eternal laws rule the rippling of waves, the growth of grass, the flight of birds, the streaming of thoughts within the mind of man. They recognized, however, that acceptance of pure determinism means abandoning all our ethical concepts of guilt and atonement, sin and virtue, and even such distinctions as important and unimportant. It means substituting for all of these values a mere cause-and-effect relationship between happenings. Responsibility would thus be completely negated, love and hate would be rendered impossible, rewards and punishments would be banned, admiration and deprecation would be outmoded, forgiveness and vengeance would be dispensed with, pride and shame would be eliminated, the whole world would be hopelessly boring. Instead of a fascinating stage for tragedies and comedies, performed by individuals, this globe would forever be the scene of a stupid, tiresome farce enacted between blind impulses which happened to be incorporated in this man or that woman. To escape from such deadening monotony, we would have to invent the concept of free will. We would need it on aesthetic grounds and as a safety valve against the despotic pressure of pure causality.

The poets of *Young Vienna* were rationalists. They insisted on subjecting all generalizations to the test of logic and experience. It is true that they recognized the limitations of reason, its inability to shape society in its image or to answer adequately man's fundamental questions. But they refused to extinguish its modest candle, though this candle shed only a little light in the infinite darkness about us — since, after all, we possess no surer source of spiritual illumination. They felt that our grief in not being lords of the lightning should not make us throw away our sole guide through the unknown, pale and glimmering though this guide may be. They preferred clarity to profundity and the honest weapons of logic to the poisonous arrows of mysticism.

The Viennese aesthetes were not pessimists, for they did not lament that this world is fundamentally tragic and that pain and sorrow dominate it. Nor were they optimists, since they did not assume the inevitability of progress or man's unceasing growth in wisdom, morality, and happiness. They were not faithful observers of established religious sects. Nor were they unbelievers, even if they continually questioned God's ways. In their opinion, the sceptic is nearer to God than the orthodox believer, because the sceptic's thoughts constantly circle about God, questioning him, doubting him, raging at him, demanding an answer of him — while the faithful adherents of ancient creeds take the status quo for granted as an inevitable product of divine design and do not feel the need of justifying God's ways ever anew.

The fame of the Viennese aesthetes was already well established when Theodor Herzl, at the turn of the century, discovered in Stefan Zweig, the nineteen-year-old son of a prosperous Jewish merchant, literary talent of a high order. As editor of the *Neue Freie Presse*, Herzl accepted for publication one of Zweig's earliest short stories and was the first person to write an appreciation of the unknown author. Herzl even hoped to win his protégé for the young Zionist movement; but in this he was unsuccessful. Reared in an assimilationist home that had profited from the fruit of emancipation, Zweig was unwilling to revert to the narrow confines of Jewish nationalism. For the ambitious youth not even the multi-national Austro-Hungarian Empire was sufficiently cosmopolitan and he was almost as much at home outside of its boundaries as within its many provinces. Although he loved his native Vienna, he did not feel himself a stranger in Paris or London, in Berlin or Rome. Travels in Africa, Asia, and America gave him world perspective. In the circle of the Belgian poet Emile Verhaeren, whom he translated into German, Zweig came in contact with the literary élite of Western Europe. Soon he began to envisage a Pan-Europe, in which political boundaries would be meaningless, and he projected for himself the rôle of sympathetic intermediary between the great European literary personalities. His Jewish background, which prevented him from taking too seriously dynastic rivalries and local super-patriotism, also enabled him to view optimistically a future of constructive work in behalf of a common European culture, the final synthesis of Hellenism and Hebraism. He drew upon Hellenic sources for his drama *Tersites* and upon Hebraic sources for his drama *Jeremias*. The latter was written in 1916 and voiced not only horror at the unnecessary holocaust of the First World War but also the comforting hope that suffering and defeat would purge the European soul of its deeply embedded imperialistic dross and bring to the fore the unadulterated gold of brotherhood, mutual tolerance, and universal enlightenment. This hope was the basis for Zweig's activity in the 1920's and 1930's. In studies on Dostoyevsky and Tolstoy, he tried to make the Russian soul more intelligible to the West at a time when Russia was regarded as a pariah among the nations. In studies on Romain Rolland, Balzac, Stendhal, Joseph Fouché, and Marie Antoinette, he continued his efforts to bring to German-speaking peoples a better understanding of their French neighbors. In studies on Dickens, Mary Baker Eddy,

Erasmus of Rotterdam, Amerigo Vespucci, and others, he appraised sympathetically the achievements of diverse peoples and ages.

In this period, when at the height of his popularity, he avoided Jewish themes, Jewish characters, and Jewish problems. To his palatial villa, atop the Capuchin Mountain overlooking Salzburg, European intellectuals made pilgrimages and came away with the impression that in him the transformation of the Jew and the Austrian into the good European seemed to have been successful.

By 1933, however, this good European was subjected to no less venomous attacks than his unassimilated coreligionists of the ghetto. His books were not spared when in May of that eventful year non-Aryan literature was tossed on the bonfires burning in Germany's main plazas. The murder of Theodor Lessing in Czechoslovakia by a raiding party from Germany clearly indicated to him his own possible fate, if he remained in his home on the German border. Involuntary exile or certain death were his alternatives. Gloom began to descend upon the optimistic patrician. In all the lands of the Continent, the good European felt harried and hurt. For a time England welcomed him, then the United States, and finally Brazil, but it was the kind and cold welcome that one accords a dignified stranger, and the appellation of refugee clung to him in all his wanderings.

It was then, in the sixth decade of his life, as loneliness gathered about him amidst the noise of cities and the bustle of busy admiring gapers, that Zweig sought to find his way back to ancestral roots. In 1937 he published *The Buried Candelabrum*, as sad an affirmation of Jewishness as ever was penned in our century.

The events of this short novel are laid in Rome and By-
zantium during the fifth century. It begins with the sacking
of the capital of the Western Roman Empire by the Vandals
in 455. Zweig has the marauders carry off, as part of their
immense booty, a candelabrum, the most sacred treasure
of Rome's Jewish community. The Jews themselves are
not the primary objects of attack on the part of the gold-
greedy army, for they are an impoverished group inhabiting
the city's slums. Nevertheless, worry weighs upon them.
They had learned in generations of bitter experience that
misfortune befalling any community or land in which they
dwelt always meant added troubles for them. In days of
splendor and prosperity their proud hosts gladly forgot them
and paid no attention to them. Patricians sought out extravagant luxuries and plebeians diverted themselves with
gambling and circuses. But whenever adversity and tragedy
threatened a land, the Jews were always blamed. If the foe
conquered, they suffered along with the vanquished; if a city
was plundered, they too were despoiled; if pestilence and
disease swept the land, they were not immune. All the
world's ills were laid at their door and against impending
violence they had no defense save prayer, since they were
everywhere a small, weak, and unarmed minority. In dark
and dangerous days, their sole escape from the brutality and
injustice of a world where might was constantly triumphant
lay in turning their thoughts from their precarious terrestrial
abode to their one, supreme, and invisible God. "For many
years, this had gone on. Now from the South and now from
East and West, there came peoples, blond and dark and
strange, but all of them rapacious; and hardly had one horde
conquered when another fell upon it. Everywhere on earth
the godless warred and did not leave the pious in peace.

Thus the godless had taken Jerusalem, Babylon, Alexandria, and now it was Rome's turn. Wherever one sought rest, there unrest prevailed; wherever one sought peace, there war came; fate could not be eluded. On this disturbed planet prayer alone offered refuge, rest, and comfort. Prayer had a marvelous power: it deadened fear by recalling great promises; it put to slumber the soul's terror by means of its singing litany; on its murmuring pinions it lifted up to God the heaviness of the heart. Prayer in need was good. Common prayer was better still, for all burdens were lighter if borne in common and the good was better in God's sight if done in unison."[2]

Prayer, however, proved ineffective against the greed of the Vandals. The Menorah — the most precious relic of a glorious past, a relic linking Solomon's temple with its latest descendants, a relic that had been dragged from country to country along with the people whose shrine it had once adorned — the Menorah had to resume its wanderings once again. Because of the supreme value of this symbol, the elders of Israel set out from Rome in the night to accompany it on its way to the galleys of the Vandals. A child went with them so that in later years it might bear testimony to the events of the fateful night. Rabbi Eliezer, the leader of this strange pilgrimage, interpreted to the young boy during the mournful hours the meaning of Israel's destiny on the stage of history.

Through the mask of this eldest of the elders there peers unmistakably the face of Stefan Zweig, the tired wanderer of the decade of Nazi-ascendancy in Europe, and in the sad words of the Ahasverus of the fifth century we can discern the final approach to the Jewish heritage on the part of the Austrian exile of the twentieth century: "It is an ancient road on which we go; our fathers and forefathers too have gone on it. For we have been a people of wanderers for endlessly long years; we are now again on the march; and who knows whether it is not our fate that we remain eternal wanderers. Unlike other peoples, we cannot call the earth we sleep on our own. Nor do we have fields of our own whereon grow seed and fruit. Only as exiles do we go over the lands, and our graves are rooted in foreign soil. But scattered as we are and thrown like weeds amidst the furrows from the morning to the midnight of this earth, we have nevertheless remained a people, a single and solitary people among the nations, because of our God and our faith in him. An invisible something binds us, preserves us, and keeps us together; and this invisible something is our God . . . All our troubles stem from our urge not to tie ourselves to concrete objects but to be and to remain seekers of the invisible. Whosoever attaches himself to the invisible is somehow stronger than those who hold to the visible, for the latter passes away and the former endures. It is for this reason, child, that we have outlasted all ages; for we are dedicated to what is ageless, and since we have kept faith with God, the invisible, He has kept faith with us."[3] While other peoples carved images of their divinities, the Jews refrained from all pictorial or sculptured representations of their God. The sacred vessels of Israel, chief among them the Menorah, were not images but symbols of ever-abiding faith. The Menorah symbolized light — the outer light that enabled our senses to become cognizant of this physical world, and the inner light that enabled our souls to attain clarity and insight into the eternal moral laws that stem from God.

To the puzzled question of the boy as to why the Jews permitted their most valuable treasures to be taken from

them again and again without offering physical resistance,
Zweig's spokesman replied that in this world right adhered
to the powerful and not to the just. Might was ever triumphant on this imperfect sphere and mere goodness was ineffective. The Jews received from God the capacity to endure suffering, but not the iron fist to enforce their right.
Why then did not God, the all-just and all-powerful, assist
them in their struggle against brute force? Why was He apparently on the side of the robbers and not on the side of the
righteous? Zweig reached a height of eloquence in posing this
question through the lips of both the boy and the graybeard
and a depth of obscurity in venturing a tentative reply.
The acts of the contemporary Nazis no less than of the
ancient Vandals were obviously before Zweig's vision when
he formulated what he called the ancient Jewish outcry:
"Why is God especially severe towards us among all the
peoples, towards us who serve Him as no others do? Why
does He cast us under the soles of others so that they step on
us, who were the first to acknowledge Him and to praise Him
in His inconceivable essence? Why does He tear down what
we build? Why does He dash our hopes? Why does He refuse
to let us rest anywhere? Why does He stir up against us one
people after another in ever-renewed hate? Why does He
test us, and us alone, again and yet again, with utmost
severity, even though we were His first choice and the earliest
to be initiated in His mystery? . . . I would be no Jew and no
human being if the question did not torture me daily, and
only in death will it be silenced on my lips."[4]

Zweig's only answer to these outcries is faith: since God's
plans are unknown to us and God's thoughts inconceivable
to mortals, comfort may be found in the hope that there is
meaning in all suffering and that all pain is atonement for

guilt. Though God's people still wanders from exile to exile, it may perhaps find itself anew some day and know peace and rest in some distant future.

Despite this vague hope, voiced on the brink of despair, Zweig's affirmation of Judaism is unconvincing. It seems as though the Viennese aesthete who had remained indifferent to Jewish fate throughout the first third of the twentieth century, neither severing his connection with the Jewish community nor participating actively in its affairs, wished to record his faith in its continued survival at a time when this survival was being questioned by many. But once this literary document was completed, Zweig resumed his attitude of aloofness from the contemporary Jewish currents. It was the survival of European culture that he despaired of during the last months of his life and it was Europe's tragedy that drove him to suicide. Because Europe was dying, he was homeless. Jewry would survive, but he was not primarily of it. The cosmopolitanism of *Young Vienna*, to which he remained ever faithful, had made way for the brutal chauvinism of Hitler's minions. Zweig was too tired to live on.

In his autobiography, published posthumously in 1943 under the title *The World of Yesterday*, Zweig described the experiences of his final months among the Jewish refugees from the European continent. These involuntary emigrants, numbering hundreds of thousands, formed, in his opinion, merely the vanguard of millions of plundered and tortured Jews who were seeking to escape from the Nazi conflagration in which they were trapped. A people had become homeless and was in panic-stricken flight — a people who were even denied the right to be a people and who failed therefore to

see any sense or meaning in their tragic experiences. It
was true that in former centuries the Jews had also often
been exiled from country to country, but previously they
had always found a bulwark in religion and knew that they
were martyrs because of adherence to a distinct faith. The
Bible was their talisman and they felt themselves to be its
chosen emissaries. The proud conviction that they were bearing witness to God's will on earth gave them the fortitude to
endure all, to put up with the Inquisition, and to face death
at the stake. The Jews of the twentieth century were, however, no longer a united people with a common mission.
They experienced their Judaism as a heavy burden rather
than as a glorious distinction. They were estranged from
their holy books and unfamiliar with their ancient sacred
language. Their deepest yearning was to be dissolved among
their neighbors, to be assimilated to the non-Jews, to be
completely Germans, Frenchmen, Englishmen, Russians.
When the new exodus struck them, they were bewildered —
for they were driven from their European homes without
being welcomed elsewhere; they were told that they could no
longer live in the lands of their birth, but were not told where
they could live; they were accused of sins and crimes, but
were offered no means to atone for these sins or to expiate
these crimes. Herded together in refugee-centers, they did
not understand each other's speech and habits or why they
were being hammered together by destiny. Zweig was one of
these bewildered souls. The catastrophe of the Hitler decade
stunned him. The possibility that Jewish existence had a
purpose dawned upon him, but real conviction was lacking.
In his last days in New York and Rio de Janeiro he still felt
himself not primarily a Jew but an uprooted European of
Viennese vintage.

Young Vienna — or shall we rename it *Old Vienna* — is now a legend. It is a legend even to the Viennese. As Napoleon put an end to the Venice of Gozzi and Goldoni, so a modern conqueror ended the glory of Vienna. The Mistress of the Adriatic knew a thousand years of splendor and is today a museum of memories and faded dreams. The Queen of the Danube seems fated for a similar destiny. On the other hand, it may chance that to the gaze of a future historian pre-Hitler Vienna will appear as the last and mellowest synthesis on the European continent of two cultural streams that long ago arose in Hellas and Judaea and that for many centuries gave to the Occident its pattern of beauty and its ideal of goodness. This pattern of beauty was shaped by Homer and Euripides, Plato and the Renaissance. This ideal of goodness was proclaimed by Isaiah and Jesus, by Judaism and Christianity. The armored men of the North, who in 1942 paraded along the banks of the Danube, seemed immune to these influences. They worshipped other gods and followed other faiths. They were said to be more virile and they claimed to die better. They were not plagued by beauty nor weighed down by morals. Their tanks scaled Parnassus and their winged monsters threatened Sinai. The Swastika flew over Olympus and the cultural splendor that was Danubian and European sought refuge in foreign exile. Zweig did not survive 1942 and the ruin of the world he had loved.

PART V

THE RENAISSANCE OF A PEOPLE

GUSTAV LANDAUER, 1870–1919

(By courtesy of Dr. Julius Bab)

CHAPTER XV

GUSTAV LANDAUER

THE intellectual ferment among the German Jews of the pre-Hitler generation led to a constant re-examination of their relationship to the Gentile majority within Germany and to the Jewish population outside of Germany. Assimilationists, Zionists, and Socialists sought to make their panaceas palatable to the sceptical generation that was coming to maturity. The critically minded were, however, wary of panaceas and refused to be enmeshed by slogans. They peered into complexities within their soul that defied simple solutions. They were not willing to eradicate or even to subordinate the Jewish or the German aspect of their being. Their difficulties and a possible overcoming of their intellectual dilemmas were delineated most sympathetically by Gustav Landauer, a profound scholar, fearless editor, and militant radical, who met a most tragic end during the turbulent days of the early Weimar Republic.

In an essay — published in 1913 under the title *Sind das Ketzergedanken?* and reprinted in 1921 — Landauer, who was not unfriendly to Zionist aspirations, sought to point out the inadequacy of Zionist ideology which called upon Jews to concentrate all efforts upon Palestine, then an impoverished Turkish province, and which completely negated their important functions in the Diaspora. As a German internationalist and as a Jewish nationalist, Landauer was well aware of his paradoxical intellectual position; yet, in-

stead of glossing over this duality in his soul, he rather
gloried in it.

Landauer loved Germany. He wanted to live for this
land of his birth and afterwards succeeded in dying for it.
He felt, however, that he could best make his contribution
to Germany and, beyond Germany, to the world at large,
not as a de-nationalized individual, but as a Jew working in
close cooperation with other Jews who were equally conscious of a common Jewish approach to the problems beset-
ting mankind. In his eyes, mankind was not an aggregate
of equal individuals but a federation of equal national
groups. Centuries of common historic experiences had done
for the Jews what a common territory did for other groups,
had given them a way of life peculiarly their own. The tendency to minimize this national configuration was unsound.
Equally reprehensible, however, was the tendency of some
Jews, who had become too conscious of their Jewishness,
to emphasize this fact on all occasions and to find complete
satisfaction in their newly acquired national pride without
translating their words and sentiments into creative tasks
and productive actions. In Landauer's opinion, the Jewish
nation, now in the process of regeneration, consisted not of
all Jews but only of those individuals of Jewish origin who
felt themselves to be members of a homogeneous group,
united by fate and history in order to perform a definite
function among the community of peoples. To be a nation
meant to be animated by a common spiritual purpose and
by a common desire to perform a specific task on this terrestrial stage. Zion came to life in Jewish hearts the moment
these tortured and yearning hearts found a common basis
for participating in their own way in the ascent of mankind.
Landauer foretold that in the none-too-distant future the

existing dynastic states and the imperialistic regimes founded
on oppression, exploitation, and violence would give way to
juster and freer governmental structures which would liberate the creative energies now dormant in many groups. And
the Jews, whether in possession of territory or not, would
be afforded an opportunity to place their sacred contributions at the service of the world at large, alongside of those
of other groups, large and small. The Jews would be redeemed when mankind was redeemed.

To the Zionists, who urged emigration to Palestine and
the revival of Hebrew as ultimately the language of all Jews,
Landauer gave the following reply: "No true person wants
to be merely a bridge for coming generations or to look upon
himself as a preface, as seed and dung. He wants to be some-
body and to accomplish something. It may well come to
pass that Hebrew will be the mother tongue of some descendant sprung from my loins. This does not affect me. My
language and the language of my children is German. I feel
my Jewishness in my gestures and facial expression, in my
bearing and appearance, and these signs provide me with
the certainty that it lives in everything I begin and am. But
far more than Chamisso, the Frenchman, was a German
poet, am I, the Jew, a German. The expressions 'German
Jew or Russian Jew' are as obtuse as would be the terms
'Jewish German' or 'Jewish Russian.' The relationship is
not one of dependency and cannot be described by means
of an adjective modifying a noun. I accept my fate as it is.
My Germanism and my Jewishness do each other no harm
but much good. As two brothers, a first-born and a Benjamin, are loved by a mother — not in the same way but with
equal intensity — and as these two brothers live in harmony
with each other both whenever their paths proceed in com-

mon and also whenever each goes his own way alone, even so do I experience this strange and intimate unity in duality as something precious and I fail to recognize in this relationship that one is primary and another secondary. I have never had the need of oversimplifying myself or of seeking a fictitious unity. I accept my complexity and hope to be a unity of even greater complexities than I am aware of."[1]

Landauer saw nothing gained in suppressing the German aspect of his personality in favor of the Jewish or the Jewish aspect in favor of the German. Upbraided that he must ever remain a mixed breed because of the duality in his soul and told that only among Eastern Jews did pure specimens of Jewry still prevail, Landauer countered with the argument that, on the contrary, Russian and Polish Jews had not one but three souls within their breasts. Their personality was fed from three sources. They were Jews and Russians or Poles or Lithuanians and also Germans of a particular kind, as evidenced by their retention of Yiddish, a Middle High German dialect. In contrast to other nations, who erected boundaries between themselves and their neighbors — boundaries that encouraged differences and provoked hostilities — the Jewish nation had taken its neighbors into its own soul and had brought about a harmonious synthesis of different strains with its own. Might not this peaceful and successful synthesis, asked Landauer, be the very mission which the Jews were fulfilling for humanity today, the very pioneering work in which they were pointing out the future direction for all?

Landauer's approach to the German-Jewish duality satisfied neither his Zionist nor his assimilationist friends. He had, indeed, challenged contradiction by labelling his views

heretical. His ablest opponent was Fritz Mauthner, a radical philosopher who sought to confound him with an excessive display of logic.

Mauthner had, in 1912, called upon all courageous German
Jews to leave their religious fellowship and to declare themselves *konfessionslos*. Without condoning anti-Semitism,
Mauthner had explained that this movement derived much
of its virulence from the strong tide of nationalism which was
sweeping over the twentieth century and also from the love
of one's mother-tongue which was outraged by the distortion
of German practiced by *mauschelnde*, or Yiddish-speaking,
Jews. With a recession of nationalism and with an increasing
respect of the Jews for the mother-tongue of their hosts, the
wave of anti-Semitism would slowly ebb.

Mauthner confessed that he was utterly without understanding of the spiritual basis of the Zionist movement. His
historic instinct told him that the erecting of a Jewish state
somewhere in some sparsely inhabited land might be a salvation for the unfortunate Russian Jews, who were as badly
treated as German Jews had been in the Middle Ages, but
that Occidental Jews of even the very slightest culture would
never dream of emigrating from their civilized European
abodes to such a Jewish state. Least of all could he fathom
the mentality of those German Jews who owed their profoundest spiritual experiences to Kant and Goethe and
Beethoven and who nevertheless succumbed to Zionist
ideology. For him, complete assimilation was the only con-
ceivable solution. This process could be hastened by some
form of compulsion or by a common decision of the Jewish
community. It was true that after a century of widespread

baptism and mixed marriages the Jews were not appreciably nearer to the desired goal of complete extinction as a recognizable group. But the blame for this deplorable fact lay not with the native Jews of Germany. Their trend towards assimilation was nullified by the infiltration of numerous coreligionists from Russia and Poland. A stoppage of this accretion from the East would be a most effective step in hastening the assimilation of German Jewry. The sealing of borders to inhabitants of a neighboring country might perhaps be contrary to Western principles of freedom. Western Jews must, however, wish for such action even more than Western anti-Semites, for they would then be in a position to draw a strict line of demarcation between their own cultured elements and an uncultured mass with which educated German Jews had nothing in common.

Holding these views, Mauthner could not accept Landauer's thesis as formulated in the essay *Sind das Ketzergedanken?* In a letter of October 10, 1913, Mauthner expressed his delight with the style and contents of the essay but not with its conclusion. "I feel myself to be a German, and a German only. I know that my brain has somewhere a duct which is called Jewish; all the worse or all the better. I cannot and do not want to change it. Your conclusion is different, and there we are at a parting of the ways."[2] Hedwig Mauthner endorsed her husband's stand and told Landauer that she recognized only human beings and not races, whether Teutonic or Hebraic. Landauer's reply was that he too did not differentiate between so-called races, but that he was not blind to differences that existed in reality. "Since mankind is not a hodge-podge, not even *tutti-frutti*, but a garden, we shall have to put up with the fact that not all trees have the same bark. If a human being feels a quality in himself which unites him with others who also feel it, then it will always be hard for an outsider to talk him out of it."[3] As for Mauthner's calling Jewishness a "cerebral duct," this very designation pointed to something that was not peculiar to himself alone but that he shared together with others. Mauthner might be happy to dispense with this cerebral duct or spiritual quality or historic relationship, but he would be doing so not on the basis of logic but on the basis of his sense of values. Landauer's own evaluation was more positive. "I do not find in our day so many communal relationships which reach back for thousands of years that I should gladly dispense with one of them, especially when I have no reason for doing so. And a relationship which, to use your terminology, is recognizable as a 'cerebral duct' is indeed real enough."[4] Differentiating between nations, nationalities, or other natural, social, and historic groups, no more negated what was common to all humanity than the distinguishing between various species of mammals effaced mammalian characteristics held in common.

Since Landauer held that a variety of opinions furthered progress, he was kind towards antagonists and tolerant of opposing views. His kindness and tolerance were withheld only from anti-Semites. When Heinrich Dehmel, son of the poet Richard Dehmel, in 1913 sought his support for a projected federation of all German Youth Movements, he was willing to lend his aid, provided that the anti-Semitic group was not invited to participate. He questioned whether an alliance was possible with a group which proscribed and outlawed another human group on the basis of an ineradicable quality, its Jewishness. "Others fight against opinions, plans, tendencies; but all of them acknowledge the possibility

that whoever is a human being can be convinced by them;
even the Socialists take for granted that an individual,
though a member of the privileged classes, may be won over.
For the anti-Semite, however, the Jew — though not the
Phoenician, Syrian, etc. — is innately an obnoxious crea-
ture."[5]

During the First World War agitation increased to limit
by legislation the influx into Germany of Jewish refugees
from the East. This agitation found some support among
Jews of Germany who feared the effect of this involuntary
migration upon their threatened legal and social position.
In an essay, entitled *Ostjuden und Deutsches Reich*, Landauer
in 1916 came to the defense of his Eastern coreligionists.
He saw no essential difference between the tradesman of the
ghetto and the Jewish businessman in the heart of the Reich.
The latter had perhaps better manners and more formal
education, but both were molded of the same unhealthy
and unpleasant pattern, products of a Europe heading towards a catastrophe. In one respect, however, the Eastern
Jew was superior: he interrupted his daily routine every few
hours in order to turn in prayer to the Almighty; he gave
precedence to religious festivals and ritual requirements over
the most important business dealings; he was ever aware of
a power beyond himself and paid reverent homage to it.
Despite his strange garb and idiom, his relationship to the
spirit of the prophets and patriarchs was undeniable. Let
not German Jews, therefore, join in the deliberations of
German politicians as to the proper steps to be taken against
the so-called Eastern menace, for such steps would ultimately be directed no less against the native Jews. Furthermore,
let not Western Jews imagine that, in offering a helping hand

to their Eastern brothers, they were merely bestowing and not also receiving. On the contrary, in the rejuvenation of all Jewry, which had become necessary, this sharing of need, material and spiritual, had definite advantages. If, as a result of this mutual contact, Western Jews came to feel that they too were strangers, lonely and outcast, in the European society that was tearing itself to pieces since 1914, then a step forward would undoubtedly have been made. Ultimately it might be all to the good even for Europe, which was hovering between decay and a possible rebirth, if the Jews could not bear to live there any longer and got out. It would not be the first time in the history of mankind that outcasts and refugees became pioneers and progenitors of a new culture.[6]

The gentle idealist, who dreamed of a rejuvenation of Jews, Germans, and all mankind, after the seemingly senseless slaughter of the First World War, saw an opportunity of carrying his humane and democratic ideas out in practice when the monarchical order collapsed in 1918 and a socialist regime assumed power. His participation in the revolutionary struggles of the young German republic came to an early end when he was dragged into the courtyard of a Bavarian prison and kicked about by German officers until their iron-shod boots extinguished the last sparks of life in his tormented body.

Ernst Toller, who barely eluded similar treatment, described the scene as follows: "Amid shouts of 'Landauer! Landauer!' an escort of Bavarian and Württemberg infantry brought him out into the passage outside the door of the examination room. An officer struck him in the face, the men shouted: 'Dirty Bolshie! Let's finish him off!' and a rain of blows from rifle-butts drove him out into the yard. He said

to the soldiers round him: 'I've not betrayed you. You
don't know yourselves how terribly you've been betrayed.'
Freiherr von Gagern went up to him and beat him with a
heavy truncheon until he sank in a heap on the ground. He
struggled up again and tried to speak, but one of the men
shot him through the head. He was still breathing, and the
fellow said: 'That blasted carrion has nine lives; he can't
even die like a gentleman.' Then a sergeant in the Life
Guards shouted: 'Pull off his coat!' They pulled it off and
laid him on his stomach. 'Stand back there, and we'll finish
him off properly!' one of them cried, and shot him in the
back. Landauer still moved convulsively, so they trampled
on him till he was dead; then stripped the body and threw
it into the wash-house."[7]

If Landauer's life and death for Germany was without lasting influence, his thinking on Jewish questions profoundly
affected the Jewish National Humanists of Central Europe.
It infiltrated into the essays of his friend Martin Buber.
It stimulated a re-examination of Zionist theory. It was
modified and deepened, but not contradicted, in the works
of Erich Kahler and Arnold Zweig.

RICHARD BEER-HOFMANN, 1866–

CHAPTER XVI

RICHARD BEER-HOFMANN

WHEN Theodor Herzl, at the close of the last century, proposed his radical solution of the duality in which Jews of the Diaspora found themselves, assimilationists and Jewish Aryans mocked at his visions. The non-German Jews, who flocked to his banner, were primarily interested in the political consequences of his thought, the homeward march of a long exiled people. The Viennese aesthetes and epicureans, who were his early associates, dismissed his Zionist theories with a shrug of the shoulders and a sceptical smile. For many years the influential Viennese organ to which he was a contributor refused to print any news or comments about his messianic complex, and he was compelled to found and to finance a newspaper of his own in order to further the spread of his ideas. A single Viennese poet of Jewish origin sensed the motivating force that prompted Herzl's dignified reaction to the German-Jewish duality. Immediately after the appearance of Herzl's pamphlet, *The Jewish State*, Richard Beer-Hofmann wrote to him: "More sympathetic even than everything contained in your book was the personality behind it. At last, once again a human being who does not bear his Judaism resignedly as a burden or as a misfortune, but who, on the contrary, is proud to be among the legitimate heirs of an ancient culture."[1] Beer-Hofmann recommended to Herzl that the Palestinian experiment should begin with the founding of a great medical university to which all Asia was to flock and which was at the same time to initiate the sanitation of the Orient.[2]

Like Herzl and Schnitzler, Beer-Hofmann stems from a patrician Jewish family. But this family had not yet succumbed to the assimilationist currents of the Austro-Hungarian metropolises. While the well-to-do Jewish circles of Vienna and Budapest were abandoning the rich heritage of their past for the doubtful privilege of being accepted on terms of social equality by the dominant German and Hungarian nationalities, the Beer and the Hofmann families clung to orthodox observances and ancestral customs. Their way of life was still simple, reserved, old-fashioned, and puritanical. Rooted in the Bohemian-Moravian provincial communities, they did not fall victim to the enervating and corrupting influences that emanated from the Danubian capitals. Even when they moved to Vienna and could share in the achievements of this highly cultured city, they gratefully accepted the new rights bestowed by the emancipation but never sought to merge completely with the German bourgeoisie. They lacked the ambition to garner social laurels by sloughing off their Jewish characteristics. They remained modestly within their own fold.

Richard Beer-Hofmann, therefore, as the sole offspring of the Beer and the Hofmann families, never experienced Judaism as a problem and never questioned the value of this heritage. It was for him rather a precious privilege, an undeserved gift, a constant source of astonishment. It has remained for him throughout his life a wonder and a delight. In contrast to the partially emancipated children of the ghetto, who stood in the shadow of the tree of Judaism and who sought to escape to an imagined pure sunlight, Beer-Hofmann possessed the personal and social gifts which enabled him to be entirely immersed in the German world. But he refused to follow the path of assimilation trodden by so many of his associates. When his education and environment removed him far from the tree of Judaism, he looked back upon it and was filled with shudders of ecstasy as he caught sight of it. Distance lent enchantment. Distance rendered possible a grasping of its total aspect. How ancient and deep-rooted, how mighty and tall, how marvelously beautiful is this tree! he exclaimed. And he never forgot to voice his thanks to his Creator, who had accorded him a heritage granted to but a few million inhabitants on this earth, a heritage which linked him with a unique people and a rare faith.

In his early novel, *Der Tod Georgs*, which appeared in 1900, Beer-Hofmann spoke through the mouth of his hero Paul and related his discovery of Judaism, a discovery which thrust him out of the artificial, unhealthy, self-centered world of dandies, aesthetes, and decadents into the community of a people which had a worth-while task to perform on earth. This task consisted in upholding both in faith and in deed, at the cost of pain and of death, the claim of justice in all ages, especially in generations beset by injustice. "Over the life of those whose blood flowed in him, justice was ever present like a sun, whose rays never warmed them, whose light never shone for them, and yet before whose dazzling splendor they reverently shielded their pain-covered forehead with trembling hands.— Ancestors, who wandered from land to land, ragged and disgraced, the dust of all the highways in their hair and beards, every man's hand against them, despised by the lowest yet never despising themselves, honoring God but not as a beggar honors an almsgiver, calling out in their suffering, not to the Lord of Mercy, but to the God of Justice.— And before them, many ancestors whose dying was a great festival prepared for others: round about them festive robes, the sparkle of noble jewels, fluttering flags and pomp and the sound of bells and the song of vesper hymns, and over all a reflection of the sinking sun and of flames kindled by royal hands — they themselves tied to stakes, awaiting the fire, in their innocence fabricating sins for themselves and calling their tortures punishment, solely in order that their God might remain a God whose justice is unquestioned.— And back of these ancestors, a people which did not beg for grace but wrestled fiercely for the blessing of its Deity, a people wandering through seas, unhindered by deserts, always as aware of a God of Justice as of the blood in its veins, calling its victory God's victory, its defeat God's judgment, selecting for itself the rôle of witness to God's power, a people of saviors, anointed for thorns and chosen for pain. And slowly releasing their God from sacrifices and burnt-offerings, these ancestors raised him high above their heads until he stood beyond all transitory suns and worlds, no longer a warrior God of herdsmen, but a guardian of all right, invisible, irradiating all.— And of their blood was he."[3]

Beer-Hofmann's discovery of the supreme value of his ancestral heritage has led him to become immersed in the severe traditions of the Old Testament prophets. Biblical sparks kindle his poetic imagination. He writes religious dramas, which delve into the fundamental question of Israel's relation to God and man and which bring new courage to his down-hearted coreligionists.

Beer-Hofmann's soul is healthy. The duality — German and Jew — which troubled so many of his contemporaries does not trouble him. His plays deal with universal themes and are addressed to readers and auditors as human beings, irrespective of boundary lines or racial, religious, and national divisions. German is the medium of his expression, and it becomes in his hands a musical instrument of delicate fiber. Austrian is the atmosphere he breathes, and it is laden with the sweet melancholy of the Danubian landscape and the fragrance of the Salzkammergut with its green lakes, white-foaming brooks, gentle hills, and snow-covered mountains. So strong is the hold of this Austrian atmosphere upon his soul that even in his last biblical drama, *Der junge David*, the Palestinian scene is infused with the aroma wafted from the land of his birth. Jewish is, however, the philosophy he expounds. The wisdom he brings to modern man is a wisdom reminiscent of the ancient prophets, whose spirit interpenetrates both the Old and the New Testaments and whose approach to life has long since become the common property of mankind. Although Beer-Hofmann uses subjects selected from widely different sources, he attains his best effects as an artist with material from the Jewish Bible.

Just as Goethe gave to the Germans, in the character of Faust, the best symbol of their longing and aspiration, so Beer-Hofmann saw in the biblical figure of David the symbolic personification of the Jewish soul in all its contradictory moods. He therefore projected a trilogy centering about this legendary character. Furthermore, even as Goethe's philosophic drama is preceded by a prologue in heaven, in which God and the archangels speak, so likewise Beer-Hofmann composed a dramatic prelude, entitled *Jacob's Dream*, in which Jacob, the ancestor of David, holds converse with God and the angels.

Two biblical episodes are selected to form the plot of *Jacob's Dream*. The first is the conflict between the brothers

Jacob and Edom which resulted from the former's stealing of the parental blessing. The second is Jacob's vision during the memorable night at Beth-El when he made his covenant with God.

The two brothers are conceived as two contrasting figures, representatives of opposing fates. Both are, however, placed in a sympathetic light and their struggle is all the more pathetic since it is preordained and inevitable. Edom, the foe of Jacob, is not a wild pogrom chieftain, but rather the proud ancestor of kings and no less necessary in the universal order than his gentler brother, the dreamer of mystic dreams. Edom is the practical son. His feet are firmly planted on the earth. His glance surveys with pride his fields and flocks. Before his arrows the wild animals fall as booty and at his command slaves gather corn and honey and wine and oil. Nor does he fail to give his tithe to God or to obey unquestioningly the religious precepts of his tribe. Jacob, on the other hand, is the eternal seeker, the eternal doubter, hounded by visions of unearthy spheres and afflicted with overmuch sympathy. Man and beast, the very stones about him and the brooks below him moan their pain to him, and their suffering reverberates in his compassionate breast. The blessing of Abraham was meant for the offspring who bears so heavy a burden and not for his contented brother. Isaac, Abraham's son, would have preferred to hand down the family blessing to Edom, the powerful hunter; but Rebecca, interpreting correctly the spirit of the ancestors, substituted Jacob for Edom, and thus Jacob became the bearer of the fate decreed for the children of Abraham.

The drama takes place on the morning and evening after this memorable event. In Beer-Sheba, on the edge of the

wilderness, the house of Isaac lies bathed in pale moonlight.
Shamartu, the slave of Edom, crouches on the wall and looks
out into the distance awaiting his master. Below him slumber Basmath and Oholibamah, the wives of Edom, strange
women from the tribes of Hitti and Hori. The gray silence of
dawn is broken by the whispered questions of the awakening
Basmath, who hours earlier had sent a messenger to inform
Edom of Jacob's theft of the parental blessing and who was
now eagerly awaiting her husband's return. If only Edom
would leave the hunt and hasten back! For Jacob was fleeing
from Canaan and might escape to Laban at Haran before
the hand of the avenging brother could overtake him.
Again and again Basmath's sharp questions cut through the
cold, cruel dawn: Edom? Edom? Finally, the long awaited
hunter bursts upon the scene, foaming with anger. He seeks
to make his way to his father, but already he is too late. Isaac
is resting under the wings of the angel of death. Jacob must
be reached and destroyed, if the effect of the blessing is to be
undone. Rebecca, fearing for her favorite son, hurls herself
in Edom's path, promising him all that his heart desires,
absolute rule over the household, over slaves and cattle and
land, if only he will leave Jacob the ancestral blessing.
"You, my Edom, are sated with possession and food and
drink and sleep and women, what need have you of the
blessing? Your joy flourishes on earth. Take your earthly
heritage." When Edom insists on knowing why Jacob was
preferred, Rebecca proudly answers that Jacob was chosen
"because he walks about full of mysterious questions, hearing
within himself the doubts, dreams, longings, and imperative
voices of his ancestors, while you rejoice in your certain
knowledge and satiety; because he does not entomb his God
in distant heavens as you do, but wrestles with Him day by

day and breast to breast; because he does not hunt and sacrifice and murder as you do, but rather pales in the presence of all suffering creatures and speaks to all of them as they to him. That is why the blessing is his — and also the burden of the blessing." At these words Edom rushes forth in rage. He has sworn not to eat or drink until he has seen Jacob's blood before him. The dogs have picked up the trail and will guide him unerringly to the fugitive.

The day is drawing to an end. Jacob in his hurried flight has reached a cliff, afterwards called Beth-El, and here he prepares to camp for the night. His sole companion on the height is Idnibaal, who for forty years has faithfully served Isaac and whom Rebecca has sent along as the guardian of her favorite son. Master and slave speak in hushed tones of the mysterious land stretching below them towards the west. There lies the once prosperous city of Ajath, now a mass of ruins, its proud kings and their prouder conquerors faded from the memory of the living. Beyond the horizon lies Jerusalem, the citadel of the Jebusites, the future capital of David's realm. The entire land has been promised by God to the seed of Abraham. Jacob, however, has no desire for its possession. He does not want to carve out for himself a kingdom on this earth, comparable to those already in existence. "The Hitti, the Perizzi, and the Kadmoni are disputing the watering places and the pastures, the Kenaani hold the seaports, the Keni occupy the fortified heights, and all these childish struggles will last only as long as the three mighty powers, Egypt, Babylon, and Phoenicia tolerate them." Surely it was not to such temporal rule that God referred when he blessed Abraham! From Jacob's lips stream words of kindness and of understanding. He who has just fled from home and who is threatened by danger and death now becomes vividly conscious of the pain of his own servant, who also was once torn from a native home and compelled for decades to obey a foreigner's commands. Jacob speaks to Idnibaal of home and love and fate. Then, having conversed with him as an equal, he can no longer look upon him as a slave and therefore sets him free. The liberated Idnibaal thereupon invokes the blessings of the gods upon the gentle, sympathetic youth and then descends from the hill.

In the nebulous light of the fast gathering dusk, the figure of Edom becomes visible. The two brothers are alone on the hill, the one prepared to kill and the other unwilling even to resist. With masterful skill the dramatist resolves their enmity into friendship, closing the scene with the rite of blood-brotherhood. This rite is to affirm the necessity of the eternal survival of both types, the unproblematic hero and the tormented dreamer, the successful man of affairs and the impractical poet. When Edom asks whether his brother regards him as in any way inferior because he finds his complete satisfaction on earth, Jacob answers in simple words that supply the solution to the entire conflict: "No! God needs me as I am, and He needs you otherwise! Only because you are Edom may I be Jacob!" Every people is a chosen people, but each is chosen in a different way and experiences a different fate. All beings are equally necessary to God and all live as they must.

Edom has disappeared in the evening mist. Jacob falls asleep and in his slumber he hears about him the voices of nature grown articulate. The brook murmurs to him and the stone whereon he lies sings of its longing and pain. Angels descend from the clouds and the presence of God fills the air. In this awe-inspiring hour, Jacob seeks an answer to the riddle of existence, seeks to discover the reason for the apparent necessity of suffering in this world. When the archangels repeat God's promise that to the offspring of Abraham will be given the fat of the earth, the dew of the heavens, corn, wine, and the cities of men, he proudly rejects their gifts and releases God from His promise. Such riches may make a person like Edom happy but not one like Jacob. "Is my blood good for nothing better than for kings?" he asks. "I do not want dominion! Doesn't God know it? Does He really think I am envious of Egypt, Babylon, or the Princes by the sea? I envy no one. I don't even envy you, archangels, your blessedness. Could I be blessed when all suffer, when all approach me by day and night, when man and beast and herb and stone moan to me with mute eyes, imploring an answer of me?" Jacob feels called upon to supply God's answer to all questions. He wants to act as God's emissary and mouthpiece. An archangel tells him that this wish may be granted. Long after Egypt shall have passed away and Babylon disappeared, the seed of Jacob will continue to wander on earth, an eternal miracle of God's eternal world. "The mighty nations will turn to dust and be blown away as dust. You alone will die a thousand deaths and will a thousand times re-arise from the dead." In a magnificent poetic vision, the Archangel Michael reveals to Jacob the future of his offspring, a people who will bear God's message to the nations and who will be the measure of all faith, hope, and pain. Samael, the angel of darkness, a defiant figure resembling Milton's Lucifer, warns Jacob against accepting such a destiny. "It is true that others will bow to your testimony, but they'll beat the mouth bloody that pronounced it. It is true that you may wander eternally. But rest? Never! And home? A word without meaning for you! Yours will be a people from which all fetch booty. To sin against you? Whom is it not permitted? . . . Every people to which you attach yourself will burn you out like a cancer. You, the beloved of God, will be hated more than a poisonous plant or a mad beast! . . . You fool, chosen to be God's whipping-post! . . . He sacrifices you. He needs you as an unbribable witness to whom He can point. Who will doubt, if you, bleeding and downtrodden, still praise Him as a just God!" Jacob, however, cannot leave God. He accepts the rôle of the Lord's chosen one with all its blessing and all its horror. Trusting in his strength, pride, and patience, Jacob is ready to help bear God's burden. Amid the wrangling of the archangels, the voice of the Lord is heard: "For my sake you may suffer unheard of pain and yet amidst tortures know that I never cast you off! I want to be so heavily indebted to you, O my son, that as atonement I may raise you up beyond all others."

Jacob's pain is his patent of nobility, the cause of his greatness and the source of his pride. Nations, weakened by excessive wealth and luxury, decay and disappear; but the sons of Jacob, whipped by ever new suffering, rise to ever new heights. And if ever they tire of their mission and are in danger of succumbing to misfortune, then new leaders arise to remind them of their rôle as God's witnesses on earth. In ages overwhelmed by materialistic ambitions, messianic heroes, such as Moses, Isaiah, Jesus, Spinoza, Herzl, born of Jacob's blood, proclaim the Jew's spiritual mission. In our day of Jewish martyrdom and deepening gloom, poets of hope are necessary to reawaken the will to live among the hundreds of thousands scattered along the world's highways. Beer-Hofmann aids in this task with his artistic apotheosis of the Jewish people.

Jacob's Dream, completed in 1915, during the First World War, was followed by *Young David*, completed in 1933, the year which witnessed the rise to power of Adolf Hitler. The burden, which God designed for the anointed and which Jacob once voluntarily took upon himself, David is again called upon to assume during the play.

The opening act takes place near the grave of Rachel, the wife of Jacob. The crossroads are alive with groups of people that come and go. Abiathar, the sole survivor of the priests of Nob who have been murdered by Saul, asks questions about Rachel and Ruth and David, about God's omnipotence and its limitations, about God's eternal justice and his apparent injustice in permitting the murder of the innocent priests of Nob. If mortals can supply no answer, Abiathar will demand one of God. But can heaven's reply be meaningful to him? "God's days are not the days of man. God measures with a different measure, and in distant days perhaps an astounded offspring hears and hardly comprehends God's answer to a question which an ancestor, moaning in pain and wild woe, once asked of heaven." May it not therefore be best for us, storm-tossed creatures, to seek a humble refuge in faith, since absolute knowledge is unattainable?

Through doubt to faith is the process by which Beer-Hofmann's characters are stabilized and matured. Abiathar's questioning of God's ways is a necessary step in his evolution as priest and religious leader. In the drama it serves as a prelude to David's more searching scepticism, which is an essential phase of his training before he can be fit for the assumption of royal power.

The testing of David forms the climax of the drama. In the war between Israel and the Philistines, he has to take sides and finds himself in a cruel dilemma. As the vassal of

Achish of Gath, he receives the command to report at the Philistine headquarters in order to join in the campaign against Israel. To disobey this command would necessitate the breaking of his oath of allegiance, an impossibility for a person of his loyal temperament. And even if he could break his oath, who would ever trust him thereafter? What friend or foe would ever regard as sacred an agreement with a person who in a critical hour was himself unfaithful to his liege lord? But, on the other hand, how could he, the anointed of his people, the national hero of Israel, assist in the slaughter of his own kinsmen and in the destruction of his own future realm?

The resolution of this dilemma is the principal theme of the stirring fourth act of the drama. Since David has sworn allegiance to the Philistines, thereby unwittingly tying the strangling noose about his neck, he must under all circumstances keep his oath until released. He will therefore go to King Achish of Gath, even though this step probably means his death. His men, however, have sworn allegiance only to him personally, only to David of Bethlehem. He will release them of their pledge. They will then be free to go to the assistance of Saul's forces and to defend their fatherland against hostile invasion. The cunning and unprincipled Achitophel warns David against setting out to certain doom. "Why do you go?" he asks in ill-concealed chagrin. "Because faith and loyalty must be maintained!" answers David. "Faith — Loyalty! They are but two words! Don't take them so seriously!" interposes the diplomat. "Merely two words, it is true — but on these the world rests!" replies David. The tragic consequences of this final decision are, however, averted at the very last moment by the arrival of a messenger from the Philistines, dispensing with David's

services on the ground that it would be too dangerous to have
in the Philistine ranks an ally who was a potential foe.
Relieved of his bondage to the enemies of Israel, David can
now follow the call of his own people. He decides to aid Saul,
though this may mean forfeiting all personal ambition for
the throne. But already it is too late. The battle between
Saul and the Philistines is fought and lost at Gilboa before
David's men can arrive.

After the death of Saul and his sons, all hopes of the
Hebrews are concentrated on David as the sole possible
savior. Before he assumes the crown, however, he passes
through profound tragedy in the loss of Maacha, his beloved
wife, and realizes that he must renounce all thoughts of personal happiness if he is to be a blessing for others. His
guardian ancestress, Ruth, who ushered in the play and who
appeared at the climax in order to admonish him to be
faithful to his truest self, now reappears at the end to encourage him to take on the responsible burden assigned to
him by a superior power. In reply to his painful question:
"What is to become of me now?" she calmly offers these
words of wisdom: "What ultimately becomes of all of us:
dung of the earth. Perhaps a song — this, too, is soon wafted
away. And yet, until then, David, you must, like God's
stars, complete your designated orbit, neither more eternal
nor more transitory than they."

The blessing and the burden of the blessing, which was
once accepted by Jacob at Beth-El, is bequeathed by Ruth
to David. As the standard-bearer of the Jewish fate, David
will now undertake his task. This task is outlined by him to
his followers in language reminiscent of *Jacob's Dream*. He
does not want to fashion another empire comparable to
Egypt or Babylon, an empire based on force and lasting only

until overthrown by a mightier force. All he desires is a peaceful breathing-spell until he can implant among his people the seed of a new faith and until a generation can grow up which does not speak in terms of territorial expansion or enslavement of neighbors, but which, on the contrary, is unhappy if it knows others to be in pain, which cannot breathe if oppression exists in its midst, which does not throw itself away on such vain objectives as splendor or domination. Even as it does not pay for an individual to live merely for himself, so too it does not pay for a people to think solely of its own aggrandizement.

Through the mouth of David, Beer-Hofmann voices his opposition to the ultra-nationalism rampant in recent years. He is sickened by the excessive brutality of his time. He refuses to be a party to the racial conceit flourishing all about him. He is a Jew and holds that the Jews are primarily a community of fate rather than a race or a religion. Few scientists, outside of the Nazi fold, believe nowadays in purity of races, nor do religious observances form an essential part of Jewish daily life in the present generation. The Jews, Beer-Hofmann insists, are a historical community held together, on the one hand, by the acceptance of certain doctrines enunciated by their prophets from Hosea and Amos and Isaiah up to the present day, and, on the other hand, by the refusal of the majority population in every country to accept such doctrines, a refusal backed up by anti-Semitic measures, from social ostracism in the most cultured lands to pogroms and mass murder in less civilized states. The Jews, Beer-Hofmann claims, not only believe, for example, that it is better to be killed than to kill, to suffer injustice than to commit injustice, but they prove, by

their continued existence down the millenniums, that non-
resistance has greater survival value than the mightiest of
armies or the strongest of navies. All empires of ancient
days, which were based on force, have crumbled and disappeared, but the Jews still live on as an eternal rebuke
to the nations that rely on the power of the sword, and will
continue to exist until these nations grow tired of bloodshed
and accept the message of peace and justice. Then perhaps
there will no longer be any necessity for the existence of the
Jews as a separate entity, because the faith of which they
are the bearers will have become the faith of all men.
Therein Beer-Hofmann echoes sentiments of biblical days,
sentiments voiced by the prophet Isaiah in verses which
the contemporary poet accepted as the motto for his religious play: "Yea, He saith: It is too light a thing that thou
shouldst be My servant to raise up the tribes of Jacob, and
to restore the offspring of Israel; I will also appoint thee
for a light of the nations, that My salvation may be unto
the end of the earth. Thus saith the Lord, the Redeemer
of Israel, his Holy One, to him who is despised of men, to
him who is abhorred of nations, to a servant of rulers:
Kings shall see and arise, princes, and they shall prostrate
themselves; because of the Lord that is faithful, even the
Holy One of Israel, who hath chosen thee."

MARTIN BUBER, 1878–

(By courtesy of the *Universal Jewish Encyclopedia*, II, 570)

CHAPTER XVII

MARTIN BUBER

RICHARD BEER-HOFMANN is the poet of the
contemporary German-Jewish renaissance; Martin
Buber is its philosopher. The conclusions that Beer-Hofmann
arrives at intuitively and records in dramatic symbols, Buber
attains as a result of laborious, profound studies and records
in the form of philosophic essays and parables. Both agree
in fundamentals. But, while Beer-Hofmann keeps strictly
aloof from the various Jewish movements that seek to advance towards the projected ideal goal, Buber has from his
youth been in the thick of the battles for the practical realization of his Jewish aims.

Buber, too, was a native of Vienna. Yet, though born
there in 1878, it was not until he entered the university at
the age of eighteen that he came under the influence of this
Danubian capital. Since his third year he had lived in
Lemberg at the home of his grandfather, Salomon Buber, a
Hebrew scholar and a leading personality of the Galician
Haskalah, or Enlightenment. During formative years in
this intellectual center of Eastern Jewry, young Buber
acquired a thorough knowledge of the Hebrew language,
religion, traditions, and folkways. The Bible was his daily
companion and remained with him as a guide throughout
life. When he later became a master of German style, he
undertook, together with Franz Rosenzweig, a translation of
the Bible into German, which has been universally acclaimed

as a miracle of fidelity and beauty. In his youth, Buber also came in contact with Hasidic groups and was initiated into their joyous mysticism. Although the representatives of *Haskalah* and of Hasidism were constantly engaged in bitter feuds, Buber saw in both of these antithetical movements precursors of Jewish regeneration, and in his mature years he strove for a synthesis of their divergent doctrines.

Student years at Vienna, Berlin, Leipzig, and Zürich gave him a rich background in philosophy, art, and literature, and for a time estranged him from Jewish problems. But the call of Herzl penetrated to him as to so many other young intellectuals and revived his flagging interest in Judaism, until it became the main interest of his life. At Leipzig he founded, in 1899, a Zionist group among the students. He participated in the Third Zionist Congress, which met at Basel in the summer of that year, and he remained active in Zionist affairs thereafter.

To Buber, Zionism is not a political party, but a dynamic attitude towards life, the creative expression of the Jewish soul, the regeneration of the eternal Hebraic idea. His Zionism is a mixture of logical reasoning and nebulous mysticism. It is linked to his religious philosophy and his messianic socialism. Though it is often re-defined in his numerous studies extending over four decades, he never doubts that it is the only lasting solution of the German-Jewish duality. Beyond all reinterpretations, he does retain a certain fundamental consistency in his point of view. He does not shun basic questions and he has the courage to offer replies.

Buber asks: why should a Jew wish to endure not merely as a human being, a human spirit, a human cell, but also as a Jew, despite the inconveniences and suffering therein involved? Buber's answer is: the individual Jew forms a link in a distinct chain of human beings who were, are, and shall be; a link in a particular fellowship of the dead, the living, and the unborn — all of whom comprise a superindividual unity. The achievements and the errors of all these people down the ages are products of the Jewish way of experiencing reality and are, therefore, part of the fate in which he, the individual Jew, is embedded. Jewish history lives within him as the tale of his own past, and Jewish destiny is his own personal destiny. The reactions of Jews in all lands and in all centuries reveal to him the dark forces operating within his own inner self and explain to him his own peculiar approach to the phenomena about him.

This knowledge is especially valuable to him, for it takes from him his feeling of loneliness, his sense of isolation, his suffering because of his strangeness. Though the land in which he dwells is not his land and the language which he speaks is not his language and the customs to which he has to conform are not his customs, nevertheless, there is a home for him and a community of beings in which he does have a share and a form of speech to which he feels himself attuned — namely, among those persons whose *Gestalt*, or type, or spiritual configuration, is moulded like his own. This common substance, this deepest layer of his personality, stems from his heredity, a rich treasure implanted in him by his chain of forebears. Their fate, their pain, their disgrace, their nobility, and their wretchedness helped to build his psychic skeleton. In him the priests, prophets, and kings of Israel still live on. His spirit still retains in its basic structure the longing for a pure and unified existence, a longing that once coursed through the veins of Abraham and Moses and David and the Essene of Nazareth. But there has also seeped into his blood the poison of all those centuries when his ancestors were divorced from the healthy rhythm of nature and trodden under the heel of oppression and forced to seek escape from frustration by over-emphasizing barren intellectualism.

The German Jew is a mixture of Jewish heredity and German environment. Both of these powerful forces claim him. He cannot, however, continue indefinitely in an unstable state of equilibrium, hovering precariously between the two. He must decide to which force he wishes to accord primacy. He must at some time make a final choice. He cannot remain German *and* Jew. He must become German *or* Jew. Once the decision has been made, he must frame his actions to harmonize with the destiny of the preferred group.

If he feels himself primarily a Jew, then he will accept the past of the Jewish people as the prelude to his own personality. He will be concerned with the present plight of the Jews in every continent and on all seven seas as with an essential part of his own immediate experiences. He will have faith in the future of Judaism, because it will be at the same time his own future. He will labor to remove from the Jewish character the dross that has accumulated in the Diaspora, for such labor will be an important phase of self-purification and a necessary step towards personal salvation.

The choice of adherence or non-adherence to Judaism is a choice which each individual must make for himself. The German or Frenchman or Englishman is not normally faced with the problem as to whether he wishes to belong to his people. Such a person lives freely, securely, naturally, on the soil of his forefathers. He participates unchallenged in the acts and thoughts, speech and habits of his ancestral group. He does not constantly question the raison d'etre of his nationality. He does not brood, why he is a German, a Frenchman, or an Englishman.

Before a Jew can be incorporated into the community of Israel, however, he has to fight a battle within himself; he has to grope his way back to his tribal roots; he has to become conscious of his Jewishness; he has to justify to himself and to others the further existence of his unique group; he has to explain why a people that has been deprived of its territory and that roams about without either a common language or a common cultural center still claims for itself an essential rôle in the future development of mankind.

In an essay, entitled *Das Judentum und die Menschheit*, published in 1911, Buber comes to grips with these fundamental questions. He asks: What is there unique and eternal about the Jewish people? What phase of human life, what aspect of the human soul is realized more purely and more intensely in Judaism than elsewhere? In what respect would mankind be poorer if the Jews had not appeared upon the world-scene or if they were now to vanish from the world's stage?

Buber's answer is as follows: The human soul has a tendency to reduce the multiplicity of spiritual experiences and the infinite possibilities immanent within us to an unceasing dynamic striving towards opposite poles, such as good and evil, heaven and earth, yes and no, salvation and damnation. In this simplified form of an eternal duality, man sees himself ever at the crossroads, exercising what freedom of choice is left him by God or fate or chance, if any, in perpetually shifting in one direction or in the other. In Judaism, this duality is more extreme, the range between affirmation and negation is wider, the swing of the pendulum between sainthood and degeneracy is greater. Beyond all duality, however, Judaism strives for unity, for a synthesis of opposites, for an amalgamation of extremes.

Judaism may be defined as a striving for unity — unity within the single person, unity between the individual members of a people, unity of all peoples, unity between mankind and all things living, unity between God and the world.

The Jewish concept of God arose from this striving for Oneness, for salvation from all duality. Hence the cardinal principle of the Hebraic faith: Hear, O Israel, the Lord our God, the Lord is One.

The striving for unity amidst the diversity of human relations resulted in the idea of universal justice, a basic idea in the Hebrew Bible. The striving to include all animate creation within a single unity gave rise to the doctrine of universal love, a fundamental doctrine in the teaching of the Jew of Nazareth. The striving to escape from the duality of this world to an absolute unity gave birth to the Messianic ideal, a cardinal ideal in the Jewish faith.

Jewish was not only the religious synthesis attempted by the early prophets but also that undertaken by primitive Christianity, which emanated from Palestine and which was not yet contaminated by the Roman way of life. Jewish was the philosophic synthesis sought in the age of Spinoza. Jewish was the social synthesis propagated in the generation of Marx, Hess, and Lassalle. Perhaps the spirit of Judaism, now on the eve of a renaissance, is preparing a synthesis of all these syntheses. For Judaism teaches that everything man does and thinks and suffers and enjoys is meaningless, unless it is welded together into a unity.

The Jews, as apostles of this faith in a universe in which duality shall cease and Oneness reign eternal, are an Oriental enclave in the Occident and are destined to act as interme-

diaries between Eastern and Western cultures. A martyrdom of two thousand years on foreign soil amidst alien
peoples has left harmful imprints upon the Jewish soul but
has not succeeded in destroying it or perverting it. This
soul can resume its creative activity as soon as it is reunited
with its native Palestinian earth. Upon the restoration of
the Jews to their Holy Land, this corridor between Europe
and Asia will again be the crossroads of peoples, will again
blossom with new vitality, and will again be a blessing for
mankind.

The first step in Israel's rejuvenation is, therefore, its return to Palestine. There it can breathe freely, it can recover
its natural voice, it can seek the harmonious expansion of
its energy, it can sweep away the dust and cobwebs accumulated during centuries of exile.

The Jews must prepare to take leave of Germany and of
Europe and to join the pioneers who have already begun
their homeward pilgrimage to Zion. "We who are under way
and deeply aware of our direction, we see this close reality,
which differs from ours but is not essentially strange to us,
and we confess that we love it: the language which trained
us to think, the landscape which taught us to see, the creative profundity of a great people to whom we are indebted
for fortunate gifts. We don't attach ourselves to the others,
but we greet them as only those can who wander towards
a goal. Friends, we are on our way, for our sake, for your
sake — for the sake of salvation."[1]

The object of Jewish colonization in Palestine, according
to Buber, cannot be the erection of another petty state
similar to the wrangling sovereignties of Europe. It cannot
be the attainment of a majority status in a limited territory
in order to be able to do unto others what is being done to

the Jews elsewhere. Colonization must rather take the form
of decentralized, autonomous working communities. These
Kibbutzim and *Kvutzot,* based on universal labor and a common
longing for self-regeneration, will form the healthy cells of
the new Jewish federated commonwealth, and this commonwealth will find its justification for existence only in so far
as it strives for more than merely its own interests. Its slogan will have to be: service to the other sectors of the population for the sake of the greater unity that is still to come.
If it pursues its own welfare, it will do so only because it
wishes to participate as a happy people in the union with
other peoples. It will, therefore, get rid of any lurking feeling
of superiority and will seek from the outset to strengthen all
links with the other groups. It will study their language
and traditions and set at rest their distrust and fears. It will
under no circumstances accept nationalism as a goal. It will
rather see in its own national consolidation, at best, a
starting-point from which to initiate an advance to a supra-
national form of life. It must adopt this approach, not only
if it wishes to be true to its historic mission, but even if it
wishes to survive at all in that part of the Orient which is
only now awakening to rabid nationalism and importing
European chauvinistic slogans.

There was room in the Near East for a new nation, a
Jewish nation, so long as the native inhabitants had not yet
reached the status of nationhood. But now that these are
organized as nations, with appetites whetted for expansion
and with articulate claims for the uncultivated tracts of
land in behalf of their own future generations, there is no
longer any room for a newcomer. The Jews can continue
to grow in the Near East only if they prove themselves of
benefit to the other peoples already resident there, if — by

investment of intelligence, energy, and capital — they become pioneers of a new cooperative supra-national economic unit, whose ties are stronger than the ties of nationalism or particularism. The Jews can exercise sovereignty only if they remain true to their ancient teaching that all sovereignties are subject to the supreme Sovereign of the world, who is also the Sovereign of their rivals and opponents, and if they remember that the Lord, who once led the children of Israel out of Egypt and is now leading them out of the Diaspora, also led the Philistines out of Kaphtor and the Aramaeans out of Kir. Israel can speak of itself as the chosen people, not in the sense that it is better than others, but in the sense that it is chosen for more difficult tasks on the world arena; namely, to be more than merely a self-contained, sated nation. As the long-suffering victim of aggressive nationalism, it recoils from exercising aggression. It returns to Palestine not in order to exploit the inhabitants in capitalistic, imperialistic fashion, but in order to resume a normal existence in a homeland which it yearns to serve with heartfelt devotion.

Buber's plea for Arab-Jewish cooperation found embodiment in the program of *Brith Shalom*, a Palestinian group that espouses a bi-national state, in which neither Arabs nor Jews shall rule or be ruled, but in which both shall join in developing the still sparsely settled territory so that, with intensive cultivation by modern methods, it shall have room for an ever-increasing population.

In Germany, Buber's ideas also fell on fruitful soil. As editor of the distinguished periodical, *Der Jude*, during and soon after the First World War and as director of the College of Jewish Studies in Frankfort, he stimulated the younger

generation of German Jews and helped to wean them from
Assimilation to Zionism. His personality and his philosophy
influenced the Jewish thinking of Arnold Zweig, Max Brod,
Franz Rosenzweig, Felix Weltsch, Hans Kohn, Kurt Blumen-
feld, and other writers of Central Europe.

On the eve of the Second World War, Buber re-formulated
the Jewish position in an open letter to Gandhi.[2] The spiritual leader of India had issued a statement, in December 1938,
setting forth his views on the persecution of Jews in Germany
and on the Arab-Jewish question in Palestine.[3] Buber, who
was a great admirer of the Mahatma and who in an essay of
1930, entitled *Gandhi, die Politik, und Wir,* had expressed
complete sympathy with the latter's religious and political
aims, felt hurt at the unjust strictures and unwise admoni-
tions contained in the widely publicized statement, and
therefore set out to correct Gandhi's wrong impression of
contemporary Jewish aspirations.

Gandhi had said that he knew Jews intimately because
of his contact with them ever since his early days in South
Africa. Some Jews had become his life-long companions.
Through them he learned of the age-long persecution of the
Jews. He found a close parallel between the treatment of the
untouchables by Hindus and the treatment of Jews by
Christians. In both cases religious sanction was invoked
to justify inhuman treatment. Despite his sympathy for
these untouchables of the Christian-dominated world,
Gandhi could not approve the Jewish efforts to leave
Germany nor endorse the Jewish cry for a national home in
Palestine. It was true that the German persecution of Jews
surpassed all previous horrors and that the tyrants of old
never went so mad as Hitler seemed to have gone. In
Gandhi's opinion, if there ever could be a justifiable war in

the name of and for humanity, then a war against Germany
to prevent the wanton persecution of an entire race would be
completely justified. But Gandhi did not believe in wars of
any kind and therefore he suggested *satyagraha*, soul-force
or passive resistance, as the most effective reply to Nazi
atrocities. No person who had faith in a living God needed
to feel helpless and forlorn. "Jehovah of the Jews is a God
more personal than the God of the Christians, the Mussul-
mans, or the Hindus; though, as a matter of fact, in essence
he is common to all and one without a second and beyond
description ... If I were a Jew and were born in Germany
and earned my livelihood there, I would claim Germany as
my home even as the tallest Gentile German may, and challenge him to shoot me or cast me in the dungeon; I would
refuse to be expelled or to submit to discriminating treatment ... If one Jew or all the Jews were to accept the pre-
scription here offered, he or they cannot be worse off than
now. And suffering voluntarily undergone will bring them
an inner strength and joy which no number of resolutions of
sympathy passed in the world outside Germany can ... If
the Jewish mind could be prepared for voluntary suffering,
even a massacre could be turned into a day of thanksgiving
and joy that Jehovah had wrought deliverance of the race
even at the hands of the tyrant. For to the God-fearing,
death has no terror. It is a joyful sleep to be followed by a
waking that would be all the more refreshing for the long
sleep." Gandhi recalled that, in South Africa at the turn of
the century, the Hindus occupied precisely the same place
that the Jews now occupy in Germany. The persecution of
Hindus had also a religious tinge. President Krüger used
to say that the white Christians were the chosen of God and
that the brown-skinned Hindus were inferior beings created

to serve the Whites. The Hindus, a mere handful, resorted to *satyagraha*, or non-violent opposition, without any backing from the outside. Only after eight years of this passive resistance did they receive aid from world opinion and from the Indian government; and this aid too was by way of diplomatic pressure. The Jews of Germany can offer *satyagraha* under infinitely better auspices than the Hindus of South Africa. "I am convinced that, if someone with courage and vision can arise among them to lead them in non-violent action, the winter of their despair can in the twinkling of an eye be turned into the summer of hope. And what has today become a degrading man-hunt can be turned into a calm and determined stand offered by unarmed men and women possessing the strength of suffering given them by Jehovah. It will then be a truly religious resistance offered against the godless fury of dehumanized man."

Buber, in his reply, pointed out that Gandhi completely misunderstood the German regime of the nineteen-thirties in assuming that it could be influenced in its racial policy by *satyagraha*. The treatment of the Jews exceeded in bestiality by far the worst excesses committed against the Hindus in South Africa a generation ago. The latter were despised by their white overlords, but they were not beyond the pale of the law; they did have certain rights; their sanctuaries were not desecrated; they were not held as hostages for the desired behavior of foreign countries. No Jew in Germany could have spoken as did Gandhi in South Africa without being killed immediately. *Satyagraha* was indeed a noble sentiment, but what possible influence could it have upon the demonic Nazi juggernaut? Martyrdom of an individual or of a group might indeed be desirable, if it served to call attention to an intolerable condition, but the martyrdom to which German Jews were subjected in concentration camps and dungeon-cells had no witnesses and, being unnoticed and unknown, could not affect public opinion or modify public policy. Gandhi, as the leader of one hundred and fifty thousand Hindus in South Africa, knew that Mother India with its hundreds of millions would ultimately stand in back of him. This knowledge that somewhere in the world there was a homeland and sympathetic kindred gave him and his followers the courage to live, to suffer, to resist, and to fight stubbornly — though non-violently — for their rights. He did not then upbraid his followers that they wanted a double home where they could remain at will. But he does presume now to tell the Jews that, if Palestine is their homeland, they must reconcile themselves to the thought that they have to leave the other parts of the world in which they were settled.

Buber asked Gandhi: supposing that on the morrow the hundreds of millions of Hindus were scattered over the face of the globe and that on the day after tomorrow another people were to settle in India, and supposing further that the dispersed Hindus were to declare that there was still room in India for the establishing of a National Home as an organic center for the scattered flock of homeless wanderers, would it be fair and just for a Jewish Gandhi to tell them, as the Indian Gandhi tells the Jews: "This cry for the National Home affords a colorable justification for your expulsion?" Would the Mahatma, who advises the Jews that Palestine is not a geographic district but an ideal within their hearts, accept the doctrine that India was not a subcontinent but merely an ideal wholly divorced from any soil? Is it not rather an ideal because it exists in reality? Is it not a symbol because it is somewhere in this world? Zion as a sacred ideal is inextricably bound up with the Holy Land, and national dispersal has a meaning only if there is a national core to serve as a common center for the dispersed. Such a center alone can bind together with a common purpose Jewish life everywhere. If Gandhi asks: why cannot Jews accept as their homes the lands in which they are born and in which they earn their living? — the answer must be: individual Jews can, but not the Jewish people. A hundred adopted fatherlands are no substitute for the one historic homeland. Hindus can be happy everywhere, but the soul of India, its specific wisdom and peculiar truth, can flourish only in the realm of the Ganges. This is equally true of the people of the Bible, who can become creative only on the soil of the Bible. There, and there alone, the longing of a hundred generations can find fulfillment and a way of life be resumed in accordance with ancient traditions.

But Gandhi raised an argument that Palestine belongs to the native Arab population and that it would be unjust and inhuman to force the Jews on the Arabs against the latter's will. Buber sought to clarify the exact meaning of "belongs." Does possession confer eternal ownership and is the status quo forever inviolable? How do peoples obtain ownership? By conquest and colonization. How did the ancient Jews come into control of the land? By conquest and colonization. How did the Arabs obtain their present position in Palestine? By conquest and colonization. How do the Jews now propose to regain their ancient soil? By colonization without the use of violence and without displacing the Arabs. Gandhi would apparently deny them this possibility and shut them out. His insisting that a land belonged to its inhabitants would lead him to defend a people whose territory was threatened by an invader; but it would also lead him, a few generations after the conquest was completed, to uphold the right of the conqueror to the land as against the claim of the displaced population. Assuming that Palestine, by intensive cultivation, could offer room both for the native Arabs and for those Jews, now homeless, who want to or have to return to their historic homeland, was it not uncharitable on the part of Gandhi to oppose Jewish national aspirations? The Jews were not coming as imperialists to enslave and to exploit the natives. They were immigrating in order to render fruitful with their sweat and blood a land that had been unfruitful for centuries and that had reverted to desert. The more cultivated the land became through Jewish toil, the more room would it have for both Jews and Arabs. Gandhi should therefore welcome such honest constructive pioneering and should seek to reconcile the conflicting rights of both groups.

Buber's reply to Gandhi expressed the sentiments not of all Jews but of an important group of ex-Germans and neo-Palestinians. In the nineteen-forties, as in the decades since 1900, his slogans still provoked discussion and controversy in the Diaspora and in the Holy Land, and contributed to the intellectual unrest that characterizes the Jewish renaissance.

In the summer of 1942, Buber, who had exchanged Germany for Palestine as his permanent home, joined with Judah L. Magnes, Chancellor of the Hebrew University, Henrietta Szold, founder of Hadassah, and others in organizing in Jerusalem, under the title *Ichud*, a political party of Jews and Arabs with the avowed aim of working for a bi-national Palestine as part of a pan-Arab federation to cooperate with the Anglo-American bloc in the reconstruction of a free, democratic, international order after the Second World War.

Chapter XVIII

PAN-HUMANISTS

PAN-HUMANISM is the attitude of those writers who, like Gustav Landauer, Richard Beer-Hofmann, and Martin Buber, affirm the desirability and even the necessity for the continued existence or the reconstitution of the Jews as a distinct people, tribe, or nation, but who see the primary justification for the survival of this unique group in its striving towards supra-nationalism, in its dedicating itself to the service of humanity at large.

Among the Pan-Humanists, the most difficult position between peoples, cultures, and languages was that maintained for decades by Max Brod, spiritual leader of the German-speaking Jews in the Czech provinces of the Austro-Hungarian Empire. When this Empire began to break up into its various national components, this editor and novelist of Prague faced the task of defining the attitude of his group towards immediate and ultimate political and cultural problems.

In July 1918, a few months before the end of the First World War, Brod called upon the Jews of Bohemia to keep aloof both from German and from Czech chauvinism, and to give primacy to Jewish national interests, in so far as this was possible within the framework of justice and of common human welfare. If, however, the interests of humanity at large conflicted at any time with specific Jewish interests,

ARNOLD ZWEIG, 1887–

(By courtesy of the Viking Press, New York)

then the latter must be subordinated; since national feeling must always yield to true humanity, which belongs to a higher category.

Brod denied that national self-preservation must lead inevitably to hatred of other nationalities and held that perhaps it was the mission of the Jews to cleanse the concept of nationalism from the filth and exaggerations of recent decades. A people could just as easily learn to love its neighbors as to hate them. A people could learn to give up voluntarily certain rights and privileges which were less valuable to it than burdensome to their neighbors. Jews had often furnished examples of this unselfish love for other peoples and, should they return to Palestine, would again demonstrate the possibility of a more moral type of nationalism. "Christian theologians treat the dispersion of the people of Israel among the nations of the earth as an act of Providence. I too see in it an act of Providence, but from another angle: we were to be dispersed among the peoples and were to experience by intimate contact and on our own body all the evils of nationalism — so that, when the time was ripe, we could found and live a new kind of nationalism in the Holy Land."[1] It was perhaps providential that upon the return of the Jews to their ancient land, they should find another people, so that the new conception of nationalism could be tested immediately. Should the Jews succeed in solving the Arab Question and in organizing a bi-national state, then they would thereby have disproved the European thesis of the inevitability of constant guerrilla warfare between different peoples who inhabit the same territory.

Brod experienced this guerrilla warfare in his native Bohemia, where Germans and Czechs vied for domination. He speaks of himself as a Jew who is at the same time a friend of the Germans and the Czechs — a friend of both but not a member of either people. Against the National-Chauvinism rampant in Central Europe, he defends the ideal of National-Humanism. Against the advocates of rugged individualism and of fascism and communism, he projects still another possibility: a relationship between man and society, whereby the former does not give up his freedom of decision even when embedded in the larger entity but rather demands: "O State, O People, admit me to all your values, to all your cultural and material treasures, so that I, the individual, and all the individuals with me, may become nobler and greater and more perfect by participating in all that you have achieved and created during the centuries and so that my moral decisions, which I must reach freely on my own responsibility, will be the result of greater fullness of knowledge and greater depth of feeling."[2]

This approach is, in Brod's opinion, typically Jewish and best exemplified in contemporary Zionism. Hence, Zionism is to him more than merely a political movement. It is the way of life for all those who accord primacy to the Jewish rather than the German or Czech phase of their personality. Perhaps, some day, a world which has experimented with Heathendom and with Christianity and which has failed to achieve a healthy relationship between individuals and peoples, will again turn to the Holy Land for guidance and will be grateful to the Jewish pioneers of a new society.

Max Brod thus continues on the path of Martin Buber. He is an exponent of cultural pluralism both in Central Europe and in Palestine, the land of his longing, whither he emigrated in 1939.

The faith, which Brod expounded in 1918, when the Austro-Hungarian Empire began to disintegrate, he reaffirmed in 1940, when all of Europe seemed to be heading to decay. In July 1940, when extreme nationalistic tendencies appeared to triumph throughout the Old World, he wrote: "The nation is not an absolute value. But internationalism of the ordinary variety, which ignores entirely the facts and the potentialities of nationhood, is a structure built on thin air. Like a harp with many strings, mankind has many national characteristics, out of the scale of whose tonalities great music is made, not by dissolving these characteristics into nothingness. National Humanism incorporates the Jewish people into the family of nations while preserving its distinctive character. This implies Jewish concentration in Palestine, since this is an essential factor for our future healthy development. It will not have us assimilated, melted down, and destroyed; but, on the other hand, it will not allow us to be driven into an arrogant posture of egotistic hostility to other nations, and particularly to our neighbors. Nations are the building-stones of humanity. A house is not built by crushing its stones, but by fitting each one into its proper place and binding them all together with mortar in accordance with a reasonable plan. So, we believe, may a structure be built in which real human beings, men who deserve to be called human, may house and live together."[3]

The Norwegian-American novelist O. E. Rolvaag interpreted Jewish participation on the world scene in a manner not unlike that of Brod and the cultural pluralists. In the novel *Their Fathers' God*, Rolvaag, in 1931, called upon his Scandinavian kinsmen in the New World to follow the example of the Jews and to effect a similar peaceful synthesis of their Norwegian and American traits. Refuting the melting-pot theory, which was then accepted by most immigrants from Northern Europe, he wrote: "And I maintain just the opposite. If we're to accomplish anything worth while, anything at all, we must do it as Norwegians. Otherwise, we may meet the same fate as corn in too strong a sun. Look at the Jews, for example: take away the contribution they have made to the world's civilization and you'd have a tremendous gap that time would never be able to fill. Did they make their contribution by selling their birthright and turning into Germans, Russians, and Poles? Or did they achieve greatly because they stubbornly refused to be de-Jewed? See what they have done in America! Are they as citizens inferior to us? Do they love this country less? Are they trying to establish a nation of their own? Empty nonsense! But they haven't ceased being Jews simply because they live here in America, and because they have adopted this country's language and become its citizens. Do you think their children will become less worthy Americans because they are being fostered in Jewish traits and traditions? Quite the contrary! If they, as individuals or as a group, owe any debt to America, the payment can only be made by their remaining Jews, and the same holds true for all nationalities that have come here. One thing I can see clearly: if this process of levelling down, of making everybody alike by blotting out all racial traits, is allowed to continue, America is doomed to become the most impoverished land spiritually on the face of the earth; out of our highly praised melting-pot will come a dull, smug complacency, barren of all creative thought and effort. Soon we will have reached the perfect democracy of barrenness. Gone will be the distinguishing traits given us by God; dead will be the hidden life of the heart which is nourished by tradition, the idiom of

language, and our attitude to life. It is out of these elements
that our character grows. I ask again, what will we have
left?"[4]

In 1936 there appeared in Switzerland, under the title
Israel unter den Völkern, an interesting study on the relation
of the Jews to their neighbors, in which this attitude of
national-humanism was ably expounded. The author,
Erich Kahler, who is best known for his philosophical and
historical masterpiece, *Der deutsche Charakter in der Geschichte
Europas,* defines the peculiar historic position of the Jews,
analyzes the source of their contemporary ills, and attempts
a diagnosis of various panaceas proposed for the coming
years.[5]

The Jews, in his opinion, differ from all the other population groups in Occidental society in that they are neither
a race nor a nation, but rather a tribal unit — the sole pure
tribe surviving in Europe. To make his viewpoint clear,
Kahler begins with definitions of race, nation, and tribe.
He shows that the concept race, which has a definite meaning when applied to horses, dogs, cows, or animals that can
be eugenically mated and bred, becomes utterly devoid of
scientific value when applied to human beings, whose primary
worth lies in their spiritual faculties rather than in their
physical components. He distinguishes between a tribe and
a nation in that a tribe is a community of kinship which
arose before the dominance of world religions, whereas a nation is a community of kinship which arose after the dominance of world religions, such as Christianity, Islam, and
Buddhism. Religions are grafted on nations, whereas they
are immanent in tribes. A nation can, therefore, change its
religion, but a tribe cannot. A tribe is a community based on

blood-kinship and centering about a divine cult. The state is of importance to a tribe only because it harbors the sanctuary of its cult, but, if this sanctuary is destroyed, the tribe is no longer tied to a definite space and may continue on its wanderings as a unity of blood and cult.

In Kahler's opinion, the Jews are the sole tribe in the Western World surviving from primeval mythical days up to our age of nations. Despite the differences in the physical makeup of Jews, their blood kinship is recognized both by themselves and by their adversaries. What these adversaries regard as a world conspiracy on the part of Jews to attain to dominance over other peoples is, in reality, nothing more that this common awareness of closeness and brotherhood, transcending all distances, languages, and nationalities.

Kahler defines Israel as a dynamic tribe that ever seeks to advance beyond mere tribal unity to a greater unity of all mankind. It is so constituted that it cannot live for itself, but must strive to go beyond itself. It finds its salvation in living for others and that is why it must live amidst others. Even its Palestinian state cannot be a typical self-satisfied state. From the moment of its regeneration, it must bring blessings to others who dwell therein. The brotherly spirit which characterizes Jewish settlements in the Holy Land will be extended to Arabs and Christians to the point of Pan-Semitism and World Brotherhood. And outside of Palestine, the Jews will still continue to function as a blessing for all nations. The road they are destined to travel has its starting point in justice and leads on to love. It is traveled by Israel's great sages from Abraham, who sacrificed his own son, to Jesus, who sacrificed himself. But, while Christianity regards the sacrifice of Jesus as a past act that brought salvation to all people for all time, Judaism insists on unceasing sacrifice day by day as its mode of living. With justice as its foundation, it strives to rear a marvelous structure of pure brotherly love and often succeeds in this difficult endeavor, as is evident in the Talmud and Midrash, in the sayings of Jesus, and in the lives of the Hasidim.

Kahler sees no essential difference between pure Judaism, as it is lived, and pure Christianity, as it is preached. He does see a contrast between Judaism and Germanism, or between Judaism and heathendom. The foes of Judaism must renounce their Christian heritage in order to be consistent in their hostility. The nations, who render lip service to Christianity at Church and on holidays but who in practice place their trust in war and mass murder, have an uneasy conscience in the presence of Jews, who do not depend upon armies or navies but who pursue justice unceasingly, practice peace on earth, and sacrifice themselves for moral values.

The emergence of the Jews from the ghetto during the past century brought three major dangers to their tribal unity. The first danger beset the emancipated Jew, who freed himself from his companions in fate and, as an isolated lonely cell, sought to make his way in the world. Released from the influence of the synagogue, which was formerly not merely a religious but also a cultural tribal center, he generally fell victim to pure selfishness, to the vilest sort of snobbery and ostentation, to shallow scepticism and impotent cynicism. He is the diabolical wandering Jew, the eternal busybody visible to all eyes, the caricature so often mistaken by outsiders as the symbol of true Judaism.

The second danger arose from too sudden and too complete national assimilation. The dynamic Jew, who had lost faith in his own people and in the traditional way of life, threw himself wholeheartedly into the service of the new national entity that at last permitted his active participation in its affairs. He sought to win the confidence of his nation by eradicating all Jewish survivals in his soul — in Germany, he became more Teutonic than the average German — until his super-patriotism began to annoy even the nationalist patriots of non-Jewish origin and they came to distrust him.

The third danger arose from too much devotion to the cause of humanity at large. The Jew dissipated his efforts in socialistic and communistic panaceas, while at the same time he abandoned his hold upon traditional realities. This is the error to which Karl Marx succumbed, but which Moses Hess, the socialistic contemporary of Marx, avoided.

The present generation in Central Europe has learned its lesson from its recent experiences. Kahler believes that it will not surrender to the above-mentioned three dangers that wrecked so many Jewish existences in the century from Ludwig Börne to Jakob Wassermann. It is more likely to follow the teachings of those seers who are rooted in Jewish traditions, without at the same time being divorced from the problems current in the world of today. Such inspiring leaders include Martin Buber — who revived for twentieth-century souls the glory of the Jewish past from the biblical struggles to the Hasidic currents, Richard Beer-Hofmann, the dramatic interpreter of Jewish heroism and the poetic preacher of Jewish nobility in attitude and action, Franz Rosenzweig, the brave thinker whose visions bridge the past and the future. A new sense of mutual responsibility permeates or should permeate each Jew today, an awareness that, in the eyes of others, everything he does or fails to do reflects upon his entire people. Though every nation is permitted its proportion of criminals and blackguards, the tribe of Israel is answerable as a whole to world public opinion for every black sheep within its fold.

In Kahler's opinion, the Jews are no longer looked upon as individuals. They no longer have privacy. What the least of them says or does has public currency and is judged as symbolic, as a word or act characteristic of the entire people. Jews must, therefore, finally realize that desertion is impossible, that indifference in this hour of their greatest need is a crime. They must lead model lives, in so far as this is humanly possible. They must be true to their past. They must not repay the hatred of others in like coin. Noble silence, dignified demeanor, greater productivity must be their answer to all attacks — and these attacks will collapse.

Jews will not cease to be. They will rather continue their existence both in the Diaspora and in Palestine. Those who live in the Diaspora, says Kahler, will have to respect and support the consecrated hearth of their tribe as a living symbol of their origin, as a place of refuge for persecuted souls, as a center from which calm strength and Jewish vital essence will radiate to all corners of the globe and enrich the dispersed flock of Israel everywhere. Those Jews, on the other hand, who live in Palestine must remain ever mindful of the fact that Zion would be but a withered relic of the past if it did not nurture its contacts with the pilgrims that are scattered throughout all continents. Palestinians must not look down upon European or American Jews as in any way less the bearers of the Jewish fate, for the latter are perhaps performing the most difficult missionary work for the Jewish idea. Certainly, two thousand years of tragic experience along the highways of the world's history and amidst strange

peoples did not have as a goal merely a reunion in an artificial petty national state or the rebuilding of a temple twice
ruined. If Jews have been thrust out upon the stage of
Europe and America, where tremendous historical forces
are at grips with each other and the future of mankind is
being forged, then they have a rôle to play there and they
must not fail to exercise their influence in accordance with
their tribal traditions.

In the whirlpool of contemporary events, Jews must seek
some hold, some guidance, some basis for faith. They cannot
find this either in the Orthodox synagogue that has ceased
to be what it once was — a school for conduct and a creative
center for communal life — or in the modernized Reform
temple that is but a pale, bloodless imitation of Christian
churches. They must fortify their faith by becoming again
the people of the Book, by seeking inspiration in those works
that record for them their way of living. These include,
according to Kahler, the Old Testament and the New, the
Talmud and the Midrash, the Cabala and the documents
of Hasidism, the myths and legends of their forefathers,
and the interpretations of their experiences by gifted Jews.
These monuments of the Jewish way of life, extending down
the millenniums in an unbroken chain from hoary antiquity
to the present day, unroll to their gaze the panorama of
Israel's unending struggle with the Eternal, Israel's ceaseless
striving for justice and brotherhood on earth. These monuments will enable each of them to understand the source of
their inner nature and to utilize their Jewish tribal impulses
in behalf of the nations among whom they dwell, driving
them on in the direction of a purer humanity.

A critical hour has come not only for Jews but for all mankind. If mankind advances along the road from selfish na-

tionalism to a more perfect brotherhood, then Jews, too, will share in this progress and will resume their beneficent activity among the European peoples. But if war, retrogression, and collapse are to be the fate of Western civilization, then Jews will at least have the comfort of knowing that they bear no responsibility whatsoever for the universal catastrophe and that they maintained to the end their post as sentinels of the higher moral values and their faith in a type of man who was fashioned in the likeness of God.

These thoughts of Erich Kahler are typical of the contemporary Jewish renaissance. They resemble ideas expressed by Ahad Ha'am and Richard Beer-Hofmann, Martin Buber and Max Brod. They find a parallel in the writings of Arnold Zweig, the novelist who attained world-wide fame with his prose epics, *The Case of Sergeant Grischa* and *Education Before Verdun*.[6]

Zweig is a profound and courageous thinker on political, social, and literary problems. Although a Zionist ever since his early days, he never nourished the optimistic belief that Palestine could completely solve the Jewish question by putting an end to the dispersion of the Jews among the peoples of the earth. But he did hold that Palestine could change the character of Jewish life everywhere by becoming once again the spiritual center of the Jews and by developing new forms of cooperative living. Palestine might even serve ultimately as a beacon for other peoples. But in the immediate future and for the majority of Jews in Germany and elsewhere, cultural pluralism offered the most satisfactory solution. Zweig best expresses this view in his detailed study, *Caliban*, which appeared in 1927, but it is echoed in all his essays written between the First and Second World Wars.

Beginning with the assumption that the assimilationist ideal, which captivated the nineteenth century, was completely bankrupt, Zweig suggests that Jews should hereafter unite in striving for cultural autonomy as the only sensible and dignified goal. Since Germany permits and even encourages the preservation of tribal peculiarities on the part of Saxons, Bavarians, Franconians, Thuringians, within the framework of the German state and of German law, why can it not accord similar permission and encouragement to the members of the Jewish tribe? Why cannot Jewish schools be founded in communities where Jews live in appreciable numbers? Why cannot a Jewish university flourish in Germany under government auspices, even as a German university flourished in Prague with the approval of the Czechoslovakian government? Why cannot cultural pluralism replace cultural monism? Surely, the hypertrophic nationalism rampant in Europe was not a healthy condition. Surely, mutual hatreds between peoples must before long bring on a crisis and yield to some form of cooperative effort. The ebbing of the violent antipathies, now at their highest crest, will inevitably result in the dwindling of neo-paganism and of anti-Semitism.

Zweig characterizes as pagan the attitude of the ultra-nationalists who want to substitute the nation for God or the universal spirit. These pagans designate as good or evil, moral or immoral, whatever seems to be desirable or undesirable for their own nation at a particular moment. In this approach, they always identify the nation with their own particular party or group. If unrestrained, they would condemn their opponents as unworthy of life and would proceed to "liquidate" all dissenters. The ultra-nationalists even claim the right to dominate other peoples and to expand their own power beyond their original borders. They pose as idealists who wish to bring the blessings of their superior culture to the world. This very justification, however, proves that even these imperialists acknowledge the good of the world or of mankind to be more important than the good of any individual nation. Mankind is a symbiosis of peoples and each nation derives its value and meaning only in relation to humanity at large.

This earth does not belong in perpetuity to any of the peoples now inhabiting its various parts. This earth has merely been leased to the diverse nations. It is, according to all myths and religions, the creation of a God or gods. It is not the creation of a human being or of an ancestor of any people. Since, therefore, all groups hold their lands in trust, they may not question the rights of others to survive thereon.

Contemporary chauvinism may shut its eyes to this self-evident truth. But, as the effect of its poison wears off, respect for the rights of foreign peoples will return. Zweig believes that a new league of nations may be formed — a United States of the World. It will then be of relatively small concern in which territorial group a person works or dwells. Today the so-called alien has no voice in the political decisions either of his own people or of the people on whose soil he has sought to take new root. These aliens and refugees and marginal persons already number millions and are constantly on the increase. An organization of peoples into a more virile League of United Nations will enable these millions to resume healthy, active participation in mankind's tasks, despite their accidental location on the wrong side of a boundary line. Indeed, once a supra-national organization has been achieved, boundaries are not likely to be regarded as so very important, and political problems that today seem well-nigh insoluble will lose their weightiness. The earth as object versus mankind as a creative organism — this problem will engage the attention of future generations. And in such an organism there will function harmoniously myriads of individual human cells, grouped in various organs, national organs whose names shall be German and Slav and Latin — and Jew.

This vision of Arnold Zweig and similar Utopias dreamed by national humanists and by Jewish sages and poets of Germany gave way to a brutal awakening in 1933 when the cohorts of Hitler began to carry out their frankly avowed program of liquidating the Jews of Europe in the briefest possible time.

A shudder ran through Jewish communities on every continent and in every land, as the Nazi solution of the German-Jewish duality unfolded itself in practice. A questioning was heard from all sides: is this the end? Is this the death of Western culture, whose fairest blossom was emancipation? — the emancipation of the individual from fears and taboos, from serfdom and bondage, from superstition and cruelty; an emancipation begun by the Renaissance and carried to fruition by the Enlightenment, blazoned on the banners of the French Revolution and inscribed in the codes of parliamentary regimes; an emancipation that broke down the walls of the ghettos and admitted to universal brotherhood commoners and pariahs no less than noblemen and patricians; an emancipation that gave to Jews and non-Jews a new sense of dignity and appraised the worth of each individual without regard to race, creed, or heritage. To share in this emancipation, the enlightened

Jews in the heart of Europe, and their brothers of North, South, and West — though not East — had denuded themselves of their ancestral wrappings and had swathed themselves in gaudy robes of Occidental fabric. And now that these new raiments were stripped from them, now that the glittering tinsel acquired in the nineteenth century was violently torn from them, along with the flesh to which it had become attached, now they stood exposed, naked and bleeding, a sorry sight for scoffers, a pitiable sight to themselves.

Many were felled by despair. A wave of suicides swept German towns, striking down some of the noblest and most sensitive spirits. This wave even lapped the shores of distant continents, claiming, among others, Ernst Toller in New York and Stefan Zweig in Brazil.

But the strong heart of Israel soon resumed its beating after the momentary severe stroke. The will to live reasserted itself everywhere. From alien altars and from foreign fleshpots, the homeward trek began. Home was not a fixed spot in an immovable territory. Home was wherever kin spoke to kin and common anguish forged common bonds. Unity reasserted itself among the dispersed and estranged. Under the hammering of misfortune there was repaired the cleavage between East and West, Assimilated and Unassimilated, Zionist and non-Zionist, Polish Jew and German Jew. And when the Second World War broke out, there was no need for a weighing of conflicting claims or a choosing between sides. The cause of the United Nations, the cause of World Democracy was the sole cause possible for Jews. The freedoms proclaimed in the Atlantic Charter of 1941 were freedoms that stemmed from biblical idealism, and the people of the Bible responded wholeheartedly. From the tundras and steppes of Russia to the deserts of North Africa and the jungles of Polynesia, their deeds of heroism shone brightly alongside of those of other groups. Stateless Jews, most of them refugees from German oppression and temporarily forced to remain aloof from the global struggle because of their status as political outcasts, clamored loudly for a Jewish army and for an opportunity to fight and to die in behalf of a cause which was theirs long before it became the cause of others. By 1944 the Jewish dead in the global conflict were numbered in the millions. Nevertheless, though the physical extermination of the biblical people was proceeding in Europe at a catastrophic pace, the remnant that survived was again sound at heart and unbroken in spirit.

In the 1940's the German-Jewish duality had become a problem of the past. The mirage that had dazzled Jewish eyes ever since the mid-eighteenth century had vanished. The Jewish renascence was in full swing.

BIBLIOGRAPHIC NOTES

A complete bibliography of German-Jewish relations from 1750 to the present is now in the process of preparation by the *Reichsinstitut für Geschichte des neuen Deutschlands*. The first volume has already appeared. It is entitled *Bibliographie zur Geschichte der Judenfrage* (Hamburg, 1938). It contains 3016 items and enumerates in chronological order all the books and articles printed up to 1848 and available in German libraries. Its value as a handbook for historians is unquestioned, despite its propagandistic purpose and its National-Socialist sponsorship. A complete bibliography may, therefore, be dispensed with in the present study. The bibliographic notes that follow are mainly guides to the original German sources of the passages quoted in the text.

CHAPTER I

1 Ellen Key, *Rahel Varnhagen*, N. Y., 1913, p. 11.
2 Ibid., p. 11.
3 Otto Bredow, *Rahel Varnhagen*, Stuttgart, 1900, p. 47.
4 Varnhagen von Ense, *Ausgewählte Schriften*, Leipzig, 1876, vol. XIX, p. 281.
5 Ibid., XIX, 287.
6 Ibid., VI, 153.
7 Rahel, *Ein Buch des Andenkens für ihre Freunde*, Berlin, 1833, p. 43.
8 Varnhagen von Ense, *Tagebücher*, Leipzig, 1865, vol. VIII, p. 401.
9 Varnhagen von Ense, *Tagebücher*, Leipzig, 1861, vol. II, p. 113.
10 S. Hensel, *Die Familie Mendelssohn*, Berlin, 1906, vol. I, p. 88.
11 Bettina von Arnim, *Sämtliche Werke*, Berlin, 1922, vol. VII, pp. 18–63.
12 *Fürst Pückler-Muskau, Tutti-Frutti*, New York, 1834, p. 94.
13 Ibid.

CHAPTER II

1 Ludwig Börne, *Gesammelte Schriften*, Wien, 1868, vol. VII, p. 37.
2 Ibid., II, 222.
3 Ibid., II, 29.
4 Ibid., II, 213.
5 Ibid., IV, 73.
6 Ibid., II, 204.
7 Ibid., VI, 13.
8 Ibid., VI, 38.
9 Ibid., VI, 9.

[10] Ibid., VI, 29.
[11] Ibid., X, 25.
[12] Ibid., X, 129.
[13] Ibid., X, 130.
[14] Ibid., VI, 233.

CHAPTER III

[1] H. H. Houben, *Gutzkow-Funde*, Berlin, 1901, pp. 154–158 and 210–223.
[2] *Klagen eines Juden*, Mannheim, 1837, p. 76.
[3] Ibid., p. 48.
[4] Ibid., p. 49.
[5] Ibid., pp. 26–28.
[6] Steinheim, *Gesänge aus der Verbannung, welche sang Obadiah ben Amos im Lande Ham*, 2nd ed., Frankfurt a. M., 1837, p. 91.
[7] J .Jacoby, *Religiöse Rhapsodien. Blätter für die höchsten Interessen*, Berlin, 1837, p. 100.
[8] Friedrich von Oppeln-Bronikowski, *David Ferdinand Koreff*, Berlin, 1928, p.174.
[9] Ibid., p. 172.
[10] Ibid., p. 190.

CHAPTER IV

[1] Heine's comments on Jews and Judaism in his works and letters have been collected and edited in chronological order by Hugo Bieber in *H. Heine: Confessio Judaica*, Berlin, 1925.
[2] H. Heine, *Sämtliche Werke*, ed. Elster, Leipzig, 1890, vol. VI, p. 315.
[3] H. Heine, *Gesammelte Werke*, ed. Elster, Leipzig, 1924, vol. IV, p. 221.

CHAPTER V

[1] Berthold Auerbach, *Das Judentum und die neueste Literatur*, Stuttgart, 1836, p. 67.
[2] Berthold Auerbach, *Briefe an seinen Freund Jakob Auerbach*, Frankfurt a. M., 1884, vol. I, p. 16.
[3] Berthold Auerbach, *Gesammelte Schriften*, Stuttgart, 1858, vol. XIII, p. 42.
[4] *Briefe*, I, 394.
[5] Anton Bettelheim, *Berthold Auerbach*, Stuttgart, 1907, p. 362.
[6] *Briefe*, II, 442.
[7] Berthold Auerbach, *Die Genesis des Nathan, Gedenkworte zu Lessings 100-jährigem Todestag*, Berlin, 1881, p. 24.
[8] Bettelheim, p. 375.
[9] *Briefe*, I, 85.

CHAPTER VI

The works of Moses Hess, to which the chapter refers, are: *Die heilige Geschichte der Menschheit*, Stuttgart, 1837. *Die europäische Triarchie*, Leipzig, 1841. *Rom und Jerusalem*, Leipzig, 1862.

Miscellaneous essays on Jewish themes collected by Theodor Zlocisti in: *Jüdische Schriften*, Berlin, 1905. Zlocisti is also the author of the best biography of Moses Hess, Berlin, 1921.

CHAPTER VII

[1] Theodor Herzl, *The Jewish State*, 3rd ed., London, 1936, p. 20.

CHAPTER VIII

[1] Leon Kellner, *Theodor Herzls Lehrjahre*, Wien, 1920, p. 108.
[2] Arthur Schnitzler, *Der Gang zum Weiher*, Berlin, 1926, p. 57.
[3] Arthur Schnitzler, *Gesammelte Werke*, Berlin, 1922; *Erzählende Schriften*, vol. III, p. 282.
[4] Ibid., III, 130.
[5] Ibid., III, 284.
[6] Ibid., III, 141.
[7] Ibid., III, 284.
[8] Ibid., III, 94.
[9] *Aufbau*, May 8, 1942, vol. VIII, no. 19, p. 17.

CHAPTER IX

[1] Walter Hartenau (Rathenau): "Höre, Israel," *Zukunft*, March 16, 1897, vol. XVIII, pp. 454–462.
[2] *Deutschlands Ereneuerung, Monatsschrift für das deutsche Volk*, November 1933, vol. XVII, pp. 732–737.
[3] Walter Rathenau, *Briefe*, Dresden, 1930, vol. I, p. 203.
[4] Ibid., vol. I, p. 220.
[5] Ibid., vol. II, pp. 129–132.

CHAPTER X

[1] Friedrich Nietzsche, *The Genealogy of Morals*, Aphorism 16.
[2] Friedrich Nietzsche, *Human All-too-Human*, Aphorism 475.
[3] Friedrich Nietzsche, *Beyond Good and Evil*, Aphorism 250.
[4] R. M. Lonsbach, *Nietzsche und die Juden*, Stockholm, 1939, p. 55.
[5] Friedrich Nietzsche, *Beyond Good and Evil*, Aphorism 251.
[6] Friedrich Nietzsche, *The Dawn of Day*, New York, 1924, pp. 210–214.

[7] Oswald Spengler, *The Decline of the West*, New York, 1928, vol. II, p. 317.
[8] Ibid.
[9] Ibid, vol. II, p. 319.
[10] Ibid.
[11] Eduard Meyer, *Spenglers Untergang des Abendlandes*, Berlin, 1925, p. 20.
[12] Theodor Lessing, *Jüdischer Selbsthass*, Berlin, 1930, p. 11.

CHAPTER XI

[1] Jakob Wassermann, *Lebensdienst*, Leipzig, 1928, p. 163.
[2] Ibid, p. 158.
[3] Jakob Wassermann, *Mein Weg als Deutscher und Jude*, Berlin, 1921, p. 96.
[4] Jakob Wassermann, *My Life as German and Jew*, New York, 1933.
[5] Jakob Wassermann, *Lebensdienst*, Leipzig, 1928, p. 28.
[6] Martha Karlweis, *Jakob Wassermann*, Amsterdam, 1935, p. 336.

CHAPTER XII

Otto Weininger's main work is: *Geschlecht und Charakter*, Wien, 1903. Valuable studies on Weininger include: Hermann Swoboda, *Otto Weiningers Tod*, 2nd ed., Wien, 1923. Paul Biro, *Sittlichkeitsmetaphysik Otto Weiningers*, Wien, 1927. Andre Spire, *Quelques Juifs et Demi-Juifs*, Paris, 1928, vol. I, pp. 165–200: "Otto Weininger."

[1] Arthur Trebitsch, *Geist und Judentum*, Wien, 1919, p. 174.
[2] Arthur Trebitsch, *Deutscher Geist — oder Judentum*, Berlin, 1921, p. 356.

CHAPTER XIII

[1] Ernst Toller, *Hinkemann*, Potsdam, 1924, p. 61.
[2] Ernst Toller, *Eine Jugend in Deutschland*, Amsterdam, 1933, pp. 276–278.
[3] Franz Werfel, "Die christliche Sendung," *Neue Rundschau*, January 1917, vol. XXVIII, pp. 92–105.
[4] Franz Werfel, *Embezzled Heaven*, New York, 1940, p. 314.
[5] Ibid., p. 282.
[6] Ibid., p. 369.
[7] Werner Sombart, *Judentaufen*, München, 1912, p. 69.
[8] Ibid., pp. 134–136.

CHAPTER XIV

[1] Jakob Wassermann, *My Life as German and Jew*, New York, 1933, p. 187.
[1] Stefan Zweig, *Der begrabene Leuchter*, Wien, 1937, p. 18.
[2] Ibid., p. 34.
[4] Ibid., p. 45.

CHAPTER XV

[1] Gustav Landauer, *Der werdende Mensch*, Potsdam, 1921, p. 126.
[2] Gustav Landauer, *Sein Lebensgang in Briefen*, Frankfurt a. M., 1929, vol. I, p. 450.
[3] Ibid.
[4] Ibid.
[5] Ibid., vol. I, p. 448.
[6] *Der Jude*, October 1916, pp. 433–439.
[7] Ernst Toller, *I Was a German*, New York, 1934, p. 249.

CHAPTER XVI

[1] Alex Bein, *Theodor Herzl*, Wien, 1934, p. 289.
[2] Theodor Herzl, *Tagebücher*, Berlin, 1922, vol. I, p. 364.
[3] Richard Beer-Hofmann, *Der Tod Georgs*, Berlin, 1900, pp. 215–216.

CHAPTER XVII

[1] Martin Buber (ed.): *Der Jude, Eine Monatsschrift*, 1917, vol. II, p. 24. A complete bibliography of Buber's works is contained in the appendix to Hans Kohn, *Martin Buber, Sein Werk und seine Zeit*, Hellerau, 1930.
[2] Martin Buber, *Brief an Gandhi*, Zurich, 1939.
[3] "Gandhi Speaks on Jewish Problems," *Christian World*, January 18, 1939.

CHAPTER XVIII

[1] Max Brod, *Im Kampf um das Judentum*, Wien, 1920, p. 41.
[2] Max Brod, *Das Diesseitswunder*, Tel-Aviv, 1939, p. 77.
[3] Max Brod, "The Individual and the Nation," *Jewish Frontier*, July 1940, p. 27.
[4] O. E. Rolvaag, *Their Fathers' God*, New York, 1931, p. 209.
[5] Erich Kahler's most important Jewish studies are: *Israel unter den Völkern*, Zurich, 1936. "Forms and Features of Anti-Judaism," *Social Research*, November 1939, pp. 455–488.
[6] Arnold Zweig's most important Jewish studies include: *Caliban*, Potsdam, 1927. *Bilanz der deutschen Judenheit*, Amsterdam, 1934.

INDEX

INDEX